5th edition

Beat Your Ticket

Go to Court & Win

by Attorney David Brown

NOLO

FIFTH EDITION	AUGUST 2007
Editor	RICH STIM
Cover Design	SUSAN PUTNEY
Production	MARGARET LIVINGSTON
Proofreading	EMILY K. WOLMAN
Index	BAYSIDE INDEXING SERVICE
Printing	CONSOLIDATED PRINTERS, INC.

Brown, David Wayne, 1949-

Beat your ticket : go to court & win / by David Brown.-- 5th ed.

p. cm.

Includes index.

ISBN-13: 978-1-4133-0698-9 (pbk.)

ISBN-10: 1-4133-0698-5 (pbk.)

1. Traffic violations--United States-- Popular works. 2. Traffic courts--United States--Popular works. 3. Pro se representation--United States--Popular works.   I. Title.

KF2231.Z9B76 2007

345.73'0247--dc22

2007007617

Quantity sales: For information on bulk purchases or corporate premium sales, please contact the Special Sales department. For academic sales or textbook adoptions, ask for Academic Sales. 800-955-4775, Nolo, 950 Parker Street, Berkeley, CA 94710.

Dedication

To my daughters, Laura and Kate, and to their mother, Nancy Brown Selvy, all of Plymouth, California.

Acknowledgment

This book could not have been published without the assistance and efforts of many people:

- First and foremost, Nolo's visionary publisher, Ralph ("Jake") Warner, a kind but demanding editor who never tolerates quitting or skimping, without whom this book would not exist.
- Spencer Sherman, the Nolo editor who magically transformed crudely crafted words into a polished product.
- Susan ("Lulu") Cornell, a dedicated Nolo editor whose excellent editorial suggestions were of great assistance in preparing the 50-state appendix.
- Peter Hartley, of Monterey County, California, my secretary/assistant who tirelessly typed various drafts of many chapters from dictation and chicken-scratching.
- George Stavropoulos, of Salinas, California, for his inspirations and for patiently analyzing the many ideas I bounced off him.
- Jane Fajardo, of Palo Alto, California. Thanks, Mom, for your loving and supportive help.
- The National Motorists Association of Waunakee, Wisconsin (www .motorists.org), a freedom-loving organization that provides first-class assistance to the motoring public.

Table of Contents

Your Legal Companion for Beating Your Ticket

1 First Things

A Tale of a Ticket 4

Are Tickets Impossible to Beat? 4

How This Book Is Organized 6

2 What Are You Charged With?

What Does the Law Say? 8

Finding Support Using Legal Research 10

3 Should You Fight Your Ticket

Understanding Traffic Offenses 16

Negative Consequences of Getting a Ticket 18

The Traffic School Option 20

Deciding Whether to Fight Your Ticket 21

Putting It All Together—How to Decide Whether to Fight or Fold 24

Defenses That Rarely Work 25

4 Lawyers and What They Can Do for You

What Lawyers Can Do 28

Types of Lawyers 29

Getting the Most Out of Your Lawyer 31

Firing Your Lawyer 32

5 Speed Violations: Understanding the Laws of Your State

Three Types of Speed Limits 34

"Absolute" Speed Limits 35

"Presumed" Speed Limits 35

The "Basic" Speed Law 39

6 Speed Detection: Pacing, Aircraft, VASCAR, Radar, and Laser— How They Work, How to Fight Them

Getting Caught 42

How Was Your Speed Measured? 43

7 Other Moving Violations

Not Stopping at Stop Signs 69

Not Stopping at a Stoplight 71

Automated Enforcement Devices ("Red Light Cameras") 73

Improper Turning 74

Right-of-Way Violations 81

Driving Too Slowly 86

Tailgating 88

Unsafe Lane Changes 90

Improper Passing 91

Non-DUI/DWI Alcohol-Related Offenses 92

8 Driving Under the Influence

Offenses and Penalties 99

How Alcohol Interacts With Your Body 103

Blood, Breath, and Urine Tests for Alcohol 108

License Suspension Penalties and Procedures 113

Dealing With a DUI Charge 114

9 First Steps to Fight Your Ticket

So You've Decided to Fight 124

Taking the First Steps 124

Using "Discovery" to Build Your Case 134

10 Preparing for Trial—Your Case

Asking for a "Continuance" (Postponement) 140

Gathering Your Notes and Research 142

Diagrams, Maps, and Pictures 142

Preparing Your Testimony 146

Preparing Your Witnesses 150

Preparing for the Prosecution's Cross-Examination 151

11 Preparaing for Trial—The Officer's Testimony and Cross-Examination

When and How to Object to Testimony.. 154

How to Cross-Examine the Officer 157

12 Trial Before a Judge (No Jury)

Introduction 182

Trial Procedure... 186

Appealing for a New Trial 200

13 Jury Trials

Introduction.. 204

Try to Settle Your Case 204

Selecting the Jury 206

Trial Procedure... 211

Preparing Jury Instructions... 216

The Judge Instructs the Jury... 217

Appeals From a Jury Verdict 217

Appendix

Traffic Court Rules for 50 States (and the District of Columbia)

Index

Your Legal Companion for Beating Your Ticket

Speeding, running stop signs, and making illegal U-turns can jeopardize the safety of everyone on the road—you, your passengers, other drivers, and pedestrians. Ticketing unsafe drivers is one means of deterring these dangerous activities. But as you're probably aware, the process of citing traffic violators is not fool-proof, and tickets are sometimes issued for the wrong reasons. A police officer may make a mistake, a camera may malfunction, or a local government—in its zeal to generate revenue—may encourage overticketing.

You're probably reading this book because you received a traffic ticket. Should you just go ahead and pay the ticket—and/or go to traffic school—and move on? If you are without-a-doubt guilty or consider the hassle factor too high, paying the ticket is probably the best course of action. For example, if you just got your first ticket in ten years and are determined that it will be ten more years before you get another, it's probably best to cough up the money and forget it.

On the other hand, if, through bad luck or indiscretion, you are facing your second ticket in three to five years, you may decide to fight it to avoid higher insurance premiums or other problems described inside. No one can guarantee your success fighting a ticket. But this book can offer some useful information that will help you assess your odds of success and make your task—should you choose to challenge your ticket—far easier. With a little research and preparation, there is a chance that a ticket you consider "unbeatable" can be beaten. No matter whether you've received your first or 22nd ticket, it is always worth carefully checking out the motor vehicle law and your potential defenses before writing out a check.

Consider these facts:

- In a small minority of cases, the police officer fails to show up in court. If so, you usually win.
- In many states, speed limits are not "absolute." If you show the judge it was reasonable to drive over the posted limit, you win.
- If you go back to the scene of the violation, you may find that what the officer said he saw was not possible from where he said he saw it.
- Many traffic laws have "wiggle room," and the officer issuing the ticket is often making a judgment call. As we'll explain, these types of tickets can sometimes be beaten.

One final note before we dive in: Procedures for fighting traffic tickets vary a lot from state to state. We can't provide 50 separate chapters with every detail from every state, but we do offer something unique: a 50-state appendix that details the most important specifics of each state's traffic laws and traffic court procedures. ●

First Things

A Tale of a Ticket..4

Are Tickets Impossible to Beat?...4

How This Book Is Organized...6

A Tale of a Ticket

It's late. You're driving home from a party. You're thinking about what a good time you had. Then you realize you've missed a turn. You're in the middle of a quiet residential district with no cars moving in either direction. All you see is a car parked a few blocks away with its lights on. You make a U-turn.

Suddenly, in your rearview mirror, you see flashing lights racing towards you. You pull over to let the police car pass. Instead, it follows you to the curb. You realize you've just been pulled over. Even before your car is fully stopped, the officer has his spotlight pointed at you. Then you hear a door slamming, the sound of pavement under boots.

Before you get a chance to ask, "What's the problem?" the officer says, "May I see your driver's license, please?" You fumble through your wallet and you hand over your license.

The officer returns to his car. His radio crackles in the night. A few minutes later he comes back and returns your license on a clipboard that also holds a traffic ticket. "You made an unlawful U-turn in a residential district," he says. "Please sign on the dotted line." When the officer goes on to explain that your signature is not an admission of guilt but merely a promise to appear in court, you meekly do as he asks. A moment later, as the officer pulls away, you eye your ticket, stunned at how quickly you've been ensnared in the justice system.

Chances are, as you drive the rest of the way home, you'll repeatedly wonder, "Why is it illegal to make a perfectly safe turn on an empty road?" Which will lead you to consider the following:

- Should I just pay the ticket and forget it?
- Is there a way to wipe this ticket off my record?
- If I pay the ticket, will my insurance rates go up?
- Do I have legal grounds to fight the ticket?
- Can I lose my license?

If you decide to fight the ticket, several things will happen:

- You will spend at least several hours and probably many more preparing to fight the ticket.
- You'll worry about making a good court presentation.
- You'll spend half a day or more going back and forth to court and arguing your case.

If you don't fight the ticket, you could end up doing some or all of the following:

- Spending money and many hours in traffic school to clear your record.
- Paying a hefty fine and having the ticket appear on your driving record.
- If you have had another recent ticket, paying higher insurance premiums for the next three to five years.
- If you have had several recent tickets, losing your driving privileges.

Are Tickets Impossible to Beat?

The answer is: absolutely not. Many tickets are given in situations where even the officer knows that a motorist who puts up a spirited defense might win. But this doesn't necessarily mean the officer will cut back in handing out marginal tickets. That's because the officer also knows that only about 3% of ticketed drivers contest their citations. And furthermore, many of those who do fight are so unprepared and nervous that they beat themselves, not their citation.

Getting a Ticket Doesn't Equal Guilt

Here is an example of why you shouldn't just assume you are guilty because you are ticketed. In San Francisco, police use automatic cameras at some busy intersections to catch red-light runners. About 30% of all those pictures used to be thrown out by the police because the picture was fuzzy, blurred, or otherwise deemed to be unusable. But in 1998 the police chief decided that everyone photographed would get a ticket—no ifs, ands, or buts. That means that 30% of these tickets are so marginal they used to be thrown away because the police themselves believed the evidence was not strong enough for a conviction.

Does it make sense for you to fight a particular ticket? Common sense would say "no" if there is a small chance of winning and "yes" if the officer clearly screwed up. Still, for most tickets, guilt or innocence is not so clear cut, meaning that you'll normally want to consider a number of factors, including the consequences of paying your fine—which is the same thing as pleading guilty.

Before assuming the ticket can't be beaten and resigning yourself to writing out that check, we encourage you to take a hard look at the facts to see if you have a reasonable chance of success. You may be surprised at the variety of legal grounds available for defeating your ticket. For example, in about one third of the states—including California, Colorado, Texas, and Massachusetts—many posted speed limits are not "absolute." This means if you were driving slightly above the posted speed limit but can convince a judge you were driving safely, you may be found not guilty. And to take another common example, where a ticket is given for an "unsafe lane change" it may be possible to show that you changed lanes with reasonable safety. That's because it involves a quick judgment call on the part of the cop to cite you—a decision you may be able to successfully challenge if the lane change did not result in an accident.

To test the legality of the ticket you received, you must learn how to research the law and court procedure. Because of the Internet, researching the law is fairly easy. Once you locate the law you are accused of violating, you should closely examine its words and phrases because, sometimes, the officer did not fully understand all of the technical aspects of the law, or worse, the officer has taken inappropriate liberties in interpreting the law.

If you are uneasy searching for legal technicalities to keep your record clear, then follow your conscience, pay your ticket, and accept the consequences. But keep in mind that exploiting legal technicalities is a common, legitimate practice for avoiding the consequences of a traffic ticket.

How This Book Is Organized

Chapters 2 and 3 provide the information you need to sensibly decide whether to fight your ticket, attend traffic school, or simply pay your fine. To help you make these decisions, Chapter 2 will also explain how to locate the law you're charged with violating, so you can analyze it and decide for yourself whether you committed the offense.

In Chapter 4 we discuss when you should hire a lawyer to represent you, particularly in serious cases like reckless driving and driving under the influence of alcohol or drugs. We also discuss how to evaluate lawyers and get help from an expert at an affordable price.

Chapters 5, 6, and 7 summarize what lawyers call the "substantive law" on most common types of traffic violations, and these chapters provide tips on how to challenge your ticket. Because speeding tickets are by far the most common, Chapter 6 focuses on how to defend yourself when your ticket is based upon various methods used by police to monitor speed, including pacing, VASCAR, radar, and laser devices.

Chapter 8 gives a few basics on the law of drunk driving (which we prefer to call "Driving Under the Influence" or "Driving While Intoxicated"—DUI/DWI). It is not intended, however, as a complete guide to the subject of defending your own DUI/DWI case—something that would take a whole book in its own right.

Chapter 9 is devoted to initial court procedures required when preparing your case—for example, obtaining the officer's notes to build your defense.

Chapter 10 helps you prepare for your day in court, including preparing your testimony and the testimony of your witnesses.

Chapter 11 helps you prepare to cross-examine the police officer.

Chapters 12 and 13 prepare you for jury and nonjury trials.

Because we want to keep this book brief, we do not cover:

- The most serious offenses, like drunk driving or hit-and-run; most people should not represent themselves against these and other charges that could land them in jail;
- Contesting the loss or suspension of your driver's licenses by the state department of motor vehicles; or
- The details of appealing to higher courts after a guilty verdict.

What Are You Charged With?

What Does the Law Say?...8

    Try the Internet 8

    Use Public and Law Libraries...9

    Read the Law Carefully..9

Finding Support Using Legal Research...10

    Finding Case Decisions...10

    Analyzing Court Decisions..12

    Can Other Laws Help Your Case?..12

What Does the Law Say?

The first thing you need to do is find out what you are charged with—not just what your ticket says, but the exact words of the law you are charged with breaking. In some states, traffic laws are set out in a "Vehicle Code," while in others they are gathered as part of a "Transportation Code," "Motor Vehicle Laws," or under some similar name. No two states have exactly the same traffic laws, but most are very similar.

Look for a number on your ticket that corresponds to the law (often called a "statute" or "vehicle code section") you are charged with violating. Sometimes it will be hand-printed by the officer in a box or blank; other times it's preprinted on the ticket, with the officer simply checking the appropriate box. In either case, near the statute number you will often find a very short description of the law (for example, "VC [Vehicle Code Section] 22350—exceeding posted speed"). For speeding violations, in most states you'll also find the speed the officer claims you were going, as well as the posted speed limit on the road where you were stopped.

Now you must look up and read the law the officer claims you violated.

Try the Internet

The fastest way to find your state's traffic laws is on the Internet. In addition to finding the law on the Internet, you can also find state and local court websites there.

To help you get started, the appendix lists the websites for each state's vehicle laws as well as court information for each state. You can usually search your state website using words or terms—for example, "Vehicle Code 15647," or you can scroll through the index of laws usually highlighted on the state's home page.

We also recommend that you consider using Google.com, the popular Internet search engine. If you are searching for a state vehicle law, try using any combination of the following elements:

- Type your state's name.
- If you know it, provide the literal name or number of the law, in quotation marks.
- If you can think of key words that identify the law, provide those as well. For instance, if the law is about speed limits in California school zones, you could probably find it by typing in the terms: "speed limit school zone California."

 CAUTION

Be sure you are reading current law. Once you've found your state's motor vehicle laws, make sure you have your hands on the latest version. This is particularly important if you use books, as described, below. Republished fairly infrequently, these law books are updated with paperback supplements inside the front or back cover.

Useful Internet Resources

Here is a list of some websites you can use to help you research your case:

- The Legal Information Institute website at Cornell Law School has links to many states' motor vehicle (traffic) codes, at www.law .cornell.edu/topics/state_statutes3 .html#motor_vehicles.
- The Legal Research Center on Nolo's website has information about conducting legal research and links to other online legal research resources, at www.nolo.com/lawcenter/statute/ index.cfm.
- Findlaw has links to state motor vehicle laws. Go to http://public .findlaw.com and type "state traffic laws" in the search box.

There are several other websites where groups and individuals provide traffic-fighting strategies and information. The ones we like best are:

- www.motorists.org
- www.mrtraffic.com
- www.speedtrap.org
- www.radartest.com

Use Public and Law Libraries

Most libraries have copies of your state's vehicle laws. This could range anywhere from a single dog-eared volume containing just the fine-print text of traffic laws to a complete multivolume set of all your state's laws. The bigger the library, the more likely it is to have a more comprehensive collection. It's a good idea to call the reference librarian to see what's available before making a trip. In most states you can usually use a courthouse or public law school law library, which will almost surely have a complete set of laws. Often the easiest way to find the text of the law you are charged with is to show your ticket to the research librarian and ask for directions to the proper book.

Read the Law Carefully

Once you find the law you are charged with, study it carefully to determine which facts the prosecution will have to prove to convict you. Many laws are complex. In fact, they are often so convoluted that it's not uncommon to find, upon careful reading, that what you did was not, technically speaking, a violation of the exact words of the statute. Always ask yourself the question: What are the elements (or parts) of the offense I am charged with committing?

For example, in most states the law making U-turns illegal reads like this:

> No person in a residence district shall make a U-turn when any other vehicle is approaching from either direction within 200 feet, except at an intersection when the approaching vehicle is controlled by an official traffic-control device.

You should break this law down into its elements by drawing a line between each clause, like this:

No person in a residence district / shall make a U-turn / when any other vehicle is approaching from either direction / within 200 feet / except at an intersection / when the approaching vehicle / is controlled / by an official traffic-control device.

Focusing on each element of a law is often the key to unlocking an effective defense. That's because to be found guilty of having made this illegal U-turn, the state must prove you violated every "element" or clause of the offense. In this case, the state would have to show specifically that:

1. You were driving in a "residence district"
2. You drove your vehicle in a 180-degree turn, or "U-turn"
3. Another vehicle was approaching within 200 feet or fewer, in front of or behind you, and
4. An "official traffic-control device" at an "intersection" was not controlling the vehicle approaching you.

If you can show that your conduct didn't violate any element of a traffic law, then the law was not violated and the charge should be dismissed. For example, you should be found not guilty if the area where you were ticketed was not a "*residence* district," or the vehicle the officer claims was approaching was over 200 feet away, *or* you were at an intersection controlled by an "official traffic control device."

This type of word-by-word reading of statutes may seem hyper-technical, but it is commonly employed by lawyers and judges. The American legal system is built on the concept that you are innocent unless the state can prove you committed some clearly defined conduct—for example, driving a motor vehicle faster than 65 mph on a public road. (Note that even if you conclude you really have violated every element of a law, your case is not hopeless. In Chapter 3 we discuss other legal challenges you can make.)

Finding Support Using Legal Research

As discussed, our first step is to dissect the wording of the violation you are charged with to see if you committed every element of the offense. If, after doing this, you are not certain you can challenge the law on this ground, there are further steps you can take to build a strong defense. The key skill to build your defense is knowing how to research and understand the laws that apply to the particular legal problem. Fortunately, legal research isn't difficult; you certainly don't need a law degree to do it. The techniques needed for even fairly sophisticated legal research on traffic tickets can be learned in several hours. An excellent tool for helping you do this is the book *Legal Research: How to Find & Understand the Law*, by Steve Elias and Susan Levinkind (Nolo). Below I'll briefly cover several key research techniques.

Finding Case Decisions

Once a law is written, judges use real-life situations to interpret it. Sometimes these decisions (called cases) will make a huge difference to your situation. For example, in all states, speeding for the purpose of being a show-off is a crime called "exhibition of speed." But an appeals court in California expanded the law to include screeching a car's tires (or burning rubber) to impress listeners who can't necessarily see you. This unusual expansion of the words "exhibition of speed" is something you would never know by reading the law alone.

In another example, Ohio's speeding law says you must drive at a "reasonable and prudent" speed. But it does not say whether it is legal to drive over the posted speed limit. A state appeals court ruled, however, that the wording of the law allowed motorists to drive above the posted speed if they are being "reasonable and prudent." Without reading the appeals court decision, the average person would not know that it was legal to drive above the posted speed limit in Ohio.

 TIP

Don't waste time researching a law that is simple and clear. If you are charged with failure to make a complete stop at a stop sign, you probably do not need to research case law. Reading the law itself is probably enough. It's usually a pretty clear law and unlikely to have been changed through court decisions. On the other hand, if the law you're charged under is a bit more complex, case law research can help you answer questions that the statutes or laws themselves don't address. For example, this could be true in a case involving a "presumed" speed law, where your right to see a copy of the officer's notes in advance of the trial has been denied.

There are a few ways to find court decisions that interpret a particular law. A common method is to look in a set of "annotated" codes or laws. This is simply a set of your state's laws that list summaries of court decisions interpreting what the law means. These summaries are found just below the text of each law. Annotated laws can be found in all law libraries, at publicly funded law schools, at principal county courthouses (usually open to the public), and at private law schools where the public is sometimes allowed access. Some larger public libraries also stock annotated codes. Annotated codes are indexed by topic and are kept up-to-date each year with paperback supplements (called "pocket parts") located in a replaceable pocket in the front or back cover of each volume. Don't forget to look through these pocket parts for any law changes or case decisions occurring since the hardcover volume was printed.

Another way to find court cases is on the Internet. Private Internet services such as LexisNexis (www.lexisnexis. com), Versuslaw (www.versuslaw.com), and FindLaw (www.findlaw.com) contain online annotated codes, but you'll have to pay a fee to access them. (We recommend Versuslaw, as it is the least expensive service, and you can use your credit card to pay for services.) You may also be able to find case law regarding certain types of motor vehicle statues by using an Internet search engine such as Google.

Analyzing Court Decisions

Once you find the law you are accused of violating in the annotated law books, skim the brief summaries of the court decisions that interpret the law. Look first for relatively recent cases that involve situations similar to yours where a judge ruled in favor of the defendant because of some circumstances that you, too, might be able to prove. Assuming you find a summary that you think might apply to you, you'll need to read the court's full written opinion to see if it really makes a point that helps you beat your ticket.

Write down the "citation" for the relevant case. This consists of a shorthand identification of the page, volume, and set of law books where the decision or case can be found. (See "How Citations Work," right.) In most states, there are two different sets of volumes of books containing the court decisions, and you'll be given a citation to each, one after the other. It makes no difference which one you use.

If you find annotations to several cases that fit your facts, look first at the most recent one (newer cases often reinterpret or supersede older ones) decided by your state's highest court (called the Supreme Court in every state except New York and Maryland). Cases from your state's intermediate level appeals courts are valid unless overruled by that state's Supreme Court. Finally, you should look at the actual case (not just the summary in the annotated codes). Fortunately, help is available:

- In the law library—Show the law librarian your citation, and

How Citations Work

Decisions of a state's highest court look like this: 155 Cal 422. The first number refers to the 155th volume of California Supreme Court decisions (Cal = California), and the second number directs you to page 422. Similarly, 55 Pa. 345 refers to the 55th volume of the decisions of the Pennsylvania Supreme Court, page 345. In addition, many case citations also may list a 2d, 3d, or 4th after the state abbreviation. Each refers to one of the chronological series of case volumes for that state. For example, the 2nd series might cover cases from 1960 to 1985, and the 3rd series 1986 to the present.

- Online—If you use one of the for-pay services, such as Versuslaw, you should be able to locate it by typing the citation into the site's search engine.

For some helpful free information online, check out Nolo's website (www.nolo.com), which contains detailed information on how to do legal research, including how to find and interpret cases.

Can Other Laws Help Your Case?

Understanding the specific law you violated—and the cases that interpret that law—is just part of your job. Since each law is written to deal with a very specific action (for example, exceeding the speed limit), other laws may also have a bearing on your case. Or put another way, the legal interpretation of one traffic law can sometimes affect another.

Here are some examples:

- Section 123.45.678 of your state's motor vehicle law forbids exceeding 25 mph in a residential district. But section 123.45.605 says all your state's speed limits are "presumed" limits. This means even though you may have technically violated Section 123.45.678, you might be able to successfully claim that it was legal to do so because Section 123.45.605 allows you to exceed the speed limit when driving safely under the circumstances (see Chapter 5 for more on "presumed" speed limits).

- You are ticketed for a violation of Section 123.45.654 of your state's vehicle code for making a U-turn in a "residential district." But Section 123.45.666 defines a residential district as an area with at least four houses per acre of land. Since you made your U-turn in an area with fewer houses per acre than are listed in statute 123.45.666, you can argue you are not guilty of *every element* of Section 123.45.654 and are, therefore, not guilty.

- You are charged with speeding based on the reading of a radar gun used by the police officer. Your ticket says you are charged with a violation of Section 123.45.765 of the vehicle code, speeding. But Section 345.67.898 of the vehicle code says an officer must follow certain procedures in using radar, and you can prove she did not follow the proper procedures (see Chapter 6 for more on radar defenses).

To find information about other laws related to your case, like these here, you will have to look in the index of the annotated codes under subjects that you believe relate to your ticket. Then you need to look up the laws related to those subjects and look for the "annotated" cases listed below the code, just as you did, above.)

Should You Fight Your Ticket?

Understanding Traffic Offenses...16

    "Civil" or "Administrative" Traffic Offenses (Some States) 16

    Traffic Offenses as Crimes (Most States) 17

Negative Consequences of Getting a Ticket..18

    Fines...18

    Insurance Rates..19

    License Suspensions 19

The Traffic School Option...20

Deciding Whether to Fight Your Ticket...21

    Prove a Necessary Element of Your Ticket Is Missing 21

    Challenge the Officer's Subjective Conclusion 22

    Challenge the Officer's Observation of What Happened 22

    Prove Your Conduct Was Based on a Legitimate "Mistake of Fact"...........................23

    Prove Your Conduct Was "Legally Justified" 23

    Prove Your Conduct Was Necessary to Avoid Serious Harm 24

Putting It All Together—How to Decide Whether to Fight or Fold.....................................24

Defenses That Rarely Work 25

Understanding Traffic Offenses

By now you should have analyzed the law you are charged with violating and have a clear understanding of all the elements you are supposed to have transgressed. Before you consume energy, time, and money fighting your case, you'll first want to think about whether it makes sense to move in this direction.

 CAUTION

Always prepare to contest serious violations. If you're charged with anything that could land you in jail—like reckless or drunk driving—it is almost always wise to at least take the first steps necessary to fight the charge. In most states this consists of telling the court clerk you want to plead not guilty and then actually going to court to enter your plea. Doing this will give you time to research the charges you face, including searching for information that might help you fight to reduce the charges to a less-serious offense through a plea bargain. It also gives you time to find and consult a lawyer, if you decide one is necessary (see Chapter 4).

A first step to doing this is to understand the category of offense you are charged with and the consequences you'll face if you fight and lose, or simply decide to pay up. Traffic offenses are classified somewhat differently in different states. You'll learn how this classification system generally works below, and more about your state's system in the appendix.

"Civil" or "Administrative" Traffic Offenses (Some States)

There is an increasing trend among states to "decriminalize" ordinary traffic violations (check the appendix to see if your state is one of them). These states call traffic violations "civil infractions," or similar terms. Although this may sound good, in some instances it can make it harder to fight a ticket. Typically, where tickets are treated as civil offenses, states make it easier to be convicted. Here's how:

- Some states with a civil system do not require proof of guilt "beyond a reasonable doubt"—you can be convicted if a judge decides that a preponderance (more than 50%) of the evidence tends to show you violated the traffic law.
- In some states with a civil traffic violation system, the ticketing officer is not required to show up at the hearing, greatly reducing your chances of casting doubt on his version of events. (Always insist that the officer appear, if you have that choice.)
- Your right to see the evidence against you in advance of the hearing (called "discovery") may be severely limited.

Even if you are charged with a civil traffic offense, you'll find much valuable information on preparing for trial in Chapters 9 and 10.

Different Standards of Proof

In states that have enacted a "civil" or "decriminalized" traffic violation scheme, the burden of proof necessary for a conviction is usually not as strict as in a regular criminal case. Most of these states apply the "preponderance" standard of proof, which is commonly interpreted to mean that more than 50% of the evidence weighs against you, or, it is more likely than not that you committed the offense. This is in contrast to the standard criminal standard of proof, "beyond a reasonable doubt," which places a much higher burden on the prosecutor.

To confuse matters further, there are a few states with civil traffic systems that use yet another standard of proof, called "clear and convincing." This means the state must prove it is "highly probable" (to quote Vermont's statute) that you committed the offense. Clear and convincing evidence is a harder standard for a prosecutor to meet than preponderance, but less difficult than beyond a reasonable doubt.

Traffic Offenses as Crimes (Most States)

In most states traffic violations are still considered criminal offenses. Typically, there are three levels of these offenses: 1) infractions, or "petty" or "summary" offenses, 2) misdemeanors, and 3) felonies. The rights you have to fight a ticket, and the way they are handled in court, depend on which level of offense your state assigns to traffic violations. The consequences will also vary.

"Petty" or "Summary" Offenses or "Infractions"

In the majority of states routine traffic violations are classified as petty or summary offenses or infractions. As these words connote, these are extremely minor criminal offenses. But fortunately, when it comes to mounting your defense, you still have the right to demand that the ticketing officer appear at trial and still may cross-examine the officer, and the prosecution must prove you guilty beyond a reasonable doubt. Unfortunately, in states that classify offenses this way, you do not have the right to trial by jury or the right to a court-appointed lawyer if you can't afford to hire one.

Misdemeanors

In most states a "misdemeanor" is an offense punishable by up to a year in jail and a fine of no more than $1,000 or $2,000. First offense charges of reckless and drunk driving fall into this category in most states. (We do not cover these more serious offenses in this book.) Ordinary traffic tickets are also considered to be misdemeanors in close to half of the states. When you are charged with a misdemeanor, you have all the rights discussed under "infractions" or "petty" offenses discussed above, plus the right to a jury trial.

Felonies

This is the most serious type of offense, usually including repeat offense drunk-driving and hit-and-run accidents causing injury or death. In some states a third or fourth drunk-driving conviction, even if it does not involve injury or death, is treated as a felony. In other states even the second DUI/DWI can be treated as a felony. Conviction of a felony can be punished by a sentence of more than a year in state prison and a substantial fine, although judges in many states have considerable discretion. We do not cover felonies in this book.

CAUTION

Charged with a felony? Get help fast. People charged with a felony need more help than this book can give. Normally you'll want to at least talk to a lawyer with lots of experience in fighting serious traffic cases. Once you are fully informed of your rights and your chances of prevailing in court, it will be time to decide whether to fight back or enter a guilty plea.

Negative Consequences of Getting a Ticket

In all states, only those convicted of the more serious traffic violations, such as drunk or reckless driving, face the possibility of going to jail. State laws do not allow a judge to impose a jail sentence for speeding or failure to stop at a signal. Even where laws do give a judge the discretionary power to jail a traffic offender (sometimes

for repeat offenders), the judge will very rarely choose to exercise it. Even though ordinary violations won't result in jail time, the other consequences of not contesting a ticket, or fighting and being found guilty, can be serious. As you doubtless know, you can face a stiff fine, a day in traffic school, significantly higher insurance premiums, and possibly even the suspension of your driver's license.

Fines

A routine ticket for speeding, failure to yield, or failure to stop at a stop sign will normally cost you between $75 and $300, depending on your state law and sometimes your driving record. If the fine isn't written right on the ticket, it's easy to learn the amount by calling the traffic court. States normally have standard fines for particular violations, based on the type of offense. In speeding cases, the fine can be based on how much you exceeded the posted speed limit. Some states can also set the fine based, at least in part, on whether you have other recent violations.

Because it's expensive for the state if you fight your ticket, courts place hurdles in the way of people who insist on a court hearing, while establishing "no muss, no fuss" options to pay your fine (often called "forfeiting bail"). But while paying up may be easy, it can have lasting negative consequences, since the violation will appear on your driving record, normally for about three years. The big exception to this rule is if you pay the fine in conjunction with going to traffic school. Completion of traffic school normally means the ticket will not appear on your record.

Insurance Rates

Depending on your state law and your insurance company policies, your auto insurance rates will normally not increase if you receive one ordinary moving violation over three to five years. But two or more moving violations—or a moving violation combined with an at-fault accident—during the same time period might result in an increase in your insurance bill. Unfortunately, because insurance companies follow different rules when it comes to raising the rates of policyholders who pay fines or are found guilty of a traffic violation, it's not always easy to know whether it makes sense to fight a ticket from an insurance perspective.

Before you can make an informed choice as to whether to pay, go to school, or fight, it makes sense to find out whether having the ticket on your record will result in your insurance rates being upped. The most direct approach is to call your insurance company and ask. Beware, though, that this approach risks alerting your insurer that you have been ticketed (something you don't want to do if you hope to successfully fight it or go to traffic school).

License Suspensions

You won't lose your license for one or usually even two tickets for a routine moving violation like speeding, running a stoplight or stop sign, or many other garden-variety traffic scrapes. That is unless you are under 18 years of age, where you could lose your driving privileges in some states.

If you are over 18 years of age and have had at least three previous convictions for moving violations in the past three to five years, you could lose your license (parking violations don't count). If you are charged with drunk, reckless, or hit-and-run driving, and have several previous convictions for moving violations, you can be pretty sure your right to continue to hold your license is in jeopardy. In most states suspensions are handled on a point system, with a license at risk of being pulled if a driver gets three or more tickets in a short period (see "How Point Systems Work," below). Check exact rules with your state's department of motor vehicles. Obviously, if you face losing your license, your incentive to fight a ticket goes way up no matter what your chances of winning.

No matter what type of point system is used, you are typically entitled to a hearing in front of a motor vehicle bureau hearing officer before your license can be revoked. At that hearing it is often a good idea to explain why at least some of the violations were the result of mistakes by the ticketing officer, but for some good reason you didn't fight the ticket. It also helps to explain the specific steps you've taken to drive more carefully and safely since the violations.

In states that assess points for accidents, this may be your first opportunity to show the accident wasn't your fault, was difficult to avoid, or was not part of an ongoing pattern of bad driving. Be prepared to do just that. Also, tell the hearing officers if it is essential that you commute to work or actually drive for your job, particularly if you will lose your job if you lose your license. Finally, if you drive 15,000 miles a year or more, you should mention this as well. Argue that since you drive more than average, your chances of getting tickets or having an accident are also above average.

How Point Systems Work

A "point" system assigns a certain number of points for each moving violation. A driver who gets too many points in too short a time loses his or her license. In some states points are also assessed for accidents, even if no court has found you to be at fault. While the details vary from state to state, most systems typically work like this:

State A: Each ordinary moving violation counts as a single point, except two points are assessed for speed violations where the speed is greatly in excess of the speed limit. A license is suspended when a driver receives four points in a year, six in two years, or eight in three years.

State B: Two points are assessed for what are classified as minor violations (an illegal turn or slightly exceeding the speed limit), with three, four, or five points assigned for more serious violations, like illegally running a stop sign or speeding. A license is suspended if a driver gets 12 points over three years.

The Traffic School Option

Almost every state allows a person ticketed for some types of moving violations to attend a six-to-eight hour course in traffic safety in exchange for having the ticket officially wiped from their record. Often attending traffic school is your best choice, even if you think you have a watertight defense. After all, while a trial is always something of a gamble, traffic school is 100% reliable in keeping the violation off your record. (As long as you remember to set your alarm clock and make it to the class.)

Policies on allowing you to eliminate a ticket from your record by going to traffic school vary from state to state. (They can also occasionally vary within a state, where local courts have some discretion to set their own policies.) For example, in some states you can attend traffic school once a year, while in others you must wait 18 to 24 months before you can eliminate a new ticket with a new trip to traffic school. And in some states you aren't eligible for traffic school if you're ticketed for exceeding the speed limit by more than 15 or 20 miles per hour.

Procedures for getting into traffic school also vary from place to place. Most courts allow you to sign up through the court clerk, but a few require that you appear before a judge to make your request. How a traffic school attendee's ticket is handled is also different in different areas. For example, in some states, courts dismiss your case when proof is received that you've completed traffic school. In other states, courts require you to pay your fine (forfeit bail) with the understanding that the conviction will not be placed on your record if you complete traffic school by a prearranged deadline. Under this system you must pay twice—once for the fine and again for the school.

In brief outline, for those who are eligible, the advantages of attending traffic school are as follows:

- As long as you show up, it's normally a 100% sure way to keep a violation off your record.
- It reduces the possibility of your license being lifted or your insurance rates going up if you get new tickets.
- If you pay attention, your driving skills may improve. (Or you may be so bored that you will drive more safely to avoid another day in traffic school.)

The disadvantages of traffic school include:

- It typically lasts six to eight hours.
- In many areas it is expensive. This is especially true if you are in a state where you must pay for traffic school plus the fine for the ticket.
- Depending on your state's rules, it may use up your traffic school option for 12 to 18 months.

TIP

Erase that ticket through online school. In some states, erasing a ticket through traffic school may even be accomplished while sitting at home. For example, California is just one of a number of states where traffic courts authorize Internet-based traffic schools (which use tests and other devices to be sure you are paying attention). This trend is almost sure to spread. But be sure

to check with the court in your particular area to make sure that an Internet-based program is acceptable. Do not pay any money to the traffic school unless you are sure that the court accepts that particular school's program.

CAUTION

You often get only one chance to opt for traffic school. By opting to fight your ticket (whether you lose or just change your mind in the middle), you often forfeit the option of having your case dismissed in exchange for attending traffic school.

Deciding Whether to Fight Your Ticket

If you nix the idea of traffic school—or you aren't eligible—you must decide whether it makes sense to fight or pay up. The decision should be based largely on your informed assessment of whether you have a good chance of beating the ticket. Here are some methods that—depending on the facts of your case—you may be able to use.

Prove a Necessary Element of Your Ticket Is Missing

As discussed in Chapter 2, your first step should be to study the exact language of the law (code section or statute) you were charged with violating. The key fact to remember: If you can prove even one element of the infraction is missing from the facts, you should be found not guilty.

Remember! No Matter Your Defense, You Normally Win If the Officer Fails to Show Up

Suppose you decide you don't have much of a defense. For example, you ran a stop sign right in front of an officer or were caught doing 90 mph on the freeway with a 65-mph limit by an officer who paced you for two miles. Obviously, the attractiveness of traffic school goes up as your chances of beating the ticket in court go down. But what should you do if you aren't eligible for traffic school? Automatically pay the ticket? You can consider one other possibility—although it is often a long shot: The officer may not show up in court. In that case, in most states your ticket will probably be dismissed. But don't count on this happening. It's true that sometimes an officer misses a court appearance while on vacation, due to illness, a scheduling conflict, or other reasons, but officers commonly show up. And the more serious the violation, the more the odds increase of an officer's appearance.

Challenge the Officer's Subjective Conclusion

Remember, in many states, with many tickets, it's perfectly possible—and sometimes even fairly easy—to challenge the police officer's view of what happened. This is particularly likely in situations where a cop must make a subjective judgment as to whether you violated an element of the offense in a situation where no accident ensued. For example, when an officer gives you a ticket for making an unsafe left turn, you may argue that your actions were safe and responsible, considering the prevailing traffic conditions. Of course, it will help your case if you can point to facts that tend to show that the cop was not in a good location to accurately view what happened or was busy doing other tasks (driving 50 mph in heavy traffic, for example). In Chapter 7 we discuss defenses to a number of other types of tickets where an officer must make a judgment call.

In about 20 states, deciding whether it is safe to exceed the speed limit is another circumstance where a subjective judgment must be made. That's because in these states the posted speed limit is not an absolute limit, but only creates a legal presumption as to the safe speed for that road. This in turn raises the possibility of challenging the officer's judgment by proving it was safe to slightly exceed the posted limit.

Challenge the Officer's Observation of What Happened

Assume now your state law requires an objective observation by the officer, not a judgment call about whether your action was safe. This would be true if you were cited for failing to come to a stop at a red light or making a prohibited turn. Defending this type of ticket often boils down to an argument about whose version of the facts is correct. For example, if you say, "The light was still yellow when I entered the intersection," the officer is likely to reply,

"It was red, red, red, ten feet before she got to the crosswalk." In disputes like this, the guy in the badge usually wins unless you can cast real doubt on the officer's ability to accurately perceive what happened. Fortunately, despite the fact that most judges tend to believe cops, there are a number of types of evidence that may work to raise at least a reasonable doubt as to your guilt.

Here are the types of evidence most likely to help you convince a judge:

- Statements of witnesses, such as passengers or bystanders, who testify to your version of events.
- A clear, easy-to-understand diagram showing where your vehicle and the officer's vehicle were in relation to other traffic and key locations and objects, such as an intersection, traffic signal, or another vehicle. Diagrams are especially important for tickets given at intersections, such as right-of-way, stoplight, or stop sign violations. (For more on preparing diagrams, see Chapter 9.)
- Photographs of intersections, stop signs, and road conditions. These can be used to show conditions like obscured stop signs or other physical evidence that backs up your case.
- Any other evidence that would cast doubt on the officer's ability to accurately observe your alleged violation. A classic way to do this is to prove his view was obscured or that his angle of observation made it impossible to accurately see what happened.

Prove Your Conduct Was Based on a Legitimate "Mistake of Fact"

Even if you technically violated a statute, consider whether you have a good defense based on the argument that your conduct was based on a legitimate mistake.

Judges are allowed some leeway in considering circumstances beyond your control. If you can show that you made an honest and reasonable error, a judge might find you made a "mistake of fact" that means your ticket should be dismissed—for example, if you failed to stop at a stop sign after a major storm because the sign was hidden by a broken branch. However, a judge would probably not buy this defense if the sign had been up for more than a few weeks, you drove that route every day, or you were traveling 50 miles per hour in a 25-mph zone.

Prove Your Conduct Was "Legally Justified"

You may also successfully argue that your actions were "legally justified" considering the circumstances of your alleged violation. For example, if you were charged with driving too slowly in the left lane, it is a legal defense in all states that you *had to* slow down to make a lawful left turn. In this situation you do not have to deny that you were driving significantly below the speed limit and causing vehicles behind you to slow down, but you can offer the additional fact that legally justifies your otherwise unlawful action. Such defenses can be very successful because they raise an additional fact or legal point, rather than simply contradicting the officer's testimony.

Here are a couple of examples of situations in which this defense might work:

- You are forced to stop on a freeway because your car began to make a loud and dangerous-sounding noise, and you feared you would put other drivers in danger if you continued to drive without checking it out.
- You swerved into the right lane without signaling a lane change to pull over because a hornet flew into your car through your open window.
- You had sudden and severe chest pain and safely exceeded the posted speed limit to get to the doctor, whose office was only one-half mile away.

Prove Your Conduct Was Necessary to Avoid Serious Harm

Emergencies not of your own making are often another legal "necessity" defense recognized in all 50 states. The key here is to convincingly argue that you were forced to violate the exact wording of a traffic law in order to avoid a serious and immediate danger to yourself or others—for example, you swerve across a double yellow line to avoid hitting another vehicle, pedestrian, animal, or other unexpected obstacle. If you had failed to take such an evasive action, you would have been at high risk of being involved in an accident.

Putting It All Together—How to Decide Whether to Fight or Fold

Here are some questions I always ask to determine whether going to court makes sense:

- Was the officer's view of what occurred obstructed by other moving vehicles or stationary objects like trees, fences, or buildings? If so, this allows you to argue that the officer could not have clearly seen the alleged offense and gives you an opening to sell your version of events to the judge.
- Did the officer stop the right car? It is quite possible in heavy traffic for an officer to see a violation committed by one white minivan (a 1995 Plymouth Voyager, for example) and to stop another (an almost identical white 1994 Dodge Caravan) farther down the road. Your ability to claim this happened (*"the officer got the wrong driver, Your Honor"*) obviously goes way up if you can show that because of a curve in the road, construction project, or just heavy traffic, the officer lost sight of the offending vehicle between the violation and pulling you over.
- Were you charged with speeding when you were driving safely, even though you were driving over the speed limit? In about 20 states, the law says it's legal to drive slightly over the posted

speed limit as long as you can prove conditions made it safe to do so. (Check the appendix to see if your state is a "presumed" speed limit state.)

- Was there an actual, provable error in the officer's approach or methodology? In citing you for speeding, did the officer correctly pace your vehicle or properly use VASCAR, radar, or laser to establish your speed? We discuss what the officer needs to prove for many types of tickets in Chapters 6 and 7.
- Do any other legal defenses exist to the law you're charged with violating? For example, if you were charged with driving too slowly in the left lane of a multilane highway, it is a legal defense (provided for in most state's laws) that you were planning to turn left.

Defenses That Rarely Work

Face it, saying "I didn't do it," or "the officer's lying," without presenting any specifics to back up your contention is highly unlikely to result in your being found not guilty. Similarly, generalized statements about the possible inadequacies of radar or laser techniques almost never result in your beating a speeding ticket. Even if you successfully point out minor inaccuracies on your ticket, such as the officer mistaking the color, make, or model of your car when writing the ticket, you will rarely get off (assuming, of course, the officer appears in court and convincingly explains why your conduct was illegal).

Below we present a laundry list of poor defenses:

- You claim you were honestly mistaken about the law (as opposed to a particular fact, as would be the case with a hidden stop sign).
- You argue your violation didn't harm anybody. The fact that your illegal conduct was not dangerous is not a winning defense, except when you are cited for speeding in states where it can be legal to exceed the posted speed.
- "The officer was picking on me." This is called "selective enforcement" and is often raised by a motorist who claims the ticketing officer ignored others who were also violating the law. To win with a "selective enforcement" defense, you have to take a huge additional step and show that the officer had a specific and improper motive to pick on you.
- Tell a sympathetic story. The fact that your child, your mother, or your parakeet was ill will not get you off.

Lawyers and What They Can Do for You

What Lawyers Can Do 28

    Consultation and Advice...28

    Negotiation...28

    Representing You in Court...28

Types of Lawyers 29

    Private Attorneys...29

    Group Legal Practices and Prepaid Legal Services 30

    Public Defenders...31

Getting the Most Out of Your Lawyer...31

Firing Your Lawyer...32

I f you have bought this book, you are probably considering representing yourself. And why not? If you are fighting a ticket that could cost between $100 to $300, it makes little sense to hire a lawyer who will charge you upwards of $150 per hour whether you win *or* lose. There are two big exceptions to this go-it-alone rule; seriously consider hiring a lawyer when:

1. Losing your license is a serious possibility, particularly if you need a car to do or get to your work, or
2. Going to jail or paying a huge fine are possibilities. This could happen if you are charged with driving under the influence of drugs or alcohol, reckless driving, or hit-and-run.

> ⓘ **CAUTION**
>
> **Get help with serious charges.** Even if you've had experience in civil court—in a divorce, name change, or a simple lawsuit—it often isn't wise to go it entirely alone when charged with a serious criminal offense, such as drunk driving. It is true that lawyers are not the only people on earth who can learn to handle a relatively straightforward trial. But it is also true that a lawyer with lots of experience in traffic court is almost sure to be a lot further up the learning curve than you are. Even if you decide it doesn't pay to retain a lawyer to represent you, paying for a couple of "lawyer coaching" sessions by someone who can help fine-tune your strategy can be an excellent idea.

What Lawyers Can Do

There are three basic ways a lawyer can help when you are charged with a traffic violation.

Consultation and Advice

The lawyer can listen to the details of your situation, analyze your legal position, and give you the pros and cons of several alternate courses of action. Ideally, the lawyer won't just give you conclusions, but enough good information to allow you to make your own informed choices. This kind of coaching is the least expensive, because it involves only an office call—or sometimes even a phone call. A charge of more than $75 for a half-hour consultation or $150 for an hour might be excessive. Find out the fee before you go in.

Negotiation

For more serious charges you may be able to use the lawyer's skill and experience to help you negotiate with the prosecuting agency. Often a lawyer's previous relationships with the prosecution and experience with plea bargaining can be helpful in limiting the price you might have to pay in terms of jail and penalties.

Representing You in Court

If you face driving-under-the-influence charges or even an ordinary ticket that could result in your license being suspended, a lawyer may be able to present a more effective defense in court than you could muster on your own. Similarly, an experienced lawyer may help you put on a more effective presentation at a motor vehicles bureau license-suspension hearing. Aside from the fact that the lawyer probably knows more than you do about effective trial tactics, it's important to understand that if the consequences of losing are truly serious, you will likely be under significant pressure and stress. This helps explain why inexperienced defendants often tend to make two big mistakes. First, they are disorganized, with the result that their version of the facts is rarely clearly presented. Second, they often focus the court's attention on reams of insignificant details, forgetting to concentrate on the one or two key points that can influence the decision. In contrast, a lawyer well schooled in traffic court knows which defenses work and which do not, and how to make a presentation in court.

TIP

Don't pay a big up-front fee. People are most scared right after they receive a serious ticket. Knowing this, some lawyers immediately ask for as much as a $5,000 retainer to be paid in advance in a serious case like drunk driving. Months later, they often advise their client to plead guilty—a result the client could have achieved on his or her own at no cost. To prevent this from happening to you, follow these rules:

- Never hire a lawyer in a hurry. Nothing serious will happen in your case for at least a week or two after you are cited (and by posting bail or pleading not guilty you can further slow things down), so take your time.
- Make sure you know what you are charged with and have followed the techniques set forth in this book to analyze your chances of winning in court.
- Make sure you hire one of the relatively few lawyers who have lots of experience in traffic court.
- Don't pay or agree to pay a big fee. Instead, pay the lawyer a small amount to help you thoroughly evaluate your case. Then, much later, armed with all the facts, decide if you want to pay more to hire the lawyer to represent you in court or represent yourself.

Types of Lawyers

Now let's look at the various kinds of lawyers and lawyer services that are available.

Private Attorneys

Most lawyers in private practice are not adequately equipped to help you mount a traffic court defense. Like physicians, most lawyers specialize. Just as you wouldn't want a foot doctor operating on your eye, you don't want a divorce lawyer defending you in a traffic or criminal case. Unfortunately, relatively few lawyers specialize in traffic ticket defense. But in every metropolitan area, a number of attorneys will routinely handle more serious vehicle code violations, such as drunk driving. These people are usually competent to advise you on how to defend yourself against garden-variety tickets. To find one of these traffic court experts, use the same sorts of commonsense techniques you use to find quality services in other fields. Ask around among lawyers, legal secretaries, or business associates for a recommendation of a traffic court pro.

TIP

Local is best. It's usually best to hire a lawyer who routinely works in the court where your case will be handled. That's because a local lawyer will know the idiosyncrasies of the judges and prosecutors who will handle your case. Just being able to chat with these folks on a first-name basis can be a huge help.

CAUTION

Beware of referral panels of local bar associations. In most parts of America, lawyers listed by referral panels are not screened. Often, attorneys who place their names on these panels are either new to the practice of law or don't have enough business. While you could get an excellent lawyer this way, you may well end up paying to educate a lawyer who doesn't know as much as you'll learn in this book.

Once you have the name of a lawyer or, preferably, several lawyers who handle traffic or criminal cases, it often makes sense to hire one for an initial consultation for an agreed-in-advance fee. Some lawyers will briefly discuss your case for free, or

charge you $50 or $75 for half an hour. For a more detailed, hour-long discussion of the facts of a serious case and presentation of the lawyer's suggestions, payment of $100 to $150 is fair. A consultation should allow you to learn important information about your case while you evaluate whether it makes sense to work with the particular lawyer. In some areas you can attempt to do the same thing by looking for a lawyer who will provide a free initial consultation, but too often you'll end up with a bottom-of-the-barrel lawyer who doesn't have enough paying clients.

TIP

From the beginning, you should make it clear if you want to participate in your defense. Some lawyers are pleased to explain all the legal aspects of your case and involve you in making good strategic decisions. Others prefer an "I'm the expert, you're the novice" approach, under which they expect you to listen and follow their advice. Especially if you are handling some or all of your own case, this second approach clearly won't work, meaning you'll need to find someone else.

Group Legal Practices and Prepaid Legal Services

A growing number of people join prepaid legal plans, which typically charge between $80 and $250 per year. Many groups, including unions, employers, alumni associations, and consumer action groups, are offering plans to their members under which they can get legal assistance for rates that are substantially lower than most private practitioners. Some of these plans are good, some mediocre, and a few are worthless. When it comes to traffic court cases, your first step is to see whether your plan provides coverage for your type of violation or one or more free consultations for any legal problem. Then, if you are eligible for help, you should be sure you are referred to an attorney with real expertise in handling traffic or criminal cases.

 CAUTION

Beware of reduced fee legal plans. Some low-end prepaid legal plans purport to give members legal services at a reduced cost. There are two problems with this. First, you have to go to a lawyer on the plan's local panel who may know little about traffic court. Second, the fee discount is often an illusion. Often, with a couple of phone calls you could negotiate the same fee with a real expert. The worst prepaid legal services plans provide for a free half-hour consultation with a lawyer, but little more. After that one meeting, you pay the lawyer by the hour, either at a standard or "reduced" fee. Since the plan reimburses the lawyer almost nothing for your consultation, the lawyer is highly motivated to talk you into buying expensive services you may not need.

Public Defenders

If you cannot afford to hire an attorney, and you face the possibility of jail time, you have the right to request help from a court-appointed attorney. Since most vehicle code violations do not result in jail time, you are not likely to get a court-appointed attorney unless you face reckless driving, drunken driving, or other very serious charges, which are not covered in this book.

The legal determination of whether or not you can afford a lawyer depends upon the requirements specified by the particular state or county. A judge may appoint a public defender or private lawyer to represent you under the following circumstances:

- You have a relatively low-paying job or are unemployed.
- Your family is living on a tight budget.
- You do not have a savings account large enough to pay a lawyer.

Getting the Most Out of Your Lawyer

In addition to finding competent and conscientious lawyers in the first place, your best approach is to pay the lawyer based on work produced, not an up-front retainer. A pay-as-you-go approach will give your lawyer an incentive to keep hustling and make it easier for you to politely but firmly fire the lawyer if you decide to end your relationship—something you have the right to do at any time.

Firing Your Lawyer

You have the right to fire your lawyer if you decide you have chosen the wrong one. You have the right to do this at any time—whether or not your bill is fully paid. It is best to do this in writing. If you fax or email your letter, follow up with an original copy and keep one copy for yourself. No need to say more than, "I no longer wish you to represent me." ●

Speed Violations:
Understanding the Laws of Your State

Three Types of Speed Limits 34

"Absolute" Speed Limits 35

"Presumed" Speed Limits 35

The "Basic" Speed Law 39

Speeding tickets are, by far, the most common moving violation. For starters, there are two things you need to know about your speeding ticket. First, were you charged under an "absolute," "presumed," or "basic" speed law? (Don't worry, we'll explain this jargon below.) Second, you need to know how the cop determined your speed—through pacing, aircraft, radar, laser, VASCAR, or other means. We discuss types of speed limits in this chapter and methods of speed detection in Chapter 6.

Three Types of Speed Limits

The 50 states basically use three types of speed limits. We call these "absolute," "presumed" (or "prima facie" in legalese), and "basic" speed limits. Because each type of speed-limit violation often requires a unique defense, it is key to understand which you are charged with violating. (See the appendix under "Speed Laws" for the rules of your state.)

Most states have an "absolute" speed law. There is no trick to how this works: If the sign says 40 mph and you drive 41 mph or more, you have violated the law.

"Presumed" speed-limit violations are a little more complicated but give you far more flexibility in building your defense. In states that use this system for all or some of their roads—California and Texas, for example—it's legal to drive over the posted limit as long as you are driving safely. For example, if you are driving 50 mph in a 40-mph zone, you are "presumed" to be speeding. But if it is 6 a.m. on a clear, dry morning with no other cars on a wide,

straight road, *and* you can convince the judge that you were driving safely given those conditions, you should be acquitted. That's because you present facts that "rebut the presumption" that by going over the limit you were driving at an unsafe speed. (We'll give you more information about this below.)

The concept of the basic speed law is even trickier. It works like this: In all states you can be charged with speeding by violating the "basic" speed law, even if you were driving *below* the posted speed limit. The ticketing officer must simply decide that you were going faster than you should have, taking into account the driving conditions at the time. Or put another way, if you are driving 40 mph in a 45-mph zone on an icy road in heavy fog, a cop could sensibly conclude that by driving too fast for road conditions you are in violation of the "basic" speed law. This type of ticket is mostly handed out after an accident.

To find out which system your state or locality follows, start by looking up your state's law under "Speed Laws" in the appendix, and then study the law itself.

Here are a few samples:

- Pennsylvania: All speed limits are "absolute."
- Texas: Almost all speed laws are "presumed."
- California: Speed limits are "absolute" on freeways but "presumed" almost everywhere else.
- Colorado: Some speed limits on city streets and county roads are "presumed." But most limits are "absolute."

CAUTION

Read the law, not just our appendix. Before preparing to defend your speeding ticket, be sure to read the exact law you're charged with violating. To find the exact speed law you are charged under, refer to Chapter 2, where you will learn the tools necessary to find and analyze the law. Unfortunately, it is sometimes hard to tell from simply reading your state speeding law whether it follows the "absolute" or "presumed" method. Here are a few things to keep in mind:

If your state's laws refer to a "maximum" speed limit, it is most likely "absolute," so that it is illegal to exceed by even 1 mph, period.

If your state's laws refer to a speed limit above which it is "unlawful to exceed," or your state's law says something like "no person shall drive in excess" of that posted or set speed limit, that speed limit is "absolute."

If the law sets speed limits but then just says it's "lawful"—in the absence of a hazard—to drive below the speed limit, without flatly saying it's illegal to exceed that limit, the speed limit is probably "presumed."

If the law says it's merely "prima facie unlawful" to exceed the posted speed limit, without reference to "maximum" limits, and it doesn't flatly forbid driving at a speed over the limit, the speed limit is likely "presumed."

"Absolute" Speed Limits

SKIP AHEAD

You may skip this section if you were ticketed on a road covered by a "presumed" speed limit.

When you're charged with exceeding a posted speed limit in an area where the limit is "absolute," the law is simple. You are guilty if you drive over the speed limit.

Your only defenses are:

- Attacking the officer's determination of your speed. To do this you must discover what method the officer used to cite you and then learn about the ways to attack that particular method.
- Claiming an emergency forced you to exceed the speed limit to avoid serious damage or injury to yourself or others.
- Claiming that the officer mistook your car for another car. With so many similar-looking cars, it is possible that a cop could see a speeding car, lose sight of it around a corner, and then wrongly pick out your car farther down the road.

In Chapter 6 we will help you build your defense by showing you how to challenge all common methods used to determine whether you were speeding. These methods will work whether you were ticketed in an "absolute" or "presumed" speeding area.

"Presumed" Speed Limits

In areas with "presumed" speed limits, the law usually reads something like this:

No person shall drive a vehicle upon a highway at a speed greater than is reasonable or prudent having due regard for weather, visibility, the traffic on, and the surface and width of, the highway, and in no event at a speed that endangers the safety of persons or property. Unless conditions require a lower speed, the speed of any vehicle upon a highway below the limits established as authorized herein is prima facie lawful. The speed of any vehicle on a highway, in excess of the speed limits herein, is prima facie unlawful, unless the defendant establishes by competent evidence that the speed in excess of said limits did not constitute a violation at the time, place, and under the road, weather, and traffic conditions then existing.

CAUTION

State statutes vary. The wording of each state's law will vary slightly, so be sure to read yours carefully.

If you're accused of violating a "presumed" speed limit, you have two possible defenses:

1. Claim you weren't exceeding the posted speed limit, just as you would if you were charged with violating an "absolute" speed law, or

2. Claim that, even if you were exceeding the posted limit, you were driving safely given the specific road, weather, and traffic conditions at the time.

Occasionally an officer will incorrectly measure your speed. (We discuss how this happens and possible defenses in Chapter 6.) But even if he does, it can be hard to convince a judge to accept your version of what happened. In short, if you were ticketed in a "presumed" speed area, it is most sensible to rely on the argument that you may have been driving slightly over the posted speed limit, but it was safe to do so considering all the highway conditions at the time. For example, if you

know you were driving 33 to 35 mph in a 25-mph zone, and the officer can probably prove it, you should concentrate your defense on showing that you were driving at a reasonable speed, considering the conditions at the time you were stopped.

TIP

Tailor your defense to what the officer says. Before you testify, you'll have a chance to listen to what the officer says and to cross-examine him. If you work quickly, you'll have the opportunity to tailor your testimony to his answers. For example, if the officer testifies he paced your car for a very short distance or simply eyeballed you and concluded you were speeding, you could attempt to cast doubt on the accuracy of the officer's determination of your speed. But if his testimony as to how he established your speed seems foolproof (he carefully paced you at a constant distance for a quarter mile), you could concentrate on arguing that you were driving safely under prevailing conditions at the time you were ticketed.

As mentioned, being charged with violating a "presumed" speed limit means you are accused of driving at an unsafe speed, considering the conditions at the time you were ticketed. But most cops don't look at it this way. They reason that if you are over the posted limit, you are a law-breaker. That's why you really do have a good chance of prevailing if you can show you were just slightly over the limit and road, weather, and traffic conditions were good.

But be aware that the "presumed" speed limit law works both ways. On a pleasant summer morning on a wide, uncrowded highway, it may be safe to drive above the posted speed limit. However, on a wet day when visibility is limited by fog, it may not be safe to drive at the posted speed limit. In short, an officer can still ticket you for driving *at or below* the posted limit, if it is unsafe to do so. This is true in all states.

Now let's focus on how you might successfully mount a defense to a "presumed" speed limit ticket. Start by understanding it is not like a typical criminal defense, where the prosecution must prove you committed an illegal act beyond a reasonable doubt. (See Chapter 13 for an explanation.) In a "presumed" speed law defense, you (the defendant) have the burden of proving your speed was safe and prudent. In other words, the speed law presumes the posted speed limit is the fastest safe speed. It is up to you to prove that going faster at the time you were ticketed is also safe.

EXAMPLE:

Bill was clocked by radar driving 43 mph on a street where 35-mph signs were properly posted. The law of his state contains a presumption that the posted speed limit is reasonable or prudent. To fight this ticket based on a claim that it was prudent to drive 43 mph, Bill will have to overcome the presumption that 35 mph was the only safe speed at the time he was ticketed. He might do this by showing there was no traffic at the time he was stopped and that the weather was clear and dry.

No question, proving that your speed was safe becomes more difficult the more your speed exceeds the posted limit. Convincing a judge it was reasonable and prudent to go 38 mph in a 35-mph zone may not be too hard. (Which helps explain why police officers rarely write tickets for speeding less than 5 mph over the speed limit.) But proving that it was safe to go 65 mph in a 35-mph zone will be close to impossible.

But remember that there are many wide, straight roads designed for safe driving at 35 to 50 mph that have lower posted speed limits because of political pressure on public officials to crack down on speeding. Your testimony, backed by photographs, could show that your speed was safe on these broad, straight roads, even though you were driving faster than the posted limit. If you have weather, visibility, and traffic factors in your favor, a judge might find you not guilty, even if you exceeded a posted speed limit.

EXAMPLE:

You are driving to work on Saturday morning at 7 a.m. (grumpy over having to work on the weekend). Realizing that you are running late (and not wanting the boss to chew you out), you are doing 35 mph in a 25-mph zone on a wide, two-lane arterial street when a cop nails you for speeding. You go to court and argue:

1. Few other cars were on the road, and
2. Traffic lights controlled traffic at all major cross streets, and

3. Visibility was great, and the sun was shining.

Regardless of whether you were driving five or 25 miles per hour over the speed limit, the strategy for attacking a speeding ticket in a "presumed" speed state is usually the same. You should attempt to prove that good weather and visibility, road configuration, and lack of traffic combined to make a higher speed perfectly safe. But it's rarely enough to simply tell the judge that the road looked safe to you. Instead, you'll want to introduce convincing proof to back up your position.

Here are important ways to build your case:

- Go back to the scene and take photos at the same time and day of the week you were cited. Also, take a photo from the driver's viewpoint. It's obviously to your benefit if you can establish the road was straight, with good visibility. It helps if you can show you were not in a residential area, where children might run out into the street or cars could back out of driveways. It could also help if you were pulled over at a time when few cars or people would normally be present (see Chapter 9).
- Diagram the road, showing the location of your vehicle, the officer's vehicle, and any other traffic. (See Chapter 9 on preparing your testimony for trial.) It helps if you were not ticketed in a busy commercial district where cars enter and exit parking lots and businesses. And it will almost

surely help if you can show you were ticketed on a wide, straight business street with a low posted speed limit early on Thanksgiving morning, when there was no vehicle or pedestrian traffic to justify the restricted speed. If you were going over the speed limit, it helps if there were few intersections along your route. If there were many intersections, be prepared to show that they were clearly controlled by lights and stop signs. (Sorry, uncontrolled intersections and speed don't go well together.)

- Although proving traffic was light is best, all is not lost if the road was busy. Indeed, the presence of heavy traffic can sometimes be a plus if you present your case skillfully. With lots of other cars on the road, your argument could be that "everyone was exceeding the speed limit by about 10 mph, and I would have endangered myself and others by driving slower than the flow of traffic." You might even want to argue that, had you driven more slowly, you would have violated your state's law on illegally impeding traffic. (Make sure you look up the exact law in your state's vehicle code and quote it to the judge. See Chapter 2.)
- Get a copy of the officer's notes (see Chapter 8) so you'll know what he's likely to say at trial. If he didn't make any specific notes about other traffic or pedestrians, curves, hills, or obstacles, he probably won't mention them at trial. This gives a good

opening to cross-examine him on those issues to show that in fact the road was relatively wide, straight, and free of obstacles (see Chapter 10).

The "Basic" Speed Law

"Absolute" speed states set an upper limit, above which your speed is considered illegal. Drive one mile over the limit and you are a lawbreaker. But these states also have a way to ticket you when you are driving under the speed limit if the cop concludes your speed was unsafe. Called the "basic" speed law, it prohibits driving at an unsafe speed, even if that speed is below the posted limit.

"Presumed" speed limit states also have the same law, although it is usually written into the "presumed" law. Or put another way, since the posted speed limit is presumed to be safe only when road or traffic conditions are good, the presumption can be rebutted by the police officer and the safe speed can be much lower.

But technicalities aside, in all states, tickets for driving under the speed limit, but too fast to be safe, are often referred to as "driving too fast for conditions."

For example, driving exactly at the 65-mph posted limit on the freeway would be really dumb amidst slower and heavy traffic, in a dense fog, or in a driving rainstorm or blizzard. In commonsense terms, such unsafe driving is unlawful, regardless of higher speed limits. Police most often rely on the "basic" speed law after an accident. They reason that you were driving too

fast, no matter how slow you were driving, because you were in an accident.

The difference between fighting one of these tickets and a speeding ticket for going over the speed limit is that here the prosecution has the burden of proving you were driving unsafely. (Again, that's because the posted speed limit is presumed to be safe.) This means the officer must testify that given the unusual road, weather, or traffic conditions, your below-the-limit speed was still unsafe. This can be tough to do unless you were involved in an accident, because the cop may be hard put to come up with enough evidence to rebut the presumption established by the posted limit. If you were in an accident, the officer will probably try to show that it was evidence you were driving at an unsafe speed, and if your speed had been lower, you would have avoided the accident.

However, you do not have to despair even if you were in an accident and are charged with violating the "basic" law for driving at an unsafe below-the-limit speed. The fact that you've had an accident is not absolute proof that you were driving unsafely. Accidents, after all, are not always caused by you violating the law. Often, they are caused when another driver screwed up.

If the police officer argues that the accident itself is *evidence* that you were driving at an unsafe speed, even though you were not technically speeding, you must be prepared to challenge him. Your best bets are normally to claim, and hopefully prove, that the accident could have occurred for a number of reasons. For example, it could have been:

- Entirely or partly another driver's fault
- The result of a freak act of nature, in the form of a sudden wind gust, a tree falling, or other natural occurrence, or
- A defect in the highway, signs, or signals, which would happen if kids stole a stop sign or a stoplight fails.

> **CAUTION**
>
> **Never plead guilty to a ticket issued to you following an accident. Seek the advice of an attorney.** Even if you don't want to fight the ticket, you should enter a "nolo contendere" plea, which is a way of not fighting the charges (see Chapter 8). A guilty plea can be used against you if anyone involved in the accident sues you for damages. By contrast, if you fight a citation and lose, a guilty verdict might be used against you in a civil lawsuit arising from the accident. If you have been involved in an accident, you may want to contact a lawyer for advice and/or representation.

Speed Detection: Pacing, Aircraft, VASCAR, Radar, and Laser— How They Work, How to Fight Them

Getting Caught 42

How Was Your Speed Measured? 43

    Pacing 43

    Aircraft Speed Detection 47

    VASCAR 50

    Radar 56

    Laser 64

Getting Caught

There may be only one way to speed, but there are half a dozen ways to get caught. Generally, police use the following methods to catch you:

- **A visual estimate.** The officer sees your car and estimates how fast you are going.
- **Pacing.** The police officer follows your vehicle at the same speed you are traveling and checks the policecar's speedometer to see how fast you are going.
- **Timing.** The officer times your vehicle along a premeasured stretch of road and is able to calculate how fast you were going.
- **VASCAR.** The officer uses a computer program to mark your time between two points and calculate your speed.
- **Radar.** The officer points a radar gun at your car and it calculates your speed.
- **Laser.** The officer points a laser gun at your car and it calculates your speed.

Not all methods are allowed in all places. California, for example, forbids the use of timing devices over fixed distances, outlaws VASCAR, and forbids radar on some roads. In Pennsylvania, only the state police—not local law enforcement—can use radar, and VASCAR can be used only if the measured speed exceeds the posted speed limit by 10 mph or more. (See appendix for details on your state.)

CAUTION

Research your own state law. If you are going to challenge the method used by the police officer to nab you for speeding, you will have to track down the state laws that authorize and control the method used against you. We explain how to do the needed research in Chapter 2.

CAUTION

Be aware of hearsay. In challenging your ticket, you will want to be aware of a key legal rule called "hearsay" that could help your case. The hearsay rule prohibits any testimony that quotes information from somebody other than the witness. This is sometimes called the "he said" rule because it forbids a witness from testifying to what somebody else said he saw. There is a huge catch to this hearsay prohibition— just like Perry Mason, you must affirmatively object or the judge will allow the testimony. Here are the most common situations in which a prosecutor is most likely to use hearsay evidence to prove a speed violation:

- An officer testifies about what another driver told her about your behavior.
- The officer who wrote your ticket testifies about what another officer told her. This is particularly likely to happen where an aircraft monitored your speed and relayed the information to a patrol car that stopped you.
- Where two officers were in a patrol car, and one of them observed your driving. The officer who did not see your driving may not testify to what the other officer told him about your driving.

How Was Your Speed Measured?

The key to challenging a speeding ticket is to know what method the officer used to determine your speed. It may not be obvious to you which method was used. First, remember to politely ask the officer when you are stopped. Second, you'll want to obtain a copy of the officer's notes before your trial (see Chapter 8 on "discovery") to learn what method was used.

Here we discuss the five most common methods of speed detection. If you know for certain what method was used to nab you, go directly to that section.

Pacing

Many speeding tickets result from the police officer following or "pacing" a suspected speeder and using his or her own speedometer to clock the suspect's speed.

How Pacing Works

With this technique, the officer must maintain a constant distance between her vehicle and the suspect's car long enough to make a reasonably accurate estimate of its speed. Some states have rules that the officer must verify speed by pacing over a certain distance. (For example, at least one-eighth or one-fourth of a mile.) In practice—even in states that don't require pacing over a minimum distance—most traffic officers will usually try to follow you for a reasonable distance to increase the effectiveness of their testimony, should you contest the ticket.

 TIP

Road configuration may help prove inadequate pacing. Hills, curves, traffic lights, and stop signs can all help you prove that an officer did not pace you long enough. For example, an officer following your vehicle a few hundred feet behind will often lose sight of it at a curve, not allowing enough distance to properly pace the vehicle. Similarly, if you were ticketed within 500 feet of starting up from a stop sign or light, the officer will not be able to prove that she paced your car for a reasonable distance.

How Pacing Fails

Now let's discuss the most common ways pacing can be shown to be inaccurate.

The Farther Back the Officer, the Less Accurate the Pace

For an accurate "pace," the officer must keep an equal distance between her car and your car for the entire time you are being paced. The officer's speedometer reading, after all, means nothing if she is driving faster than you are in an attempt to catch up with you. That's why an officer is trained to "bumper pace" your car by keeping a constant distance between her front bumper and your rear bumper. Doing this correctly requires both training and good depth perception, and it becomes more difficult the farther behind the officer is from your car. (The most accurate pace occurs where the officer is right behind you.) But patrol officers like to remain some distance behind a suspect, to avoid alerting a driver who periodically glances at his rearview and sideview mirrors. So if you know an officer was close behind you for only a short distance, your best tactic in court is to try to show that the officer's supposed "pacing" speed was really just a "catch-up" speed. You will want to ask the officer the distance over which she tailed you. If she admits it was, say, only one-eighth mile (between one and two city blocks), it will

help to testify (if true) that you noticed in your rearview mirror that the officer was closing the gap between your car and hers very quickly. This would have the effect of giving her a high speedometer reading (represented graphically on the next page).

Your goal is to use the speeds that the officer testified to for her car while she was pacing you to argue that she used her speed

The Math of Pacing

V_{you} = your speed

V_{cop} = the officer's speed as she closes

D_{you} = the distance you travel during the "pace"

D_{cop} = the distance the officer travels during the "pace"

D_{cop0} = the distance the officer was behind you, when she started the "pace"

t = the time the officer took to start from D_{cop0} behind you, to catch up to you, and wind up on your tail.

This formula can prove the officer improperly paced you. But there is one problem. The judge may not allow it as evidence. Normally, in court, legal rules of evidence require a mathematician or expert to use this kind of testimony. But you may be able to present it in your closing argument, where the rules of evidence don't come into play.

Here's how it's derived:

Speed equals Distance divided by Time, and Time is equal to Distance divided by Speed. In mathematical symbols, since $v=d/t$, then $t=d/v$. The time, t, over which the pacing occurred will be the same for you and the officer. Therefore, this time t will equal both (D_{you}/V_{you}) and (D_{cop}/V_{cop}), which are equal to each other, both being equal to time t. Therefore, (D_{cop}/V_{cop}) = (D_{you}/V_{you}). It's also true that if the officer drove faster to gain on you, then $D_{cop} = D_{you}$ + the distance the officer was originally behind you (D_{cop0}). Also from rearranging (D_{cop}/V_{cop}) = (D_{you}/V_{cop}), we get $D_{cop} = (D_{you} \times V_{cop})/V_{you}$. These last two D_{cop} equations are equal to each other, so, $D_{you} + D_{cop}$ behind = (D_{you} and V_{cop})/V_{you}. Rearranging this last equation gives: $V_{you} = (D_{you} \times V_{cop})/(D_{you} + D_{cop}$ behind). Dividing both numerator and denominator by D_{you}, we get: $V_{you} = V_{cop}/[1 + (D_{cop}$ behind$/D_{you})]$.)

Pacing Formula

First, the officer starts following you:

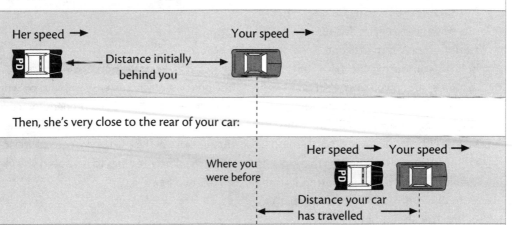

Then, she's very close to the rear of your car:

The faster the police car is bearing down on you, the more distance it will cover over any time interval. The mathematical relationship between the officer's speed and yours—the distance the officer initially was behind you, and the distance your car traveled after the officer began following you—can be expressed by the formula:

$$\text{Your speed} = \cfrac{\text{Officer's speed}}{\left[1 + \cfrac{\text{Distance the officer was initially behind you}}{\text{Distance your car traveled until she was on your bumper}}\right]}$$

Here's an example of how this formula works. Assume the officer was going 75 mph on the freeway. (They do it all the time.) She started out one-quarter mile behind you and tailed you for one and one-half miles. Finally, she bore down on you. She will say that, since her speed was 75 mph, your speed was 75 mph too. However, your speed works out to:

$$\text{Your speed} = \cfrac{\text{75 mph (officer's speed)}}{\left[1 + \cfrac{\text{¼ mile initially behind you}}{\text{1½ miles you drove as she followed you}}\right]} = 64.3 \text{ mph}$$

Obviously, this would have the effect of giving her a higher speedometer reading than yours.

while closing in on you as you were driving under the speed limit. Here is how to do this:

1. Read the material on how to cross-examine the officer in Chapter 11.

2. Pin down the officer during cross-examination on the distance she was behind you during the pace and the distance she paced you. (See above for how to do this.) At that point, you can use a calculator to figure—based on the officer's answers, pacing and tailing distances—whether these speeds and distances, inserted into the formula, will result in a speed that is below the speed limit.

3. Later, when your turn comes to testify, emphasize (if true) how you initially saw the patrol car some distance back in your rearview mirror, then saw it bear down on you quickly.

4. Be sure to also testify (if true) that you periodically glanced at your speedometer, which indicated a steady speed, and that you didn't slow down when you saw the patrol car.

5. During your final argument, you should emphasize the point that your testimony and the officer's both show that she was actually closing in on you when she claimed to be measuring your speed, not truly pacing you at a constant speed. Then, if the above formula will result in your speed being below the limit, explain that there is a simple mathematical formula to show your true speed. Show how it is derived (see above), and how, when the numbers are plugged in, it shows

your speed was below the speed limit. (See Chapter 12 for closing arguments before a judge and Chapter 13 for closing arguments before a jury.)

TIP

Practice, practice, practice. If you are pretty sure your defense will turn on whether the officer really paced you properly, practice explaining the speed formula ahead of time. Bring a large piece of thick white paper to court, so that after the officer testifies to her speed you can plug in this number.

Pacing at Dusk or Night

Pacing is much more difficult in the failing light of dusk or in complete darkness, unless the officer is right on your tail. In darkness, the officer's visual cues are reduced to a pair of taillights. Also, if an officer paces a speeder's taillights from far back in traffic, she'll have trouble keeping the same pair of taillights in view. In Chapter 10, we include a few cross-examination questions to bring this out during the trial.

Road Conditions Can Affect Pacing

Pacing is easiest and most accurate on a straight road, with no hills, dips, or other obstacles and where the officer can see your vehicle continuously as she follows you. This allows her to keep her car at a constant distance behind you while she paces your speed. Hills, freeway interchanges, dips, curves, busy intersections, and heavy traffic make for a poor pacing environment. All of these obstacles can be used to challenge the accurate pacing of your vehicle.

Aircraft Speed Detection

Many drivers are ticketed for speeding when a ground patrol unit is alerted to their speeds by a radio report from an airplane. Obviously, this is especially common in states with lots of wide-open highway. If your ticket was based on information from one of these aircraft patrols, there are several possible ways you may be able to challenge it.

How Aircraft Speed Detection Works

There are two ways an aircraft officer determines your speed. The first is to calculate your speed by timing how long it takes for your vehicle to pass between two highway markings at a premeasured distance apart. The second involves a kind of "pacing" of the target vehicle, but from the aircraft. The pilot uses a stopwatch to time its own passage over highway markings that are a known distance apart. Then the aircraft is used to pace your vehicle's speed. As we'll see, this second method is less accurate and therefore easier to attack.

Under either system, if a car is found to be speeding, a waiting ground patrol car is radioed. If that ground patrol car does not independently verify your speed, your chances of successfully fighting your ticket go up. For starters, that's because both the aircraft and ground officer will have to be present in court. The aircraft officer must testify as to how he measured your speed, and the ground officer must say that you were, in fact, the driver. If the pilot appears in court but the ground officer does not,

the prosecution cannot prove its case in the majority of states that treat traffic cases as minor criminal violations. In part, this is because you are not required to testify, because the Fifth Amendment to the Constitution gives you the right to remain silent. However, in states that treat traffic violations as "civil offenses," you may not have this right to remain silent (see Chapter 3).

 TIP

Ask for a dismissal if either officer fails to appear. If both officers are not in court, ask the judge to dismiss the case. If the prosecution tries to introduce an absent officer's police report or other written record into court in place of live testimony, simply object on the basis that it is hearsay. Without an officer present, the written report is inadmissible hearsay testimony. For more on how to object and insist that the case be dismissed, see Chapter 11.

Even if both officers show up, you still may have a decent opportunity of winning a case where an airplane is involved. To maximize your chances, ask the judge to exclude one officer from the courtroom while the other is testifying. (See Chapter 12 for more on why and how to do this.) Don't worry, you are not being impolite but only exercising your right to prevent the two cops from taking cues from each other's remarks.

How Aircraft Speed Detection Fails

Fortunately for you, there are several good ways to challenge tickets based on an aircraft's measuring your speed.

Stopwatch Error/Reaction Time

If the timing is not performed properly from the aircraft, the speed of your vehicle will be wrong. Since this speed is calculated by dividing distance by time, the shorter the distance your speed was measured over, the more likely it is that a timing error on the part of the sky cop will result in a too-high speed reading. If the officer hesitated even slightly before pushing the timer as you passed the first ground marker, the measured time would be shorter than the true time your vehicle took to traverse the distance to the second marker.

EXAMPLE:

Officer Aircop sees Dawn Driver pass between two markings an eighth of a mile apart. At a speed of 65 mph—the speed limit—Dawn's car should cross the two marks in 6.9 seconds. But if Officer Aircop starts the stopwatch a second too late or stops it a second too early and gets 5.9 seconds, he incorrectly figures Dawn's speed to be (0.125 mile/5.9 sec.) x 3,600 = 76 mph.

The longer the distance between the ground markings, the more accurate the officer's reading is likely to be. A one-second error in starting the stopwatch will result in only about a 1-mph error, where the distance between markers is a mile. (See Chapter 10 for cross-examination questions that highlight this error.)

Difficulty in Keeping Your Car in View

If two markers are a mile apart, it takes a car doing 75 mph some 48 seconds to travel between the two markers. It's hard to stare continuously at anything for that long, especially from a plane. If many other cars are on the road, it would be easy for the sky officer to lose sight of your car while he is looking at his flight instruments.

You should raise this possibility on cross-examination by asking the airplane officer about procedures during her flight. Your goal is to get the officer to admit that she did not continuously watch your car during the pacing. Hopefully, you will learn that the officer must keep a log for every vehicle she paces, recording the vehicle's basic description, the time between the two points, and the calculated speed. In short, the officer is usually also keeping track of other cars. If you establish this during cross-examination, you can argue in your final argument that the officer might have started to pace your car, but mistakenly focused on another car that looked like yours after looking up from taking notes. (See Chapter 10 on cross-examination.)

Using the Aircraft to Pace You

The second method by which an officer in an aircraft can determine your speed involves two steps: (1) timing the aircraft's passage over two separate highway markings a known distance apart to get the aircraft's speed and then (2) using the aircraft to "pace" your vehicle. For example, if the aircraft passes over two markings a mile apart in 60 seconds, the aircraft's speed is 1 mile/60 seconds, or 0.0167 mile per second. Since there are 3,600 seconds in an hour, this 0.0167 mile per second is multiplied by 3,600 to get miles per hour, or 60 mph. If the car below stays ahead of the aircraft, it's going 60 mph; if it's pulling away, it's going faster. The officer in the plane then radios this information to the officer on the ground. This method is less accurate than timing a car's passage between two points for the following reasons:

- **Inconsistent distance while pacing.** It's much more difficult for an aircraft pilot than for the driver of a police car to maintain the same distance behind the paced vehicle.

- **Inaccuracy in ascertaining reference points from the air.** For the officer in the air to determine his speed, he has to time the passage of his plane over two markers several thousand feet below. This is done by starting a stopwatch as the plane passes the first marker on the roadway and by stopping the watch as the second marker is crossed. The speed is then determined by dividing the distance between the markers by the elapsed time. This sounds reliable enough, but it often isn't. For starters, it is difficult for a pilot to know exactly when he passed a spot on the ground. An inconsistency in the aircop's body position within the aircraft, by even a few feet, as he times the passage, can add several miles per hour to your estimated speed.

- **Wind conditions can also affect the speed of the aircraft.** If a headwind comes up after the aircraft has timed its passage over two markers its airspeed would be decreased. That would make it appear to the aircop as if you were going faster than you actually were.

Problems Identifying the Vehicle

After testifying about how the speed was computed, the aircraft officer will next testify about radioing the information to the ground officer who stopped you. Here you'll again want to raise the possibility that the ground cop stopped the wrong car. Given that license plate numbers are too small for the airborne officer to see, and many modern cars look very much alike, this is a real possibility.

 TIP

Ask the pilot how many cars he fingered for speeding. Often aircraft officers relay information on several speeding cars at the same time. This, of course, increases the possibility that the ground officer might confuse different cars. If the ground officer is excluded from the courtroom, she will take the copy of the ticket with her, since she issued it. This means the aircraft officer won't be able to use the ticket to "refresh his memory" while testifying. In Chapter 10 we discuss cross-examination techniques, including suggested questions for this situation.

More About Aircraft Tickets

When the aircraft officer identifies a car going too fast (either by pacing it or measuring its speed between two marks), he normally records the time, speed, vehicle color, and type, along with brief notes on the car, in what's usually called an "observation log." As noted in Chapter 9, you have the right to request a copy of this log before trial. It really does pay to examine this log. Here are some things to look for:

- References to multiple vehicles, thus raising identity problems
- Hard-to-believe identical speeds for multiple vehicles
- Short distances between markers, creating a greater chance for reaction-time errors, and
- Long distances between markers, raising possible vehicle-identity problems.

You may also see that the timing occurred over less than a minute, or even that your car was described as being a different make or color than it really is. Obviously, tidbits like these are extremely useful to prepare questions that cast doubt on the reliability of the pacer's observations.

If the patrol officer on the ground testifies that he independently checked your speed by means of pacing, try to establish that he overly relied on the radio report and didn't really pace you for an extended period. See Section 1, above, for how to challenge the accuracy of pacing.

Converting Miles Per Hour to Feet Per Second

Some judges will insist that you explain your math when you talk about translating miles per hour into feet per second. Here is how to do it: There are 5,280 feet in a mile, so one mile per hour is 5,280 feet per hour. Since there are 60 seconds in a minute and 60 minutes in an hour—or 60 x 60 seconds in an hour (3,600 seconds)—one mile an hour, or 5,280 feet per hour, is really 5,280 feet per 3,600 seconds, or 1.47 feet per second. If one mile per hour is 1.47 feet per second, you multiply the speed, in miles per hour, by 1.47, to get the speed in feet per second.

MPH	Ft/Sec
20	29.4
30	44.1
40	58.8
50	73.5
60	88.2
70	102.9

VASCAR

Most states allow police officers to catch speeders using technology called VASCAR (Visual Average Speed Computer and Recorder). Despite the fancy name, VASCAR amounts to a stopwatch coupled electronically with a calculator. The calculator divides the distance the target vehicle travels (as recorded by the stopwatch) by the time it took to travel that distance. For example, a car passing between two points 200 feet apart, over two seconds, is traveling an average speed of 200/2 or 100 feet per second, which converts to 68 miles per hour.

How VASCAR Works

VASCAR is not like a radar or laser gun, which gives a readout of a vehicle's speed by simply pointing and pulling the trigger. A VASCAR unit requires far more human input than radar or laser guns. As we will see, this also greatly increases the possibility of mistakes.

VASCAR works like this: The officer measures the distance between the two points by using a measuring tape or uses her vehicle's odometer, which is connected to the VASCAR unit. When the officer sees the target vehicle pass one of two points, she pushes a button to start the electronic stopwatch, then pushes it again to stop it when the vehicle passes the second point.

EXAMPLE 1:

On a busy street, the officer uses a tape to measure the distance between two road signs, which comes to 234 feet. She then goes back to her car and dials this number on her VASCAR unit. When a car passes the first sign, the officer presses the "time" switch, then presses it again when the car passes the second sign. If the elapsed time is 2.75 seconds, the VASCAR unit calculates the average speed as 234 feet divided by 2.75 seconds, or 85.1 feet per second (57.9 mph).

EXAMPLE 2:

Another officer picks one point at a marked crosswalk and another at a manhole cover in the street. The officer drives the distance between the two points, making sure to press the distance button on the VASCAR unit when she drives over the crosswalk and again when she reaches the manhole cover. The odometer connected to her VASCAR unit measures a distance of 0.12 mile or 633 feet and records this in its memory. The officer then picks a hidden spot where she has a clear view of both points, and waits. A motorcycle passes the crosswalk line, and the officer clicks the "time" button, then clicks it again when the vehicle crosses over the manhole cover 6.78 seconds later. The VASCAR unit calculates the speed as 633 feet in 6.78 seconds, or 93.4 feet per second (63.5 mph).

A VASCAR unit is normally connected to an officer's odometer to allow her to measure a distance between two preselected points while driving past them. This also allows her to use the unit while moving. VASCAR units are engineered to take into account the police unit's speed and the suspected vehicle's speed by pressing the "time" switch twice as your car passes the two preselected points, and by pressing the "distance" button twice as her car traverses those same two points.

The officer can use a VASCAR unit in five ways:

- While stationary. The officer manually measures a certain distance with a tape or other measuring device, dials that measurement into the VASCAR unit, then clicks the "time" switch when the car passes the first and second distance marks.
- While stationary, after having driven a set distance in her vehicle and using the odometer to enter that distance into the VASCAR unit. Again, the cop clicks the "time" switch when the car passes the first and second distance marks.
- While following you and allowing the VASCAR unit to take into account that her patrol car is also moving.

  EXAMPLE:

  While 200 feet behind you on a downgrade where the officer has a good field of vision, he watches you pass a no-parking sign and clicks the "time" switch. He pushes the "distance" switch as he passes the same sign, then pushes the "time" switch again after you pass a shadow made across the road by a telephone pole. Finally, he pushes the "distance" switch a second time as he passes that same phone-pole shadow. The VASCAR calculator divides the distance by the time to calculate the speed.

- While ahead of you, by pressing the "distance" switch twice as she passes between the two points, then the "time" switch twice as she watches you—in her rearview or sideview mirror—pass over the same two points.
- While driving in the opposite direction, by clicking the "time" switch as you pass a point well ahead of her and by simultaneously pressing the "time" and the "distance" buttons as your cars go past each other—setting the second point. Then the officer presses the "distance" switch as she reaches the first point where she started to time you. (She then makes a quick U-turn to pull you over.)

VASCAR is obviously a much more flexible tool than pacing, since the officer does not have to be going the same speed as you are or follow you over any particular distance. As long as she manipulates the "time" and "distance" switches correctly and consistently, while accurately observing when your vehicle and hers pass over the same two points, she can accurately track your speed.

But fortunately (from your point of view) using VASCAR correctly isn't easy. For example, it is no easy thing to accurately push the "time" and "distance" buttons while observing the target pass between two points, at least one of which is almost sure to be far away from the officer. And, of course, doing this accurately is even harder when the patrol car is moving.

How VASCAR Fails

Because speed is defined as distance traveled per unit of time, timing an object's passage between two measured points seems foolproof. But because VASCAR measurement depends entirely on human input—accurately pushing the button for "time" and "distance"—it is easy for errors to creep in. The most common three mistakes that can cause error in a VASCAR measurement are:

- The inability of the officer to accurately see when a distant car passes a distant point
- The officer's reaction time (how long it takes her to push the button when a car passes a marker), and
- The accuracy of the odometer on the officer's car.

In its Legal Defense Kit for defending traffic tickets, the National Motorists Association of Waunaukee, Wisconsin (www. motorists.com) includes a scientific study entitled "An Error Analysis of VASCAR-Plus," by Kenneth A. Moore of JAG Engineering, Manassas, Virginia. Through numerous calculations, charts, and graphs, Moore demonstrates that VASCAR is most prone to error where the distance between the two clocking points is 1,500 feet or more. (He also agrees that it is prone to error below 500 feet.)

The possibility of VASCAR error is so well known that Pennsylvania lawmakers have taken action. Pennsylvania law (Title 75, Section 3368) forbids a VASCAR speeding conviction—where the speed limit is less than 55 mph—if the VASCAR speed readout isn't more than 10 mph over the limit. That's another way of saying, "We don't trust the accuracy of a VASCAR unit that says '44 mph' when the speed limit is 35."

Different Types of VASCAR Errors

Short Distances. At short distances—generally fewer than 500 feet—reaction-time error is most likely to produce an incorrect VASCAR result. If the officer is late to the trigger when you cross the first measuring point, but accurate as you cross the second point, you will be clocked as going faster than you actually were. For this reason, a federally commissioned study of VASCAR recommends that to obtain accurate VASCAR readings, officers measure speeds over elapsed times of at least four seconds for stationary police units and five seconds for moving units.

The name of this study is "Analysis of VASCAR" and it is available for download from the U.S. Department of Transportation's On-Line Publications website, at http://isddc.dot.gov. To find the study, go to the site's main search page and plug in the publication's number (DOT HS 807 748) or the keyword "VASCAR."

Long Distances. When VASCAR is used at distances over 1,500 feet, reaction-time errors are less of an issue. (Half a second one way or the other won't make much difference.) Here, significant errors usually result because the officer simply doesn't see when you pass the marker point farthest from her car because it is too far away.

If you're charged with speeding and the officer used VASCAR, you should try to bring up these possibilities for inaccuracy at trial. The best way to do this is to cross-examine the officer, knowing what questions to ask (see Chapter 11).

Officer's Observation of Distant Point

When an officer times the passage of a car between two points, she must accurately record when the car passes each. This becomes more difficult the farther the officer is from either point. This is especially true at dusk, at night, and during bad weather, particularly fog or rain. For example, while VASCAR can be used at night, the officer must be able to see when vehicle headlights pass objects that may be illuminated poorly or not at all. Obviously, this is far more difficult than watching a car pass two nearby points at noon in good weather.

EXAMPLE:

At dusk, the officer is parked near the first point—a crosswalk. The second point—a phone pole—is 500 feet away. The officer can see and accurately react to your car passing the crosswalk near him. But due to poor visibility and a poor visual angle, he slightly misjudges when you passed the distant shadow of the telephone pole. It took you six seconds to drive that distance (your speed was 500/6=83.3 feet per second, or 56 mph). However, because the officer misjudges when your car passed the second point, he clicks the VASCAR "time" switch after only five seconds and your speed is calculated erroneously at 500/5=100 feet per seconds or 68 mph. In short, his one-second error results in your speed being recorded as 12 mph too fast.

It follows that in court, whenever a VASCAR ticket turns on an officer's ability to record when your car passes a distant spot, you'll want to challenge her testimony that she could see your vehicle clearly. (See Chapter 11 on cross-examination.)

Officer's Reaction Time

Reaction time is the time between observing something and responding to it. Especially where the distance between the two points is only a few hundred feet, an officer's reaction time will greatly affect the speed calculated by the VASCAR unit. Here's why: The shorter the distance between the two points, the lower the elapsed time a speeding car will take to pass through those two points. For example, if the distance is only 100 feet, the car will pass the second point in only a second or two, meaning a reaction-time error of only a few tenths of a second will affect the accuracy by 20 or 30%. On the other hand, if the distance between the two points is 1,000 feet—which takes 15 seconds for a car going 40 mph to pass—a reaction-time error of a few tenths of a second will affect the accuracy by only 1 to 2%.

EXAMPLE:

The speed limit is 45 mph. The distance between the two points is 100 feet, and your car covers that distance in 1.54 seconds. Your speed is 100/1.54=64.9 feet per second, or 44.2 mph, which is legal. But if the officer pushes the "time" switch 0.124 seconds after you pass the first point (the average reaction time of race car drivers) and then she records your passage past the second point more accurately (which is likely because she can anticipate, rather than react), the VASCAR elapsed time will be 1.42 seconds. Your speed will be incorrectly read as 100/1.42=70.4 feet per second, or 48 mph, which is illegal.

In promotional materials, VASCAR manufacturers claim reaction time isn't a factor, because they assume that the officer will anticipate, rather than react to, your car passing each point. They also argue that any delayed reaction will be the same for each click of the VASCAR unit, thereby canceling out the error. This is faulty reasoning. There's no guarantee that the officer will delay the same interval when pushing the button as you pass the first and then the second points. In fact, she may do a much better job at the second point because her eyes have now been fixed on your car for quite some time, making her better prepared to press the button. The result can easily be that she's erroneously shortened the time and, thereby, increased your recorded speed.

Reaction-time error is likely to be worst in the situation where the officer's vehicle is approaching yours from the opposite direction. For example, if you're doing 65 mph northbound, and an officer is doing the same speed southbound, your closing speed is 130 mph, or 191 feet per second. If you're 500 feet away, the officer has little more than two seconds to look ahead, watch your vehicle pass one point, hit the "time switch," then hit the "time" switch again simultaneously with the "distance" switch as your cars pass each other. The officer then has a few more seconds to hit the "distance" switch a second time, hopefully just as she passes the same point you passed when she hit the "time" switch the first time. Operating VASCAR in the opposite direction is so difficult to do well that some police agencies discourage officers from using it this way.

Your main goal is to attack the officer's reaction time through cross-examination (see Chapter 10), focusing your questions on the difficulty in timing a car's passage past a distant point. When it is your turn to testify, tell the judge in detail (if true) that your speed was at or under the limit—or safely above it in a "presumed" speed limit state. Finally, be prepared to argue during your closing argument (see Chapters 12 and 13) how your testimony as well as the officer's responses to your cross-examination questions raise a reasonable doubt over whether you were violating the speeding law.

Odometer Error

The VASCAR unit's accuracy depends on the accuracy of the police vehicle's odometer, except where the distance between the two points is independently measured with a tape and dialed into the VASCAR unit. That is because the VASCAR gets its distance information via the patrol vehicle's speedometer/odometer, to which it is connected.

As the patrol vehicle moves forward, the cable linking the VASCAR unit to the speedometer/odometer turns, calculating how far the vehicle has moved from Point A to Point B. It is supposed to be recalibrated at least once a year. Tire wear and pressure can affect the accuracy of a speedometer. These factors will also affect odometer accuracy, because the odometer and speedometer both run off the same cable.

For example, low tire pressure and tire wear on the police vehicle can result in a tire with a slightly smaller circumference than a new and properly inflated tire. The smaller wheel must make more revolutions to cover the same distance as a new tire. This results in erroneously high speedometer readings and in an exaggerated odometer distance reading. Since speed is distance divided by time, an erroneously high odometer distance fed into the VASCAR unit will result in an erroneously high speed reading.

This type of error, however, is usually fairly small. For example, a 24-inch diameter tire that has lost 1/4-inch of tread will be 23.75 inches in diameter, a mere 2% less, so that the recorded distance and speed will be only 2% high. Still, this type of error, when added to other types of errors—like the ones listed above—may well result in an erroneous VASCAR reading. So, during cross-examination, ask when the VASCAR unit was last tested. If it was not tested recently, or the officer does not know when it was tested last, you should attack the accuracy of the test in your closing argument. (See Chapters 12 and 13.)

Radar

Because so many speeding tickets involve the use of radar measurement systems, let's briefly examine how radar works. Of course, the point of doing this is so you'll be well positioned to cast doubt on the accuracy of your radar ticket. It can sometimes be an uphill battle trying to convince a judge that a sophisticated electronic radar device is fallible. But it is definitely possible to do this. After you've read what follows, you'll know more about radar than most judges and some police officers, and may be able to use your knowledge to beat your ticket.

CAUTION

Don't confuse radar with laser. You need to determine how you were caught. You can ask the ticketing officer what method she used, and testify to that in court. Or you can demand to see the officer's notes, which will indicate what method was used to clock your speed. While radar and laser detection systems work in a similar way, the way to fight them in court has significant differences. Be sure you know which one was used against you.

How Radar Works

The word "radar" is an acronym for "Radio Detection And Ranging." In simple terms, radar uses radio waves reflected off a moving object to determine its speed. With police radar, that moving object is your car. Radar units generate the waves with a transmitter. When they bounce back off your car, they are picked up and amplified by a receiver so they can be analyzed. The analysis is then reflected in a speed-readout device.

Radar systems use radio waves similar to those involved in AM and FM radio transmissions, but with a higher frequency— up to 24 billion waves per second as compared to one million per second for AM radio. Why so high? Because the higher the frequency, the straighter the beam, the truer the reflection, and the more accurate the speed reading. It's important to know this because, as we discuss below, the primary defense to a radar speeding ticket is to attack its accuracy.

To better understand how radar works, remember what it was like to blow peas out of a straw as a kid. If you blew the peas at the trunk of a stationary car, they would (at least theoretically) take the same amount of time to bounce back and hit you in the forehead. If the car had been moving away from you, the peas would each take a longer time to hit and bounce back. The radar beam sends out billions of electronic pulses (like peas) per second and sends back reflected waves whose pulses are slightly farther apart.

The greater the difference between the transmitted and reflected waves, the greater the relative speed or difference of speed between the target vehicle and the police car.

Although radar signals can be bounced off stationary or moving objects, they cannot be bent over hills or around curves. To clock your speed with radar, this means

you must be in an officer's line of sight. However, don't expect to see the radar unit. Officers can hide it behind roadside shrubbery or stick it out unobtrusively from behind a parked car.

Unfortunately for errant motorists, modern radar units are fairly easy to operate. Officers using them do not have to be certified or licensed. But it's also true that to operate radar units with a high rate of accuracy under all sorts of road and weather conditions takes practice and skill. The best way to learn is with the help of an experienced instructor. It follows that it will usually look bad in court if an arresting officer admits she's never had any formal instruction in the use of radar equipment. Realizing this, most officers will say (either when making their presentation or in answer to your cross-examination questions) that they have taken a course in how to use radar. It's important for you to know that this course can range anywhere from a short pep talk by a company sales representative to a few hours or even a day of instruction at a police academy. Either way, most officers don't receive comprehensive instruction on the important fine points of using radar.

This gives you the opportunity to use cross-examination questions to try to pin the officer down (see Chapter 11) on just how few hours she actually spent on good instruction. Assuming you succeed in doing this, you'll then want to make the point, during your closing argument, that the officer could well have misused the unit. For example, the officer may not have realized that at a distance of a few hundred feet, a radar beam is wide enough to cover four lanes of traffic, and thus might have clocked a nearby vehicle instead of yours. And as we discuss in the rest of this chapter, there are a number of other ways officers commonly produce false radar readings.

How Radar Is Used/Types of Equipment

Although many brands of radar units are in use, they all fall into two types: car-mounted units that can be operated while the officer's vehicle is stationary or moving, and hand-held radar "guns" often used by motorcycle officers in a stationary position. Let's briefly look at the distinguishing characteristics of each with the idea of using our knowledge to mount an effective defense.

Car-Mounted Units

Most radar antennas used in patrol vehicles are shaped something like a side-mounted spotlight without the glass on the front. They are usually mounted on the rear left window of the police car facing towards the rear. If you're sharp-eyed and know what to look for, you can sometimes see one sticking out from a line of parked cars.

But no matter where the antenna is mounted, the officer reads your speed on a small console mounted on or under the dash. The unit has a digital readout that displays the highest speed read during the second or two your vehicle passes through the beam. This means that once you go through the radar beam, slowing down does no good. These units also have a "speed set" switch that can be set to the speed at which the officer has decided a ticket is appropriate.

This allows the officer to direct his attention elsewhere while your car travels through the beam. If the speed reading exceeds the "speed set" value, a sound alarm goes off. The officer looks at the readout, then at your car, and takes off after you.

Most modern police radar units can also operate in a "moving mode," allowing the officer to determine a vehicle's speed even though her own patrol vehicle is moving. In moving mode, the radar receiver measures the frequency of two reflected signals: the one reflected from the target vehicle—as in the stationary mode—and another signal bounced or reflected off the road as the patrol vehicle moves forward. The frequencies of these two signals indicate the relative speed between the officer's vehicle and the target, and the officer's speed relative to the road. The target vehicle's speed is then calculated by adding or subtracting these two speeds, depending on whether the two vehicles are moving in the same, or opposite, directions. This calculation is done automatically, by the electronics in the radar unit.

EXAMPLE 1:

Moving radar from opposite direction: A police car is going north on a two-lane road at 50 mph. Your vehicle is heading south at 45 mph. This means the vehicles are closing in on each other at a combined or relative speed of 95 mph. The radar unit in the 50-mph patrol car with its beam pointed at your car will receive a reflected radar signal indicating a 95 mph combined speed, as well as a signal indicating the officer's

50-mph speed relative to the road. After the police vehicle's 50-mph speed is subtracted from the 95-mph relative speed, your actual speed of 45 mph is obtained.

EXAMPLE 2:

Moving radar from same direction: A radar-equipped patrol car is traveling 50 mph. A truck is traveling 70 mph in the same direction as the officer. The officer would like to know how fast that truck is going. Since both vehicles are going in the same direction, with the truck pulling away from the patrol car, the relative speed between the two vehicles is 20 mph. The radar beam reflecting back from the road shows the officer's 50-mph speed. The unit adds the 20-mph difference between the truck and the officer to this 50-mph speed. The result is a reading showing that the truck is going 70 mph.

Hand-Held Radar Units

Hand-held radar guns are used most often by motorcycle officers. A radar gun is simply a gun-shaped plastic mold containing the transmitter, receiver, and antenna. The antenna is normally mounted at the front of the gun, and a digital speed readout is mounted on the back. A trigger is included, allowing the officer to activate the radar beam only when she sees a car that appears to be traveling fast enough to spark her interest.

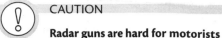

CAUTION

Radar guns are hard for motorists to detect. Radar detectors have a difficult time detecting hand-held radar devices. While car-mounted police radar units often transmit a steady signal that can be detected hundreds of feet or even yards down the road, radar guns usually do not transmit steady signals. (The convenient trigger on the hand-held unit allows the officer to activate it only when the targeted vehicle is close enough for the officer to clearly see and aim the gun.) So, when the officer finally pulls the trigger and your radar detector beeps a warning, it's usually too late to slow down.

How Radar Fails

Contrary to police department propaganda, new technology has not completely ironed out problems known to cause radar malfunctions. Most screwups result from the radar's operation in real-world conditions, which are often far less than ideal. And, of course, human error can also cause radar devices to fail.

One good way to point out all the pitfalls of radar readings is to subpoena the radar unit's instruction manual. (See Chapter 9 for how to do this.) The manufacturer will usually include a page or two on inaccurate readings and how to avoid them. If you study the manual, you may find a way to attack its reliability in court using the manufacturer's own words.

TIP

Make sure the manual is complete.
Police departments have been known to tear out pages that discuss common radar screwups from the radar manual before responding to a subpoena. So be sure to look to see if any pages are missing and, of course, point out any gaps you discover.

The following are descriptions of common malfunctions and sources of inaccurate readings.

More Than One Target
Radar beams are similar to flashlight beams —the farther the beam travels, the more it spreads out. And this simple fact often results in bogus speed readings, since it's common for a spread-out beam to hit two vehicles in adjacent lanes. Most radar units have beam angle or spread of 12 to 16 degrees, or about 1/25th of a full circle. This means the beam will have a width of one foot for every four feet of distance from the radar antenna. Or put another way, the beam width will be two lanes wide (about 40 feet), only 160 feet distant from the radar gun. Thus, if you're in one lane and a faster vehicle is in another, the other vehicle will produce a higher reading on the officer's radar unit, which the officer may mistakenly attribute to you.

The mistaken reading of another vehicle's speed is especially likely to occur if the other vehicle is larger than yours. In fact, the vehicle contributing to the officer's high radar reading needn't even be in another lane; if a larger vehicle, such as a truck,

is rapidly coming up behind you in your lane, the officer may see your car while her radar is reading the truck's speed. Inability of the equipment to distinguish between two separate objects is called lack of "resolution."

TIP

At trial, ask the officer if his radar unit was on automatic. The chances of registering the speed of the wrong car go way up when an officer, who is stationary, points his unit at a highway and puts it on the automatic setting. This is true because the officer isn't pointing at a specific vehicle, and the beam angle width means the unit could be picking up one of several cars going the same, or even opposite, directions. In this case, ask the officer whether there was other traffic in either direction. If his answer is "yes," ask him which direction. If there was traffic in the direction opposite you, follow up and ask him whether the unit responds to traffic in both directions. (See Chapter 10 for sample cross-examination questions of this type.) Either way, if there was other traffic, be sure to raise the possibility in your closing argument that the radar unit clocked the wrong vehicle. (See Chapters 11 and 13.)

Wind, Rain, and Storms
Although metal reflects radar beams better than most surfaces, pretty much any material will reflect radar waves to some extent. In fact, on windy days, windblown dust or even tree leaves are often read by radar devices. And sometimes these spurious readings can be attributed to your vehicle. You may have read newspaper

stories about radar trials in which a hand-held radar gun was pointed at a windblown tree resulting in the tree being "clocked" at 70 mph!

Windblown rain can also reflect enough energy to give false signals, particularly if the wind is strong enough to blow the rain close to horizontal. The more rain or wind, the more likely an erroneous radar reading will result. Pre-thunderstorm atmospheric electrical charges can also interfere with a radar unit. That's because electrically charged storm clouds can reflect a bogus signal back to the radar unit even though they are high in the sky. If such a storm cloud is being blown by the wind at sufficient speed, a false radar reading may result.

Typically, you would attack the radar use by referring to the manual during cross-examination and getting the officer to admit that the manual says errors can occur due to adverse weather conditions. Then in your final argument, you might say something like this: "Your Honor, the officer testified that the radar unit's accuracy can be affected by windblown rain and storm clouds, and she also admitted that at the time, there were clouds and rain."

Calibration Problems

Every scientific instrument used for measuring needs to be regularly calibrated to check its accuracy. Radar equipment is no exception. It must be checked for accuracy against an object traveling at a known (not radar-determined) speed. If the speed on the radar equipment matches the known speed, the unit is properly calibrated. In practice, the best way to do this is to use a tuning fork as the moving object. While this may seem a far cry from a moving car, the use of a tuning fork is scientifically sound; tuning forks, when struck against a hard object, vibrate at a certain frequency which we hear as an audible tone.

More About Tuning Forks

Tuning forks are supplied by the manufacturer of the radar equipment and certified to correspond to the speed marked on the fork. According to most operation manuals, a radar unit should be calibrated with the tuning forks before and after every shift. Ideally, several tuning forks vibrating at different speeds should be used to check the radar unit's accuracy. Since tuning forks can easily become inaccurate, it's important that they be protected from damage. (A good scratch or dent can render one inaccurate.) Keeping the forks in a sturdy box usually protects them.

It is time-consuming to use a tuning fork as a calibration device. So a second, but far less accurate, method has been developed to check the accuracy of radar units. This consist of flicking on the "calibrate" or "test" switch built into the radar unit itself and seeing if it calibrates properly. The unit reads a signal generated by an internal frequency-generating device, called a "crystal." The resulting number is supposed to correlate with a certain predetermined speed.

Unfortunately, there is a big problem with this sort of calibration testing. There are two types of circuits in the unit, frequency circuits and counting circuits. Flicking the calibration switch tests only the counting circuits. In short, if the frequency circuit is not calibrated, the radar unit may well be inaccurate. The Connecticut case of *State v. Tomanelli*, 216 A.2d 625 (1965), indicates that the use of a certified tuning fork is the only scientifically acceptable method of calibrating a radar unit.

The fact that an internal "calibrate" test isn't a substitute for a tuning fork explains why it's so important in any traffic trial involving the use of radar to cross-examine the officer and see whether she really did use a tuning fork before you were ticketed. Typically, they are required to use the tuning fork at the beginning and end of their shifts. If she says "yes," move on to another question. But if she says she didn't, then it's time to ask more specific questions. (See Chapter 10 for suggestions on cross-examination questions on this point.) Of course, if you discover that a tuning fork wasn't used, you'll want to emphasize this as part of your final argument.

False Ground Speed Reading in Moving Radar

A radar unit used while a patrol car is moving must take into account:

- The speed of an oncoming vehicle relative to the patrol car, and
- The speed of the patrol car relative to the ground.

Above, we discussed common ways that a moving radar unit can incorrectly attribute high speed to your vehicle. Here we deal with the notion that radar units can also misjudge the patrol car's speed. This can most easily occur if the radar unit mistakes a signal reflected back from a nearby car or truck for the signal reflected back from the ground.

EXAMPLE:

A patrol car is doing 70 mph southbound and passing a truck going at 50 mph. You are going 65 mph northbound, in the opposite direction. Your car approaches the officer's car at a combined speed of 70 + 65, or 135 mph. The officer's unit detects this 135-mph speed and should subtract his 70-mph ground speed, to get your true speed of 65 mph. Instead, the officer's ground-speed beam fixes on the truck ahead and measures a false 50-mph ground speed. It subtracts only 50 mph from the 135-mph, to get 85 mph for your speed, even though you're doing only 65 mph.

Pulling You Over As Part of a Group of Cars

In situations where several cars proceed over the speed limit, some especially zealous officers will take a radar reading on the "lead" vehicle and then pull it over, along with one or two followers. In court, the officer will try to use the reading for the first vehicle as the speed for everyone else. She may even be up front about this, saying that she saw the vehicles behind following at the same speed. ("There was no change in bumper-to-bumper distances".) Or she may even claim that she also used her radar unit to measure the speed of second and/or third cars. ("When they passed through the beam, there was no change in the reading.")

Either way, this is shaky evidence. To be really accurate, the officer would have had to simultaneously note the lead car's reading while also keeping a close eye on the other cars. (This is something that is especially hard to do if the officer's car was also in motion.) If the driver of the second car can truthfully testify as to how the lead car was going faster and increasing the distance, it should be a big help to establish reasonable doubt in court. And the use of radar to measure the cars is also problematic, since by doing so the officer admits several cars were close together and that she was trying to measure all their speeds almost simultaneously. Here are some possible defenses:

- If you were the driver of the lead car, you may be able to claim that the officer inadvertently locked onto a higher reading of the second or third vehicles that were gaining on you. If the second or third vehicles were larger than yours, the chances of a false reading on your car go up, because the larger vehicle will reflect a stronger signal. In this situation it may help the driver of the lead car if he or she can truthfully testify to seeing (in the rear or side mirror) the second vehicle quickly gaining from behind and suggest that the radar reading was really for that vehicle.
- If you were the driver of one of the vehicles behind the lead car, the vehicles in front of you may have been traveling faster (as lead vehicles often

do). If that vehicle was larger than yours, or closer to the officer's vehicle, this would result in that vehicle's reflected radar signal being stronger. You could argue here that the radar unit read the speed of the car ahead of you, not your slower speed.

About Radar Detectors

No discussion of radar would be complete without a few words on the technology of radar detectors—little black boxes that consist of a sensitive radio receiver adjusted to pick up signals in the radar frequency range. But instead of powering a loudspeaker, this type of radio circuit activates a beeper or light to warn that your speed is being monitored. Many of the commercially available detectors have a sensitivity control that can be adjusted to give the best compromise between trying to detect even faint, far-away police radar signals and attempting to screen out off-frequency signals that come from sources other than police radar.

Radar detectors are illegal in Virginia and the District of Columbia but legal in all other states for most drivers. However, federal regulations, which apply in all states, prohibit commercial big-rig drivers from using them. Where radar detectors are illegal, you can usually be ticketed for having one and have it confiscated. Often this occurs when officers use what, for lack of a better term, are called radar-detector detectors. These are, in essence, radio receivers that pick up the low power signal emitted by most radar detectors.

Even when radar detectors are perfectly legal, some people believe that officers are more likely to issue a ticket—as opposed to a warning—when they see a radar detector in your car.

Laser

Laser detectors are the most recent addition to the traffic officer's arsenal of speed-measuring devices. Built to look and act like a hand-held radar gun, a laser detector uses a low-powered beam of laser light that bounces off the targeted vehicle and returns to a receiver in the unit. The unit then electronically calculates the speed of the targeted vehicle. Laser detectors are supposedly more accurate than radar units.

One advantage for police officers of the laser gun is that the light beam is narrower than a radar beam, meaning that it can be more precisely aimed. This is true even though laser detectors use three separate beams, because the combined width of the three beams is still much narrower than a single radar beam at the same distance. This technology reduces, but does not eliminate, the chance that the speed of a nearby car will be measured, instead of the speed of the car at which the operator aims the gun. Still, there is room for error. Here's why:

Laser detectors measure distance (between the gun and the target car) using the speed of light and the time it takes the light, reflected off the target vehicle, to return to the laser gun. The detector makes about 40 of these distance measurements over a third of a second, then divides the light's round-trip distance by the time, to get the speed. This means to be accurate the officer must hold the combined beams on the same part of the car during the test. While this is easier to do with radar because of its wide beam, it is tricky to do this with a narrow laser beam. Moreover, it's impossible to be sure that it's been accomplished, because the officer can't see the beam. As a result, the laser detector's measurement is highly subject to error.

EXAMPLE:

Officer Krupke fixes her laser gun on Jane's car, which is traveling 60 mph, about 90 feet per second. It travels about 30 feet in the one-third of a second measurement the laser device uses. If the laser beam starts at the windshield and travels to the bumper, it adds about four feet to the 30-foot distance that the machine otherwise would have measured if it had stayed pointed at the windshield. It would incorrectly calculate that Jane went 34 feet, or 102 feet per second, or 68 mph in the one-third of a second it took to measure the speed of her car. The result is that the laser unit registers Jane's speed 8 mph faster than it was actually going. (See Chapter 10 for specific questions to ask when cross-examining the officer.)

It's also possible (especially in heavy traffic) for one beam to hit the target car and another beam to hit a nearby car. The chances of this happening increase with traffic density, and the distance between the laser unit and the measured vehicle. If the two cars are traveling at different speeds, the laser detector will read incorrectly.

Other Moving Violations

Not Stopping at Stop Signs 69

    You Stopped Farther Back 70

    The Stop Sign Was Obscured 70

    Newly Installed Stop Signs 71

    The Limit Line Was Faded 71

Not Stopping at a Stoplight 71

    Your View Was Better Than the Officer's 72

    The Officer Didn't See Your Red Light 73

Automated Enforcement Devices ("Red Light Cameras") 73

Improper Turning 74

    Failing to Stay to the Edge of the Road to Turn 75

    Turns Prohibited by Signs or Marked Lanes 75

    Prohibited U-Turns 76

    Unsafe Turns and Lane Changes 79

Right-of-Way Violations 81

    Right of Way at Intersections 82

Driving Too Slowly 86

    Driving Too Slowly in Left Lane 86

    Impeding Traffic 87

    Failing to Use "Turnouts" 88

Tailgating 88

Unsafe Lane Changes 90

Improper Passing 91

    Endangering Those You Pass 91

    Unsafe "Blind" Passing 91

    Passing on the Right 92

Non-DUI/DWI Alcohol-Related Offenses 92

    Open Container on Driver's or Passenger's Person 92

    Open Container Kept in Vehicle..93

    Drinking in Vehicle 94

    Illegal Drug Use/Possession..95

In most states moving violations other than speeding tickets are treated as petty offenses or infractions not punishable with jail time. Your chances of successfully beating one of these tickets often depends on your ability to show:

- You did not violate every element of the law as written.
- The officer was unable to clearly observe the alleged offense from where he was located.
- The officer lost sight of your vehicle between the time the offense was committed and the time you were stopped, opening up the defense that he mistook your car for the offending car.
- You made a reasonable mistake based on genuinely obscured signs or signals.
- You technically violated the law, but did so in an emergency situation.

> **TIP**
>
> **Tickets involving judgment calls are often beaten.** Statutes that prohibit "unreasonable" actions, like unsafe lane changes or turns, are based on subjective judgments. This gives you the chance to argue that what you did was safe and reasonable under the circumstances. The officer, of course, will probably claim just the opposite. But if you can present evidence supporting your claim that you acted reasonably (and show that the officer didn't have as good a view of the traffic situation as you did), many judges will give you the benefit of the doubt.

> ### Tickets Issued After Accidents
>
> Police officers are rarely present when an accident occurs. Therefore, most tickets written after an accident are handed out without firsthand knowledge of what happened. To figure out what happened, the officer must rely on the positions of the collided vehicles, other people's statements, and possibly your own admissions. Beware! Your own damaging statements can be used against you later in court. Therefore, it is unwise to admit any fault or to discuss what happened with the officer, the other driver, or anyone else. Instead, it's perfectly legal (and can't be held against you later) to simply tell the officer that you're upset and don't wish to discuss what happened until later.

Not Stopping at Stop Signs

Most stop sign laws say something like:

> The driver of any vehicle approaching a stop sign at the entrance to, or within, an intersection, shall stop at a limit line, if marked, otherwise before entering the crosswalk on the near side of the intersection. If there is no limit line or crosswalk, the driver shall stop at the entrance to the intersecting roadway or railroad grade crossing.

To be found guilty of this offense, in most states all the following conditions (legal elements) must be satisfied:

1. You must drive a vehicle and approach a stop sign.
2. The stop sign must be at the entrance to or within an intersection or railroad grade crossing.

3. You must fail to come to a complete stop at:

    a. A limit line (a white stripe painted at or near the beginning of the intersection), if it exists

    b. A crosswalk, if any

    c. The entrance to the intersection or railroad crossing, if there was no marked limit line or crosswalk.

Here are the most successful defenses.

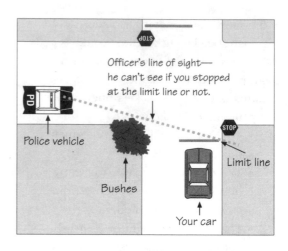

You Stopped Farther Back

Most statutes say you must stop at the limit line, crosswalk, or entrance to the intersection. Practically, this means you must stop slightly before you reach this line. Some conscientious drivers, however, stop farther back from the white marker line or crosswalk. In these cases, an officer hiding behind a bush 50 feet down a side street might not be able to see whether the driver stopped or not.

To mount this defense, first request a copy of the officer's notes (see Chapter 9). Then go back to the scene of the ticket and take pictures from exactly where the officer was sitting. Especially if you can document a visual obstruction—and convincingly testify you did stop—this defense is often a winner. Of course, it's a big help if you can produce a passenger or other witnesses who will sign on to your version of the facts.

The Stop Sign Was Obscured

Here you concede that while you may have run the stop sign, it wasn't your fault.

This can occur if the stop sign is hidden by storm-blown branches, twisted the wrong way by kids, or obscured for any of a variety of reasons. Called a "mistake of fact" defense by lawyers, what this amounts to is your claim that, given the information you had, you made a reasonable mistake and are therefore not guilty. But realize you have to prove your mistake was truly reasonable—it's never enough to say it was "a little hard to see the sign, Your Honor."

    TIP

Pictures are worth a thousand words. Pictures taken from different angles or distances are more convincing than your testimony. For example, if a stop sign is hidden from view by overhanging branches until a few feet before the intersection, take pictures from inside your vehicle (with someone else driving) as the car approaches the sign. Snap one from a distance of 75 feet, and others from 50, 25, and ten feet away from the sign. (Write on the back of each the exact distance from the sign.) In court, you may show your pictures to the judge and explain that they reveal the sign was obscured until it was too late to stop at the intersection. (See Chapter 12 on how to admit evidence.)

> **TIP**
>
> **To video or not to video.** Lots of judges are hostile to videos. Most traffic-court courtrooms are not equipped with video players and monitors, and even if they are, judges may resent the time it takes to set up and watch a video. Certainly, few judges will be willing to peer through the viewer of a portable video camera. If you really feel you need to make your point with a very short video, contact the clerk well in advance to find out whether the judge will let you show it in court.

> **CAUTION**
>
> **Ignorance is no excuse, even in a mistake-of-fact defense.** It is not a mistake-of-fact defense to say you did not know it was illegal to do something illegal (roll through a stop sign, for example). You were taught the rules before you got your license, and you are expected to know them. A mistake-of-fact defense works only if you reasonably lacked a piece of factual and important information when you broke the traffic law. This would be the case if a traffic sign was missing or seriously obscured, but not if it was obvious and you just failed to see or abide by it.

Newly Installed Stop Signs

Another possible mistake-of-fact defense exists if you are ticketed for blowing through a newly installed stop sign. No question, it is easy to miss a new sign on a familiar road. But this has a hope of working only if you can prove the sign really was recently installed and that you used the road frequently before the sign was installed. It will also help if you can introduce pictures into evidence showing the sign was also hard to see from a distance (just around a curve, for example).

The Limit Line Was Faded

Crosswalks and limit lines fade. If you are ticketed at a stop sign for stopping a little too far into an intersection, you may win if you show that the limit line or crosswalk was too faded to see clearly. Here again, a picture is truly better than a thousand words. (See Chapter 10 on introducing photographs into evidence.)

Not Stopping at a Stoplight

Most state laws on stoplights read something like this:

> A driver facing a steady circular red signal shall stop (1) at a marked limit line, or (2) if none, before entering the crosswalk on the near side of the intersection or, (3) if none, then before entering the intersection.

The legal elements of this offense are basically the same as for driving through a stop sign, with one big exception. Stop signs stay red all the time, but traffic lights change colors. Of course, it's always legal to drive safely through an intersection when the light is green or yellow. In fact, in most states, as long as the front of your vehicle entered the intersection (passed the crosswalk or limit line) before the light turned red, you haven't broken the stoplight law.

Here are the most successful defenses.

Your View Was Better Than the Officer's

The only time an officer has a really good view of when your car entered an intersection is when he is sitting directly to the side of, and close to, the intersection (usually either standing on the corner or in a car on the cross street near the corner). But chances are the cop was someplace else—sitting across the street in a parking lot, perhaps.

Cross-examine the officer as to exactly where he was when he says he saw you run the red light. Ask the officer whether other cars were in a position to obscure his view of the intersection. (See Chapter 11 on cross-examination.) Then, when it's your turn to testify, provide detailed testimony, making it clear where you were when you saw the light turn yellow, and how far you were across the intersection when it turned red. (See Chapter 10 on preparing your testimony.) Make a simple diagram like

the one below (adapted for your particular situation, of course) and show it to the judge. (See Chapter 10 for how to do this.) And especially if the cop really did see you from a bad angle, work in the wide receiver analogy—it's a real winner with jock judges.

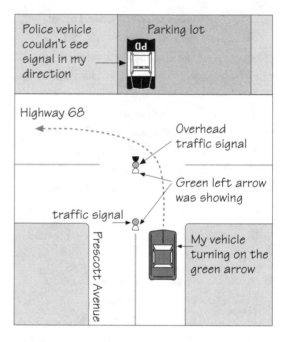

TIP

Bring a witness to court. When a judgment call is involved (such as the location of your front bumper when a light turned red), two observers are always far better than one. If someone riding in your front seat can testify that the light was still yellow when you entered the intersection, you should present her as a witness.

The Officer Didn't See Your Red Light

When a light turns green, we assume the light for cross-traffic has simultaneously turned red. For example, if an officer approaches an intersection with a green light and sees you drive across the intersection, he will assume you ran a red light and won't later check to be sure that the light changes were synchronized. Sometimes they aren't. If you can go back to the scene and document that the light was mistimed, you should be entitled to acquittal. And don't dismiss this possibility—neither machines nor the people who time them are infallible.

 CAUTION

Never claim a yellow light was too short. Traffic engineering practices require the duration of yellow lights to be at least the time it takes to stop if driving at the speed limit. This might tempt you to tell the police officer who stops you or the judge at trial that the yellow light was too short ("fewer than three seconds, Your Honor"). The problem with this defense is you come very close to admitting that you were driving too fast to stop in time, or entered the intersection when the light was red. No joy there.

Automated Enforcement Devices ("Red Light Cameras")

A new twist in defending against red light tickets has occurred in recent years, with the introduction of photographic automated enforcement systems, also known as red light cameras. These devices work by triggering a camera as a vehicle passes over a sensor in the intersection when the light is red. The camera takes pictures of the vehicle's front license plate and driver. A citation is then mailed to the vehicle's registered owner, supposedly after a police officer checks the photo of the driver against the driver's license photo of the registered owner.

In most of the states that allow photo enforcement of red lights, the law states that the driver, not the vehicle's owner, is liable for the ticket. (New York treats red light camera violations like parking citations, making registered owners responsible without regard to who was driving when the camera snapped the photo.) In states where the driver—not necessarily the owner—is responsible for the ticket, and the owner was not driving at the time of the violation, the owner can fill out an affidavit, swearing that he or she wasn't driving when the violations occurred.

The first step to take in fighting a ticket issued by a red light camera device is to get the photographs. In some states, those photos will be mailed to you along with the citation. In other states you will have to make a "discovery" request to get them. When you get the pictures, examine them to see if the picture of the driver bears any likeness to you, and whether the license plate number can be read clearly. For example, Maryland Sen. Alex Mooney successfully fought a ticket for running a red light in 2003 despite a red light camera showing his car speeding through an intersection. Why? Because

Mooney was able to prove to a judge that a car thief was behind the wheel of his car.

At a trial, the government (whether represented by the police officer or a prosecutor) must present evidence on how the device works and that it was working properly on the day the citation was issued. The prosecution must also present the camera's photos showing the vehicle's license plate and the driver, along with the driver's license photo of the vehicle's registered owner.

If the images are clear, you can consider mounting the following defense: If no employee from the company that maintains the red light camera device shows up to testify, you should object to the photos being admitted into evidence, saying, *"Your Honor, since no one has appeared to authenticate the photographic evidence, I object to such evidence for lack of foundation."* If the photographs are excluded, there is no evidence to convict you. (On the other hand, if the judge allows the photos in evidence over this proper objection, you may later have a basis for an appeal if found guilty.)

If the photos are allowed into evidence but the images are not clear, you can consider challenging the photo's clarity, arguing that the evidence is not convincing enough to convict you. You should not agree to testify unless you can truthfully say that you were not driving the vehicle at the time the picture was taken.

If you ran the light to avoid a serious accident or harm to others, you should make that argument, and it's possible that the judge may find that you acted out of "necessity," which may be reason enough to find you not guilty.

Red Light Cameras—Here to Stay?

Although red light cameras are in use in at least 15 states, they are far from universally accepted. Several signs point to a backlash against this automated enforcement system:

- At least five state legislatures (including Alaska, Nebraska, New Jersey, Wisconsin, and Utah) have banned photo enforcement.
- In 2001, a judge in San Diego dismissed 292 red light camera tickets on the grounds that the photos were untrustworthy because Lockheed-Martin, the company that owned and operated the devices for the city, was paid $70 from each $271 fine.
- Anger mounted in Washington, D.C., when police admitted that a red light camera had not been placed in the proper location within an intersection, yet motorists who had been ticketed from that camera and paid the fine were not offered refunds.

Improper Turning

There are many ways to be ticketed for making improper turns. One of the most common is making an improper U-turn. Here we provide information on defending against a wide array of these violations.

Failing to Stay to the Edge of the Road to Turn

Most state laws read like this:

The driver of a vehicle intending to turn upon a highway shall do so as follows:

(a) Right Turns. Both the approach for a right-hand turn and a right-hand turn shall be made as close as practicable to the right-hand curb or edge of the roadway.

(b) Left Turns. The approach for a left turn shall be made as close as practicable to the left-hand edge of the extreme left-hand lane or portion of the roadway lawfully available to traffic moving in the direction of travel of such vehicle, and, when turning at an intersection, the left turn shall not be made before entering the intersection. After entering the intersection, the left turn shall be made so as to leave the intersection in a lane lawfully available to traffic moving in such direction upon the roadway being entered.

The term "as close as practicable" is your best friend in defending against this violation. You will want to present evidence that shows why what you did was the most "practicable" thing to do under the circumstances. These include:

- Avoiding cars parked at the curb
- Steering clear of traffic pulling out of parking spaces
- Avoiding roadside construction, and
- Avoiding pedestrians.

Turns Prohibited by Signs or Marked Lanes

Here are edited versions of the three most common laws that make it illegal to make certain types of turns.

When turning movements are required at an intersection, notice of such requirement shall be given by erection of a sign, unless an additional clearly marked traffic lane is provided for the approach to the turning movement, in which event, notice as applicable to such additional traffic lane shall be given by any official traffic control device.

When right- or left-hand turns are prohibited at an intersection, notice of such prohibition shall be given by erection of a sign.

When official traffic-control devices are placed as required by law, it shall be unlawful for any driver of a vehicle to disobey the directions of such official traffic-control devices.

Basically, all these laws forbid right, left, or other specified turns when "notice" of special turning requirements is given by a sign, signal, or white arrow painted on the road surface. For example, a sign at an intersection may prohibit all U-turns and left turns during certain hours.

Here is one possible defense: You claim you weren't given proper notice of the prohibited turn. For instance, assume you receive a ticket at an intersection where the sign or signal prohibiting a turn was difficult to see because it was turned the wrong way, obscured by a pole, or not visible for some other reason. You argue and prove "reasonable notice" was not given, and the judge dismisses your case.

EXAMPLE:

You're driving home from your new job westbound on a road you have never been on before. It's 4:45 p.m. on a Wednesday in November, and the sun is setting. You enter an intersection and turn left. The setting sun happens to be right next to the sign that says, "No Left Turn 4:00 PM–6:00 PM MON–FRI." Because of the strong glare, you don't see this sign until you have almost completed the turn. In court, you show the judge a photo you took the next day showing the sunset obscuring the sign. You argue that given the circumstances, the sign was poorly engineered. On cross-examination, the officer admits the sign was right where the sun was. You win.

Prohibited U-Turns

In most states, U-turns are almost always illegal in business districts. In residence districts and other areas, they are likely to be legal except where traffic conditions make them unsafe. Because possible defenses to U-turn tickets greatly depend on where a turn was made, let's look at the most common situations.

> **CAUTION**
>
> **U-turn laws vary considerably from state to state.** Be sure to read the law you're charged with violating to see exactly what its elements are. Then try to figure how you can convincingly claim you didn't violate at least one of them.

U-Turn in Business District

Most state U-turn statutes say something like:

> No person in a business district shall make a U-turn, except at an intersection or on a divided highway where an opening has been provided.

In most states it is usually legal to make a U-turn unless you are in a business or residential district (see below) or a sign prohibits it. A "business district" is typically defined as a place where over 50% of the property fronting the street is "in use for business" along a specified length, often defined as several hundred feet and often longer. Even in a business district, it usually is legal to make a U-turn at a stoplight as long as you begin your turn in the far-left lane.

Your best defense to a charge that you made a U-turn in a business district is usually that you weren't, in fact, in such a district. Typically, this involves two steps: First, looking up your state's definition of the term business district (see Chapter 2 on how to find the right law) and then going back to the scene of your turn to see if the location meets your state's technical definition.

> **TIP**
>
> **The officer must prove you were in a business district.** Because making a U-turn in a business district is a key element of the offense you are charged with, it should be up to the officer to prove it. It follows if the officer provides no proof, you should win your case. Often it's best not to bring up this point until after the prosecution has finished presenting evidence, because you do not want to tip off the other side to your strategy. Instead, this point should be made in your direct testimony and closing argument. For example, you might say, "Your

Honor, the only reason my U-turn is said to be illegal was that it supposedly occurred in a business district. But Officer Kwota didn't say a word about what kind of area it was." And then, if true of course, you could continue, *"In fact, while there are some businesses in the area where I made my turn, I do not think the state proved that it falls within the definition of a 'business district' under the law of this state."*

U-Turn in Residence District

Most state laws read something like this:

> No person in a residence district shall make a U-turn when any other vehicle is approaching from either direction within 200 feet, except at an intersection when the approaching vehicle is controlled by an official traffic-control device.

To be convicted of this, the prosecution must prove that you did all of the following things (violated all of these legal elements):

1. You were driving in a "residence district," which is usually defined elsewhere in your state laws or code; you'll want to use the appendix to find where the "rules of the road" or similar laws are located in your state's vehicle code, then look it up and read it carefully

2. You made a full 180-degree or U-turn

3. Another vehicle was approaching (not merely stopped) within the distance specified by the law, and

4. You were at an intersection not controlled by an "official traffic-control device" (sign or signal).

The Poor Person's U-Turn Is Okay

Dividing your U-turn into several parts makes it legal. It is legal if you turn into a driveway or parking lot, make a full stop, then back out into traffic to complete the U-turn. Think of it this way: The left turn into a driveway is legal. Backing out of the driveway is legal, as long as you stay to the shoulder of the road, stop, activate your left turn signal, and enter traffic when safe to do so. And best of all, it's a way to make what amounts to a U-turn while keeping all those green portraits of Andrew Jackson safely in your pocket.

The best ways to beat this violation are to raise doubt as to whether another vehicle was approaching within the distance specified in your state law or whether the area was a "residence district." To demonstrate that other vehicles were not within the specified number of feet at the time you made your turn, it often helps to use maps or drawings containing a distance scale. (See Chapter 9 on introducing diagrams and maps into evidence.) One way to do this is to enlarge a city map to help show the judge where your car and the other vehicle were, noting that no vehicle was within 200 feet of you. Or you can draw your own map, carefully indicating the distances.

Or, you can use pictures of the street when no other traffic is present on it. That way you can mark, on the photograph, with felt-tipped or ballpoint pen, the spots where the other vehicles were. You can testify that you went back to the scene and measured the distances from where your car was to those points when you started the U-turn.

If your state law sets a more relaxed U-turn standard in rural or other nonresidential areas, you may want to try to show there weren't enough residences within the area for it to be a residence district. But be careful not to open up the possibility that you turned in a business district, which will almost always have even tighter U-turn rules.

U-Turns on the Highway (Not in Residence, Business, or Other Restricted Districts)

The law usually reads like this:

> No person shall make a U-turn upon any highway where the driver of such vehicle does not have an unobstructed view for 200 feet in both directions along the highway.

This law applies to areas of any highway that are not labeled a "residence," "business," or other specified district. Here you are free to make a legal U-turn, provided you have an unobstructed view for the number of feet specified in your state law. It doesn't matter whether other vehicles are approaching within that distance, so long as you can see them clearly and it's safe to make the turn. You can often use maps, diagrams, or pictures to demonstrate that you could see more than the distance specified by law. (For defenses to a charge that your turn was unsafe, see below.)

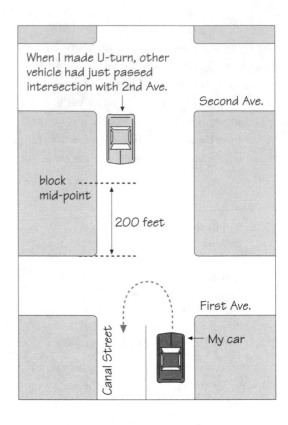

When I made U-turn, other vehicle had just passed intersection with 2nd Ave.

Second Ave.

block mid-point

200 feet

First Ave.

Canal Street

My car

U-Turns Across a Traffic Island

A "divided highway" is often a road with a traffic island or other physical barrier in the middle, separating the two directions of traffic. It's obviously against the law to make a U-turn over a physical barrier. Because it is very dangerous and potentially damaging to the vehicle, few sober drivers attempt it. However, a divided highway can also be designated by a "painted traffic island" consisting of two sets of double yellow lines at least two feet apart. And it's far more common for drivers to cross this type of artificial barrier.

A typical state law reads as follows:

> Whenever a highway has been divided into two or more roadways by means of intermittent barriers or by means of a dividing section of not less than two feet in width, either unpaved or delineated by curbs, double-parallel lines, or other markings on the roadway, it is unlawful to drive any vehicle over, upon, or across the dividing section, or to make any left or U-turn except through a plainly marked opening in the dividing section.

In other words, you can't legally cross two pairs of double white or yellow lines two or more feet apart or a highway divider strip, except at an opening or a place where the double-double lines drop to one set of double lines (or, in some states, become intermittent).

Your best defenses:

- The two sets of parallel lines were less than two feet apart. At your trial you can challenge the officer to say whether he measured the distance between the lines or just estimated them. Although technically this is a decent defense, most judges probably won't go for it (they will assume the two sets of lines were the correct distance apart) unless you measure them and prove they were not. Since people who paint highways aren't perfect, it can pay to wait until traffic is light and get out the old measuring tape.

- There appeared to be a break in the double-double lines to accommodate a driveway. Pictures help a lot with this one, although sometimes you can challenge an officer on cross-examination and get him to admit he can't remember. If so, when it comes to your turn to testify, you'll want to claim that the officer's inability to remember raises a reasonable doubt as to your guilt.

- You were forced to divert over a set of double lines to avoid a dangerous traffic situation. The burden of proving any "emergency defense" is squarely on you. Be sure your emergency really relates to road conditions (you had to avoid an out-of-control truck) and not just your personal situation (you needed to stop to adjust your seatbelt).

Unsafe Turns and Lane Changes

In addition to the specific turn laws outlined above, most states also have a catchall category called "unsafe turns or lane changes." Here is a typical statute.

> No person shall turn a vehicle from a direct course or move right or left upon a roadway until such movement can be made with reasonable safety and then only after the giving of an appropriate signal in the event any other vehicle may be affected by the movement.

In theory, at least, it is up to the prosecution to prove facts that, taken together, demonstrate that you were not driving safely. But in a real courtroom, the ticketing officer will probably just testify that your actions were dangerous. Although this is a conclusion—not really proof—it is usually enough to shift the burden of proof to you. (The judge will now expect you to show your actions were safe.) It is, therefore, important for you to be prepared to produce evidence that this was the case. Following are some suggestions on how to do this.

Turning Left Against Oncoming Traffic

It is legal to make a left turn in front of oncoming traffic if you can do so with reasonable safety. If ticketed, you can start by testifying that, because your turn did not cause an accident and the other driver did not have to swerve or brake sharply, your turn was safe. In addition, you may wish to point out that there was enough distance between your car and an oncoming car to make the turn safely. One good approach is to use a little mathematics to show the judge how much time you had to make your turn. Start by understanding that six car-lengths equals about 100 feet. Assuming the car approaching yours was traveling at 25 mph (or 37 feet per second), you would have about three seconds for you to make your turn. Twelve car lengths (or 200 feet) would allow about six seconds, and so on. You should explain that with the help of a diagram as part of your direct testimony and reiterate it in your closing argument.

> **TIP**
>
> **Testify if the other driver signaled you to proceed.** If the reason you made your illegal turn was because another driver signaled you to go first, you should testify that the other driver nodded or otherwise told you to go ahead with the turn.

Pulling in Front of a Vehicle Going the Same Direction

The law in most states also prohibits pulling out in front of another vehicle in an unsafe manner. This can happen when you turn right or left at an intersection in front of another car that is too close to your vehicle. And, of course, it can also occur when you change lanes abruptly, especially when you don't signal. Officers who cite for this offense will usually testify that your actions caused another car to slow abruptly, indicated by brake lights and quickly reduced speeds.

Your best defenses are typically to show:

- You allowed enough space—diagrams and photos can help. (See diagrams in this chapter and Chapter 10.)
- The other driver did not come to a screeching halt (if true) and no accident occurred.
- The other driver overreacted by braking or swerving unnecessarily.
- The other driver was exceeding the speed limit.
- The officer had a poor view of the incident.

This last point can be the most important. Unless the officer was right behind your vehicle, in the case of a lane change, or sitting at the intersection in the case of a too-fast merge, she might not have been in a good position to be able to judge the relative speeds and positions of both vehicles. In short, you would argue the officer could not see if you performed an unsafe maneuver as part of presenting your testimony—backed up by a diagram—that your turn was safe.

Pulling Onto a Road and Backing Up Unsafely

Typically, your state's law will say something like:

> No person shall start a vehicle stopped, standing, or parked on a highway, nor shall any person back a vehicle on a highway, until such movement can be made with reasonable safety.

To win you must present testimony that you took reasonable precautions before you pulled onto the road and started backing up.

Start by explaining in your testimony what you did and why it was sensible and safe under the circumstances. Assuming your conduct might reasonably have looked dangerous to the officer, be ready to explain that the problem was really caused by the unpredictable or antisocial actions of the other driver. (Remember, this person won't be in court to contradict you.) This would be true if another vehicle suddenly did something truly dangerous, like exceeding the speed limit or making a high-speed turn. If possible, present convincing eyewitness testimony to back up your story. Plan to use a diagram or map to help show why your conduct was safe. (See Chapter 9 on preparing and using diagrams.)

Failing to Signal a Turn

Your state law will say something like this:

> Any signal of intention to turn right or left shall be given continuously during the last 100 feet traveled by the vehicle before turning.

Officers write many turn signal tickets claiming the offenders didn't signal for 100 feet before making a turn. (Incidentally, it's fine to use hand signals—they're just as legal as electric signals.) These tickets are tough to beat—it's your word against the officer's. Also, keep in mind that the fact that your dashboard turn signal is clicking does not mean your turn signal lights are blinking. Your lights may be out. In that case, you may claim that you made a reasonable mistake-of-fact (you shifted your signal lever but didn't know your signal lamp had burned out). But this defense can also backfire because you would have to prove that you learned of the broken bulb immediately *after* you were ticketed. If you knew or should have known about the defective signal before getting the ticket, you will lose your case.

Right-of-Way Violations

Tickets in this category are usually issued when, in the estimation of an officer, a driver rudely fails to yield to other motorists or pedestrians when required. Unfortunately, if the officer shows up in court, he is likely to remember this type of incident and make a forceful presentation. For example, he may explain in great detail why your failure to let an elderly person cross the street in a crosswalk was a dastardly act.

Here is a rundown of the most common violations for failing to yield to other vehicles, along with suggestions on to how to fight them.

Right of Way at Intersections

State laws typically read:

> The driver of a vehicle approaching an intersection shall yield the right of way to any vehicle that has entered the intersection from a different highway.

These statutes do not mean you have to wait until the intersection is completely clear before entering. Instead, they simply prohibit deliberate crowding or interfering with other vehicles already in the intersection. Fortunately, whether you really did improperly fail to yield the right of way to another driver is commonly a judgment call, meaning you usually have a pretty decent shot at beating this type of ticket.

EXAMPLE:

You cautiously enter an intersection, even though there is another vehicle ahead of you. You wait a few seconds before you see that its driver is not sure whether to go straight or turn. To exit the intersection for safety reasons, you cut to the left of the vehicle and make your left turn. In court, you would testify that you first slowed to allow the other driver to leave the intersection. But when he didn't, you realized you were in danger of blocking other traffic and creating a dangerous situation, so you proceeded as cautiously as you could to leave the intersection. In short, with the help of a diagram, you could demonstrate that the other car, not your vehicle, caused the confusion in the intersection.

Failure to Yield at Uncontrolled or Four-Way Stop

There are laws controlling actions at intersections that have four-way stop signs or no lights or signs, called "uncontrolled" intersections. They typically say:

> When two vehicles enter an intersection from different highways at the same time, the driver of the vehicle on the left shall yield the right of way to the vehicle on his or her immediate right.

This ticket involves a violation at an intersection that has:

1. No traffic signal, stop sign, or yield sign
2. Four stop signs, one facing in each direction, or
3. Stoplights that, for an unknown reason, are inoperative.

Start by understanding that the first car stopped at a four-way intersection has the right of way. And that if two cars arrive at the intersection at the same moment from different directions, the vehicle to the right has the right of way.

The legal elements of this violation normally include all of the following:

1. The vehicle was "approaching a four-way intersection."
2. The intersection had four stop signs, one for each street in each direction. Or the intersection had no yield sign, stop sign, or operative traffic light on any street approach.
3. Another vehicle entered the intersection from "a different highway." (That is, not directly across from you, but to your right or left.)

4. The other vehicle entered the intersection first or, if you both entered at the same instant, the other vehicle entered from the street or road to your right.

5. You failed to yield to the other vehicle.

This kind of ticket is often written after an accident. It follows that if you tell the officer that the other car entered the intersection first or that it arrived at the intersection to your right at the same time you arrived, you have all but admitted your guilt. Instead, to prevail, it's normally important to be able to claim you entered the intersection first, or would have if the other driver hadn't rolled through a stop sign. Obviously, it is a huge help to have a witness if you made a real stop while the other driver faked it.

TIP

A picture or diagram can help you out. A diagram or picture of the intersection, showing where your car collided with the other car, may be helpful in showing that the other driver rolled through the stop sign. For example, if you can show the collision occurred farther from the point where you entered an uncontrolled intersection than from where the other vehicle entered it, that supports the idea that you were in the intersection longer—or first. That would mean you had the right of way.

Failing to Yield at a "T" or Three-Way Intersection

At three-way (or "T") uncontrolled intersections (or where the two roads are controlled by stop signs), the rules are a little different. The driver on the road that dead-ends must always yield to the other driver (the one crossing the T), no matter who got to the intersection first.

Here the law typically says:

> Where two vehicles enter an intersection formed by a continuing highway and a terminating highway, at the same time and from the different highways, the driver of the vehicle on the terminating highway shall yield the right of way to the driver of the vehicle on the continuing highway.

The elements of this violation are:

1. A "T" or three-way intersection is formed by one road that terminates and another that goes through.

2. The intersection is not controlled by stop signs, or it has stop signs in all three directions, or an inoperative stoplight.

3. You were driving on the road that ends at the intersection.

4. Your vehicle and the other entered the intersection at the same time, and

5. You failed to yield to the other vehicle.

Again, as is true for a four-way intersection, your main defense to this charge is that your vehicle entered the intersection first.

Failure to Properly Yield When Making Left Turn

Most state laws read like this:

> The driver of a vehicle intending to turn left on a highway, or to turn left into public or private property, or an alley, shall yield the right of way to all vehicles approaching from the opposite direction that are close enough to constitute a

hazard at any time during the turning movement and shall continue to yield the right of way to the approaching vehicles until the left turn can be made with reasonable safety.

To be convicted, the prosecution must establish all of these elements:

1. One or more vehicles were approaching from the opposite direction.
2. Approaching traffic was "so close as to constitute a hazard" at any time during the turning movement.
3. You made the left turn anyway without "reasonable safety."

As with many other types of illegal turn tickets, this one involves a judgment call from the ticketing officer that your turn was "unsafe." It follows that in mounting your defense, it is often wise to focus your defense on the words "reasonable safety." For example, you might argue to the judge that if no other car had to suddenly brake or swerve to avoid hitting your turning car, there is at least a "reasonable doubt" as to whether your driving was unsafe. (See Chapter 13 for a discussion of why establishing "reasonable doubt" should lead to your acquittal.)

Failing to Yield at Stop and Yield Signs

Even though you may have stopped as required at a stop sign, you may still be ticketed if you fail to properly yield to another driver who has the right of way. In most states, the elements of this violation are:

1. After encountering a stop sign or a yield sign, you entered an intersection.

2. One or more other vehicles approached on an intersecting street or road.
3. Approaching traffic constituted a hazard, and
4. You continued through the intersection anyway.

EXAMPLE:

After signaling your intention to turn right, you stop at a stop sign. You turn even though a car is approaching from the left on the cross street. The other car must brake to avoid rear-ending you. You get a ticket.

Your defenses:

- The other vehicle appeared to be turning left, right, or stopping so that it shouldn't have presented a hazard.
- The other vehicle sped up suddenly just as you entered the intersection, creating a hazard where none should have reasonably existed (people really do this!).
- You were lawfully in the intersection (after having stopped) before the other driver got close to it.
- Obstructions on either side, such as hills or bends in the road, meant you couldn't see traffic from that direction, and that, given those obstructions, the other driver was driving too fast, thus creating the hazard.

As you can see, your defense should normally be based on raising the likelihood that another vehicle—not you—caused the dangerous situation. Or put in reverse, you want to convince the judge or jury that you acted with "reasonable safety." One way to do this is by clearly demonstrating that you had a better view of the developing situation than the officer did. For example, you might be able to testify that several other cars were between the officer and the intersection and, therefore, you were closer to what was occurring. Supplement this with pictures and diagrams showing where you were in relation to the other vehicle. (See Chapter 10.)

Yielding to Pedestrians

Let's now discuss the most common tickets issued for failing to yield to pedestrians:
This law typically states:

> The driver of a vehicle shall yield the right of way to a pedestrian crossing, or trying to cross, the roadway within any marked crosswalk.

In most states the elements of this violation are:

1. You drove a vehicle.
2. You approached a marked crosswalk.
3. There was a pedestrian crossing or trying to cross, and
4. You failed to yield to the pedestrian by either refusing to stop (even though there's no stop sign or traffic light) or coming very close to running the pedestrian down.

The law in some states contains an additional requirement that you must yield to a pedestrian within any "unmarked crosswalk" at an intersection. In short, the law assumes that a crosswalk exists at any corner where two roads meet. If you get a ticket for failing to yield to a pedestrian who is not in a marked crosswalk, it is very important to check the exact wording of your state's law on this point. For example, you'll learn that if there is a crosswalk on one side of a major intersection and no crosswalk on the other, pedestrians are required to use the marked crosswalk side. In this case, it is not a violation to cross in front of a pedestrian on the non-crosswalked side. (See Chapter 2 on how to find the exact law you are charged with violating.)

To consider other ways to defend against this type of ticket, it will help to look at a real-life situation. Assume, as you approach a corner, a pedestrian begins to cross the street, walking slowly from your right to your left in a crosswalk. You see you have plenty of room to drive by safely after the pedestrian passes by. So you drive through the intersection while the pedestrian is still in the crosswalk. You are stopped and ticketed.

To contest the ticket, start by focusing on the exact words (legal elements) in your state's law. For example, in some states the law makes it clear that it is legal to cross through an intersection after a pedestrian has passed the path of your vehicle even if they are still in the crosswalk. But in other states, the pedestrian must be entirely off the street before you can proceed. If you are in a state that allows cars to proceed while pedestrians are still in the crosswalk, your defense should focus on proving that you gave the pedestrian plenty of room to pass by and then proceeded safely across the intersection. In states that absolutely prohibit you from moving across the intersection until the pedestrian has cleared the crosswalk, you must try to prove that you did wait for the pedestrian to leave the street and the officer just didn't see clearly.

Driving Too Slowly

There are several circumstances in which drivers may be ticketed for illegally blocking or impeding traffic by driving too slowly or failing to yield to a long line of vehicles behind them. Let's look briefly at the most common.

Driving Too Slowly in Left Lane

Your state's law will say something like:

> Any vehicle proceeding upon a highway at a speed less than the normal speed of traffic moving in the same direction at such time shall be driven in the right-hand lane for traffic or as close as practicable to the right-hand edge or curb, except when overtaking and passing another vehicle proceeding in the same direction or when preparing for a left turn at an intersection or into a private road or driveway. If a vehicle is being driven at a speed less than the normal speed of traffic moving in the same direction at such time, and is not being driven in the right-hand lane for traffic or as close as practicable to the right-hand edge or curb, it shall constitute evidence that the driver is operating the vehicle in violation of this section.

In plain English, this law means if you're poking along, you had better be in the right-hand or slow lane unless you're preparing to turn left.

The elements of the violation are:

1. You drove at a speed "less than the normal speed of traffic," and

2. You didn't drive "as close as practicable to the right-hand edge or curb."

Of course, if you read your statute carefully, you'll likely find that there is one big exception to this move-to-the-right-if-you-are-driving-slowly requirement. As long as it is permitted, you have the right to move to the left to pass an even slower vehicle, even if doing so means you are briefly driving slower than the normal speed in that lane. For example, if you are driving 35 mph in a 45-mph zone and there is a farm tractor, an oversize motor home, or some other slow vehicle in the right lane doing 20 mph, it's okay for you to be one lane to the left to pass it.

The best way to defend against this ticket is to prove:

1. In an "absolute" speed limit state (see Chapter 5 and the appendix) you were traveling at the posted speed limit.

2. You were preparing to make a left turn (if true).

3. You were passing even slower-moving traffic to the left and were prepared to return to the slow lane as soon as it was safe.

4. Your speed, although below the posted limit, was the only safe speed for that road under the conditions you were driving through, which could include rain, wind, darkness, or other dangerous conditions.

5. You were blocking the traffic behind you only because, in fact, it wasn't safe to go any faster.

In court, the officer must testify only that you were driving below the speed limit, or, in a "presumed" speed limit state, at a speed slower than other safe-driving traffic.

It is then up to you to show a legal excuse for your action—for example, road conditions required that you slow down, or the glare from a reflected window prevented you from seeing clearly.

Impeding Traffic

This offense is similar to driving too slowly in the left lane. The difference is that you can be charged with the offense even if you're in the curb lane or the only lane on a one-lane road.

A typical impeding traffic law says:

> No person shall drive upon a highway at such a slow speed as to impede or block the normal and reasonable movement of traffic, except when reduced speed is necessary for safe operation, because of a grade, or compliance with the law.

The elements of this violation are:

1. You drove on a highway at a speed less than the "normal and reasonable" speed of traffic.
2. Your reduced speed was not made necessary by safe operation or a grade, and
3. You were not speeding.

The success or failure of your defense will normally pivot on whether you can convince the judge that your view of events was more reasonable than that of the officer's. Your best defense is to show that your slow speed was reasonable because of road, weather, or traffic conditions. An officer trying to make this one stick will likely testify that you were driving below the speed limit and holding up a long line of frustrated, finger-gesturing, horn-honking drivers. The law will excuse your slow driving if you can show:

- You were traveling at the posted speed limit, or safely above it in a "presumed" speed-limit state, or
- You were driving slower than the posted speed, but lower speed was "necessary for safe operation" of your vehicle.

During cross-examination ask the officer, "How fast was traffic moving when I was stopped?" If he says he can't remember (but can remember that cars were trying to get past you), you should prevail if you can testify that you were driving at the speed limit while the cars trying to pass you were attempting to violate the posted limit.

But if you were driving much under the posted limit, this first defense won't work. In this situation, be prepared to testify and document—with photos or diagrams—that poor road conditions, bad weather, steep grades, or sharp curves made a higher speed unsafe. Although personal reasons normally won't help, this is one circumstance where I have occasionally seen a judge side with a motorist who tells a good story. If, for example, you were carrying 12 dozen cartons of raw eggs to an Easter celebration or moving your grandmother's 100-year-old dishes over a poorly paved road, it won't hurt to work it in to your testimony.

TIP

Rough pavement can be a reason to go slowly. Speed limits are normally posted based on an assessment of how fast it is safe to go on a particular road. Occasionally, however, conditions change for the worse after the speed limit is posted. This is particularly likely if construction or heavy wear has degraded the road surface. So if the pavement was in bad shape, make sure you document it with photographs and argue that it was unsafe to go faster than your speed.

Failing to Use "Turnouts"

A turnout is usually a patch of pavement on the right side of the road where slow drivers can pull off the road to let faster drivers go past. If you're driving slowly and there are a whole lot of drivers behind you wanting to go faster, you normally have a legal duty to pull over and let them go by.

Here, a typical state law reads like this:

> On a two-lane highway where passing is unsafe because of traffic in the opposite direction or other conditions, a slow-moving vehicle, including a passenger vehicle, behind which five or more vehicles are formed in line, shall turn off the roadway at the nearest place designated as a turnout by signs erected by the authority having jurisdiction over the highway, or wherever sufficient area for a safe turnout exists, in order to permit the vehicles following it to proceed. As used in this section, a slow-moving vehicle is one that is proceeding at a rate of speed less than the normal flow of traffic at the particular time and place.

The elements of this violation include:

1. You were driving a "slow-moving vehicle," meaning you were driving slower "than the normal flow of traffic" at the time.
2. You were on a highway with two lanes, one in each direction.
3. There were at least five other vehicles behind yours that all slowed down because of you (this number can vary from state to state), and
4. You failed to pull over at a marked "turnout" or other widened area to the right where you could safely pull over.

Driving slowly because of safety concerns, such as a degraded pavement, is not a defense to this charge, since you could still have used the turnout. Your only available defense is normally that, for some good reason, you were unable to pull over safely to let the other traffic past. For example, you may not have been able to use the turnout because you were pulling a trailer, trying to avoid a hole in the road, or afraid of slipping on snow or ice.

Tailgating

We all hate it when someone rides our bumper. And with good reason. Driving too closely behind another vehicle really is dangerous. That's why the traffic laws of all states prohibit this conduct. Most define the violation as follows:

> The driver of a motor vehicle shall not follow another vehicle more closely than is reasonable and prudent, having due regard for the speed of such vehicle and the traffic upon, and the condition of, the roadway.

Here are the elements of this violation:

1. There was a vehicle in front of you, in the same lane, and
2. You followed more closely than reasonable, given the road, weather, and traffic conditions.

The key to winning a case for tailgating is to prove that your distance behind the other car was reasonable and prudent given the circumstances at the time. The big word here is "circumstances." If you are 15 feet behind another vehicle traveling at 70 mph, your actions are not reasonable or prudent. But if traffic is creeping along at 10 mph, a distance of 15 feet behind the car in front of yours is reasonable. Now suppose traffic is proceeding at 25 mph. Is 15 feet still a reasonable and prudent distance to follow the car ahead? Probably not. The normal safety guideline is that a driver should leave one car length between his car and the car in front of his for every 10 mph. So, to be safe, a car traveling 60 mph should normally have at least six car lengths of empty space between him and the car in front of him.

TIP

Convince the judge your tailgating was temporary. Every driver has experienced situations where another car suddenly slows down, with the result that you have to quickly adjust your speed by also slowing down. In this case, an officer might see you before you have completed your adjustment, making it falsely appear you were tailgating. If this was what happened to you, you should testify along these lines.

"I was traveling at 50 mph, according to my speedometer, with the rest of traffic. I allowed at least five car lengths of space between the front of my vehicle and the pickup truck in front of me. However, when that truck abruptly slowed to about 35 mph, for no apparent reason, the distance closed to about two car lengths. Before I could slow further, to lengthen the distance to three or four car lengths, the officer behind me pulled me over. I tried to explain to the officer that because there was no objective reason, such as heavy traffic, for the truck to slow down, I couldn't have anticipated it, but he wouldn't discuss what really happened."

Tailgating tickets are occasionally given when a driver rear-ends another vehicle. In this instance, the officer usually has not witnessed the accident and cannot testify that he saw you tailgating. Fortunately, there are ways to defend against this type of ticket. For example, the accident might have been caused by the other driver stopping too quickly or pulling into your lane too close to your car. In short, it's your job to convince the judge in your direct testimony that there was a non-tailgating explanation. And when you cross-examine the officer, you'll want to establish that because she didn't see what happened, she can't rule out the fact that the accident was not caused by your tailgating. Because the other driver won't be present and the cop showed up later, this is often fairly easy to do.

Unsafe Lane Changes

Most state laws say something like this:

> Whenever any roadway has been divided into two or more clearly marked lanes for traffic in one direction, the following rule applies: A vehicle shall be driven as nearly as practicable entirely within a single lane and shall not be moved from the lane until such movement can be made with reasonable safety.

You can be cited for an unsafe lane change under the rule that prohibits unsafe turns, or under this more specific violation, which has the following elements:

1. The road had two or more lanes for traffic in the same direction.
2. Lane boundaries were clearly marked, and
3. You either failed to drive "as nearly as practicable" within the lane or changed lanes without regard for "reasonable safety."

Police will readily and properly pounce on a driver who weaves in and out of traffic without signaling, especially if he cuts off another car, forcing it to abruptly brake. Often the officer will watch for brake lights flashing on cars in your vicinity to determine if you are endangering others with your frequent lane changes. Your defense to this one should often be based on the fact that there can be many reasons for a driver to touch the brakes, and that your lane change may have had nothing to do with it. For example, a car could have been traveling much faster than the speed limit before you pulled into its lane, causing it to brake sharply. Or a car in front of you may have braked sharply, forcing you to

make a quick lane change. Because all these circumstances are difficult to see from a distance or a bad angle, you'll have a good chance to sell the judge on why your lane change was safe under the circumstances.

TIP

Establish where the officer was when you changed lanes. Most drivers are on their best behavior when a police cruiser is close. So officers end up issuing many violations that they view from a distance, meaning their ability to judge the nuances of whether particular conduct was safe or not is poor. If this was true in your case, use your chance to cross-examine the officer to ask questions like these:

"How far behind the other vehicle were you when you observed it brake?"

"After I changed lanes, you were behind the other car, weren't you?" [If "yes," follow up with] *"At that moment, you couldn't see the distance between my car and the other car, could you?"*

"I assume you weren't pacing the vehicle you claim I turned in front of?" [If "no," follow up with] *"Then you don't know how fast it was going, do you?"*

Then work the officer's admissions into your testimony that your conduct was safe and that the officer's conclusion that it wasn't isn't reliable.

EXAMPLE:

You're driving 65 mph on the freeway in the right-hand lane. To avoid cars entering from an upcoming on-ramp, you decide to move into the center lane. Preparing to change lanes, you flick on your left turn signal and look in your rear- and side-view mirrors. You see another car in the middle lane, but it's about eight car-lengths back, so you make the lane change. As you do, the apparently inattentive driver of the other car speeds up, with the result that your vehicles are very close together. You are ticketed for an illegal lane change.

In court, explain that you were going at or near the speed limit and were changing lanes to avoid a dangerous merge situation. Also, testify—if true—that just after you signaled your lane change, the other driver sped up. (Since the other driver won't be in court, only the police officer will be there to contradict you.) In short, any unsafe conditions were brought about by the other driver's unsafe conduct, not your lane change.

Improper Passing

Unsafe passing is dealt with in several common ways in most states. Here are the contexts in which unsafe passing is made illegal.

Endangering Those You Pass

The violation:
In most states, you are forbidden from *"interfering with the safe operation of any vehicle"* that you pass, and any vehicle coming from the opposite direction on a two-lane highway.

The defense:
The ticketing officer must have some evidence of your unsafe passing. You must cause an accident or nearly force another car off the road before an officer has enough evidence to write you a ticket, particularly if he did not see you pass other cars on the road. If a car approaching you had to put on their brakes and slow slightly to allow you to complete your passing attempt, this is not necessarily a violation, because the other driver may have slowed down unnecessarily. But if you force them off the road, you probably have little defense.

Unsafe "Blind" Passing

The violation:
This law forbids you from passing in the oncoming traffic lane when *"approaching the top of a hill or a curve, so as to create a hazard"* to vehicles that might approach from the other side.

The defense:
This law does not require that you put another driver into jeopardy to be convicted. It is sufficient that you created the possibility of a collision by attempting to pass on a blind curve or in some area where your view of the road ahead is obscured. Your defense should be aimed at challenging the officer's recollection of how far you were from the hill or curve when you passed the other vehicle. You could argue (if true) that the car you were passing sped up suddenly, making it impossible for you to complete your maneuver before reaching a blind curve area. Remember, the officer has

the burden of proving each element of the violation.

Passing on the Right

The laws in most states prohibit passing on the right, except under the following circumstances:

- The passed vehicle is about to turn left. (You still can't drive onto the unpaved shoulder of the road.)
- The street or road is wide enough to accommodate two lanes of traffic.

Even if passing on the right is allowed under one of the above exceptions, you must do so "under conditions permitting such movement in safety."

Non-DUI/DWI Alcohol-Related Offenses

States define alcohol-related offenses in several ways and use several different laws to punish drivers and passengers who carry or use alcoholic beverages while driving. Driving Under the Influence (DUI) and Driving While Intoxicated (DWI) offenses are serious offenses that often require the assistance of an attorney. (We briefly cover the subject in Chapter 8.) There are, however, some alcohol-related violations that fall into the "infraction" or "petty" offense category covered here. These include drinking while driving (but not being legally drunk) and having an open container of alcohol in your vehicle. Even if you are not charged with DUI/DWI, some insurance companies will raise your rates

or cancel your insurance for convictions of these violations. It follows that there is a big incentive to fight these tickets or, if possible, have them dismissed by attending traffic school.

Open Container on Driver's or Passenger's Person

This is the most common alcohol-related offense where the driver is not charged with DUI/DWI. Most state laws say something like this:

> No person shall have in his or her possession, while driving a motor vehicle upon a highway, any bottle, can, or other receptacle containing any alcoholic beverage that has been opened, or a seal broken, or the contents of which have been partially removed.

The elements of this violation are all of the following:

1. You drove a motor vehicle.
2. You drove on any public road or "highway." (Private roads or parking lots don't count.)
3. You kept a container, such as a bottle, can, or glass, on your person, which means you held it in your hand, kept it within your reach, or kept it in a pocket or purse.
4. The container held any amount of an alcoholic beverage when the officer found it, although simply the odor of an alcoholic beverage is not enough, and
5. The seal, if any, on the bottle was broken, or the container's contents were "partially removed."

You can bet, in most states, if an officer finds an open container in your vehicle, she is going to charge you with the most serious offense she can. If she rules out DUI/DWI, an "open container" violation is a way for her to cite you for a less-serious offense.

This offense requires that the ticketing officer connect the open container to the person cited. The open container must be within the control of the driver, or within his reach. If there are open containers in the vehicle, but not close to the driver or any other passenger, the driver may still be cited for keeping an open container in the vehicle.

If you are cited for having an open container on your person, and you have no good defense, it may be worth attempting to negotiate accepting a lesser violation, like simply having an open container in your vehicle. (See Chapter 13 on how to plea bargain.)

When a passenger has an open container in the vehicle, both the passenger and the driver can be cited: the passenger for having or drinking from an open container, and the driver for allowing an open container in the vehicle. The driver's only valid defense is that he had no reason to know the passenger had the open container.

EXAMPLE:

You and your friends are on the way to the beach with a few unopened sixpacks of beer. Unbeknownst to you, one of your friends in the back seat can't wait and quietly opens a can of beer before you get there. When an officer pulls you over for an expired registration, he notices the open beer can in the back and tickets you, the driver. Your defense is that you didn't have any reason to know your passenger made that stupid move.

Open Container Kept in Vehicle

Almost all states forbid driving with an "open container" of an alcoholic beverage in your vehicle. In a few states it is legal for a passenger, but not the driver, to drink an alcoholic beverage while the vehicle is in motion. Although having an open container is a less-serious offense than drinking from one, a conviction can still seriously affect your license status or insurance.

Most state "open container" laws say something like this:

> It is unlawful for the registered owner of any motor vehicle, or the driver, if the registered owner is not then present in the vehicle, to keep in a motor vehicle when the vehicle is upon any highway, any bottle, can, or other receptacle containing any alcoholic beverage that has been opened, or a seal broken, or the contents of which have been partially removed, unless the container is kept in the trunk of the vehicle, or kept in some other area of the vehicle not normally occupied by the driver or passengers if the vehicle is not equipped with a trunk. A utility compartment or glove compartment shall be deemed to be within the area occupied by the driver and passengers. This section shall not apply to the living quarters of a motor home or camper.

The elements of this offense are all of the following:

1. You were a driver or owner of a vehicle.
2. You were in the vehicle.
3. The vehicle was "upon any highway," but not necessarily driven by the registered owner.
4. There was a container, such as a bottle, can, or glass somewhere in the vehicle other than the trunk. (For vehicles without trunks—such as pickups and hatchbacks, the container must be "in some area of the vehicle not normally occupied by the driver or passengers," but not in the glove compartment.)
5. The container held some amount of an alcoholic beverage when the officer found it.
6. The seal, if any, on the bottle, etc., was broken, or its contents were "partially removed," and
7. The container was not in the living quarters of a motor home or camper.

About the only real defense to this is the mistake-of-fact defense that says you didn't know the open container was in the vehicle. This is justified only if a passenger really did open a bottle or can without your knowledge (especially if she will come to court and say so).

Drinking in Vehicle

Every state forbids drivers—and most states forbid passengers—from drinking any alcoholic beverage in a moving motor vehicle. You can be guaranteed that a police officer will administer an alcohol test on a driver caught with an open container on his person, and will probably administer the test if he finds an open container anywhere in the passenger area.

Even if you pass that test, you are not out of the woods. Every state has a law allowing you to be charged with drinking in a vehicle, even if you pass the sobriety test. However, the officer must be able to testify that he actually saw you raise the bottle or can to your mouth and drink from it. If your breath smells of alcohol, that alone is no proof you drank while driving the vehicle, even if you were carrying an open container. After all, you could have had a drink before you got into the car. Even so, you can still be convicted, in most states, of the lesser offense of having an open container in your vehicle.

 CAUTION

Myth of the road. It is a myth that some states, like Texas, allow you to drink and drive as long as you stay below the official blood/alcohol level for intoxication.

Illegal Drug Use/Possession

This is a serious crime, akin to DUI/DWI. A federal law requires states to lift driver's licenses for six months after any drug conviction. Some states have refused to enact this federal requirement. But in states that have enacted such a law, you can lose your license for having drugs in your car, even if you are not charged with driving under their influence. It may make sense to check with an attorney if you are charged with this type of violation.

Driving Under the Influence

Offenses and Penalties...99

    Driving Under the Influence...99

    Driving While Blood Alcohol Is 0.08% or Higher 101

    Penalties... 102

    Felony DUI.. 103

How Alcohol Interacts With Your Body 103

    Absorption Into the Bloodstream 103

    Elimination From the Body.. 104

    Calculating Approximate Blood Alcohol Levels............... 104

    Effects of Alcohol 106

Blood, Breath, and Urine Tests for Alcohol 108

    The "Implied Consent" Law.. 108

    The Chemical Tests: How They Work, How They Fail 109

License Suspension Penalties and Procedures 113

Dealing With a DUI Charge.. 114

    Evaluating Your Case... 114

    Getting a Lawyer.. 116

    Plea Bargaining.. 116

    Pretrial Court Proceedings... 117

    The Trial 119

One of the most serious driving offenses is that which we call "drunk driving." In some states it's referred to as Driving While Intoxicated (DWI), but you don't have to be intoxicated or "drunk" to be convicted of this offense. For this reason, many people call this offense Driving Under the Influence (DUI), the term we use in this chapter. Because this charge is so serious, and because factual and legal issues in such cases can be very complicated, we don't intend here to tell you how to conduct your own defense to this kind of charge—that would take a book in its own right. Here we simply give you the basic information you will need to understand your options and deal intelligently with your lawyer, if you decide to hire one.

Under many states' laws, this class of offense not only includes driving while "under the influence" of alcohol and/or drugs (legal or illegal), but also includes driving with a blood alcohol level exceeding 0.08%, whether you were feeling any "influence" of the alcohol or not. The two offenses, driving under the influence and driving with a blood alcohol exceeding a certain level, are treated equally seriously. And because DUI is considered much more serious than ordinary traffic offenses, a person charged with even first-offense DUI has a right to a jury trial in almost every state. (Hawaii, Louisiana, and Nevada are exceptions.)

Though much of this book is designed to help you handle your own traffic court case, you should be more cautious about handling your own DUI case, since the stakes are very high. In most states, the maximum sentence is six months or a year in jail, and even a first conviction will usually result in some jail time, a large fine, and a driver's license suspension. Second and third offenses often result in jail sentences of several months to a year. In addition, your insurance may be canceled or, at least, the rates drastically increased. And a drunk-driving charge stays on your driving record for many years.

Before you read further, we wish to emphasize general rules that you should understand when dealing with the subject of DUI:

1. You will almost always be better off taking the blood, breath, or urine test when it is requested by the police.
2. Your chances of beating a DUI charge are exceedingly slim if the chemical test result is substantially over the limit (0.08% alcohol by weight).

Read the rest of this chapter with these two points firmly in mind.

Editor's Note: The subject of driving under the influence stimulates much passion. Obviously, it would be a safer, saner world if it were possible to stamp out the practice of driving while intoxicated. But, as with many issues in criminal law, driving under the influence is not always black and white. And because every criminal defendant is presumed innocent until convicted, this book seeks to provide information about the law so that those accused of violating DUI/DWI laws can assess their chances and defend themselves, if required.

Offenses and Penalties

In this section, we explain the elements of several different types of DUI offenses. At the end of this chapter, we include a state-by-state chart comparing the various DUI/DWI offenses.

Driving Under the Influence

Most states' laws forbid driving "under the influence of an alcoholic beverage," driving under the influence of a drug, and driving under the combined influence of an alcoholic beverage and any drug. The elements of this offense are:

1. You drove a vehicle—that is, you steered and controlled it while it was moving, and

2. At the same time, you were "under the influence" in that your ability to drive safely was affected to an appreciable degree by an alcoholic beverage you drank, a drug that you took, or the combination of the two.

Driving

The first element—"you drove the vehicle"—is usually not in dispute. Even when it is, it can be proved in court by "circumstantial" or indirect evidence. In one case, for example, a person accused of drunk driving had been discovered passed out in a car with its engine running. The jury was allowed to infer from the running engine that he had been driving.

Sometimes a drunk driver and a sober (or, at least, less drunk) passenger will try to switch places in their seats just before the officer approaches the car. This tactic almost always fails to fool the officers and can often make the situation worse if the officer later testifies in court as to all the "furtive movements" occasioned by this awkward and desperate ploy.

In sum, the defense that you weren't driving (or that no one saw you drive) can sometimes be a fairly difficult one. You should definitely talk to an attorney experienced in drunk-driving defense if you think you might be able to use it.

Simultaneous Driving and Intoxication

Though it may sound obvious, both the driving and the under-the-influence elements must occur at the same time for a person to be guilty. For example, if you gulped down a double martini just before you started to drive and drove only a few minutes before being stopped and arrested, you might have been sober enough while driving. However, by the time a blood sample is taken a half hour later, it may show a substantial alcohol content. In other words, if your blood alcohol level was rising because of drinks you had before you started to drive, your blood alcohol content (BAC) may have been lower while you were driving than when you were tested later. (This is often referred to as the "rising blood alcohol" defense.)

A more unusual, yet similar, situation occurs when a driver who has had nothing to drink gets into an accident and then walks into a nearby bar to get a drink and calm his nerves. This is a terrible idea, because when the police arrive to investigate the accident, they smell alcohol on his breath and arrest him. By the time he submits to a chemical test of his blood or breath, the alcohol will have worked its way through his body, and he will be erroneously charged with having driven under the influence. But we use this extreme example to illustrate the idea of a "rising-blood alcohol" defense.

It is important to understand that the delay between the time a person was driving and the time she gave a blood or breath sample can affect the outcome of the case. Once you stop drinking, your blood alcohol level decreases as time passes. This means that it was higher when you were driving than when the blood or breath sample was taken. Indeed, prosecutors use this fact to their advantage. For example, if your BAC was measured at 0.07% one hour after you were stopped, the prosecutor can argue to the jury that an hour before the test, when you were driving, your BAC was 0.09% and "burned off" to 0.07% by the time you were tested. That's because alcohol levels in the body fall at approximately 0.02% per hour, as the prosecution will tell the jury.

Being "Under the Influence"

You don't have to be drunk to be "under the influence." (In a sense, the phrases "drunk driving" and "driving while intoxicated" are both misnomers.) The question is whether your ability to drive was "impaired" so that you weren't as cautious or alert as a nondrinking person would have been in similar circumstances.

How is this determined? Well, the arresting officer will testify about your driving behavior that led him to stop your car, your symptoms (slurred speech, red eyes, dilated pupils, flushed face, strong alcoholic beverage odor on breath, unsteadiness on feet after getting out of car, and so on), and your inability to pass the roadside coordination test. The coordination test may involve saying the alphabet, closing your eyes and touching one index finger to the other or to your nose, counting forwards and backwards using your fingers and thumb, patting one palm rapidly with the front and back of your other hand, balancing on one foot, the well-known walking a straight line (usually a sidewalk cement line), and so on.

Finally, "scientific" evidence—the concentration of alcohol in your blood or breath shortly after you were arrested— allows the judge or jury to infer, perhaps after hearing the testimony of an "expert witness," that you were under the influence while driving. However, this kind of evidence isn't absolutely necessary to convict you. Many people who have refused to submit to blood or breath tests for alcohol have been convicted of driving under the influence solely on the basis of the testimony of police officers that they drove erratically or flunked coordination tests.

Blood Alcohol Levels

All states require a person arrested for driving under the influence to give a blood, breath, or urine sample to be tested for alcohol content—when asked. Your refusal to do so will result in a driver's license suspension of three to 12 months, depending on the state—in most cases even if you're eventually found innocent of the charge. Because of this, most people submit to the tests. As a result, the prosecution is usually armed with "scientific" evidence of a defendant's supposed intoxication. The more alcohol in your blood, the more likely it is that you were under the influence. But it is important to realize that you can be convicted of driving under the influence even though your blood alcohol level is fairly low—particularly if you drove erratically, slurred when you spoke, or staggered around. As we'll see, some people are more intoxicated at a given blood alcohol level than are others.

To make it easier for a judge or jury to decide whether you were "under the influence," all states' legislatures have come up with a set of "presumptions" that are based on the amount of alcohol determined to have been in your blood while you were driving. The jurors do this by considering the chemical test evidence.

A jury will be instructed at trial that if they determine your blood alcohol level, while driving, to have been 0.08% or more, they must presume you were under the influence. This means that the jury must find you guilty unless you raise a "reasonable doubt" as to whether you really were under the influence. But, in the states that also make it an offense to drive with blood alcohol in excess of a certain level, you still can be found guilty of that separate offense, as we'll see below.

If your blood alcohol content (BAC) is found by a jury to have been less than 0.05%, the law "presumes" that you were not under the influence. This means that unless there's other strong evidence against you (such as testimony that you were erratically weaving all over the road), you should be acquitted. Prosecutors will almost always drop the charge when the BAC results come out this low.

Drugs: Legal or Illegal

All states also make it illegal to drive under the influence of a drug, or under the combined influence of alcohol and a drug.

Most folks are surprised to learn that the "drug" doesn't even have to be an illegal one. You can be arrested and convicted for driving under the influence of legally prescribed tranquilizers or painkillers, or even over-the-counter nonprescription drugs, like antihistamines or other decongestants, if they adversely affect your ability to drive.

Driving While Blood Alcohol Is 0.08% or Higher

Many states, in addition to prohibiting driving under the influence, also flatly prohibit anyone with a blood alcohol concentration of 0.08% (eight one-hundredths of one percent by weight) or more from driving, or more, whether or not any driving is impaired.

The elements of this type of offense are:
• You drove a vehicle, and

- Alcohol was present in your blood at a concentration of 0.08% or greater *while you were driving.*

What this law means is that regardless of whether you have been "driving under the influence," you can still be found guilty of the offense of driving with a BAC of 0.08%. In states with this type of law, the jury will usually be given a choice of finding a defendant guilty of driving under the influence and/or driving with a blood alcohol level of 0.08% or higher. So, even if you and your witnesses could convince a jury that your ability to drive was superb and that you were just as cautious and conservative a driver as a person who'd had nothing to drink, the jury can still find you guilty of what we call "drunk driving" if it believes your blood alcohol was 0.08% or more while you were driving. The penalty in most cases is the same whether you are convicted of one or the other, or both.

EXAMPLE:

Tom Tippler, just out of a late business meeting, was driving down the freeway at 9:00 p.m. Although he'd had two stiff Mai Tais at Pete's Plateau, his reflexes and muscular coordination were close to normal because, quite frankly, he drank like that every day and his system was used to it. When he leaned over to light a cigarette, his car swerved just a bit inside his lane. A zealous police officer pulled him over, smelled the alcohol on his breath, and asked him what he'd had to drink. Tom replied truthfully, and the officer arrested him. A blood sample he gave showed an alcohol concentration

of 0.09%. Even if the jury believes Tom's business associates when they testify to his apparent total sobriety when he left them, it may still convict Tom of driving with a blood alcohol level of 0.08% or more—if the jurors believe Tom's blood alcohol level was 0.09%, or even 0.08%, while driving.

Penalties

In all states, first-offense driving under the influence is a misdemeanor punishable by up to six months in jail (or more under certain circumstances). Subsequent offenses are punishable by up to a year in jail. Many states' laws also provide for minimum jail sentences of at least several days on a first offense.

In addition to jail sentences, courts can and do impose high fines, ranging from $500 to as much as $2,000. Courts, and more increasingly state motor vehicles departments (DMVs), now impose substantial driver's license suspensions even on a first offense. Many states also provide for increased punishment if you refused to take a blood, breath, or urine test, and such increased penalties are usually in addition to the license suspensions typically imposed for such a refusal.

Because state laws vary widely, these general statements are all we can say here about DUI sentences and penalties. Keep in mind that in addition to these penalties, your insurance company may cancel your policy or drastically increase your rates.

Felony DUI

If you kill or injure anyone as the result of driving while you are under the influence of alcohol (or while your blood alcohol is 0.08% or more in those states that punish driving with a certain BAC), you can be found guilty of a felony and could go to state prison for years. Prior convictions for misdemeanor under-the-influence or over-0.08% will usually result in a greater prison sentence. In some states, a third or fourth DUI can be charged as a felony, even when no one is killed or injured.

This is all we'll say about felony drunk driving. Needless to say, no one should ever attempt to handle a felony charge without a lawyer, and anyone accused of felony under-the-influence or over-0.08% driving should use this book only as a very limited introductory resource.

How Alcohol Interacts With Your Body

Just as the amount of gasoline in your fuel tank depends on how often you fill it and how much you burn off as you drive, the amount of alcohol in your bloodstream is determined by a balance between how fast alcohol is absorbed into your blood and how fast it's eliminated from it. Elimination occurs when most of the alcohol is "burned" or "oxidized" in your body, while the rest of the alcohol is excreted in breath, urine, and perspiration. Since alcohol is eliminated from the bloodstream at a fairly steady rate, the degree of intoxication depends a lot on

the rate of absorption. If alcohol is absorbed rapidly into the bloodstream, the blood alcohol level will get high fast—and so will you. If it is absorbed slowly enough to be eliminated before it builds up, you won't feel very high.

Absorption Into the Bloodstream

When you take a drink, the alcohol is absorbed into the blood through the mucous lining of the entire gastrointestinal tract: the mouth, the esophagus, the stomach, and the small intestine. The rate of absorption increases as the drink moves down the tract. Absorption from the stomach into the bloodstream (by way of blood-carrying capillaries in the stomach lining) is faster than from the esophagus or mouth. The street wisdom, which says that drinking on an empty stomach will get you higher, faster, is true because there is nothing else in your stomach to compete with the alcohol in terms of getting absorbed. The fastest rate of absorption is from the upper end of the small intestine.

For an "average individual," about 60% of the alcohol consumed at a given time will have been absorbed into the bloodstream a half-hour later. About 90% will have been absorbed in an hour, and all of it will have been absorbed in an hour and a half. However, this is just for an "average" individual with an "average" stomach food load, drinking "average" drinks. In fact, the rate of alcohol absorption depends on all sorts of things: the quantity of alcohol ingested, the concentration of alcohol in the drink, the rate of drinking, and the nature and amount of diluting material already in the stomach.

Elimination From the Body

Alcohol is eliminated from the body in two ways. Ninety to ninety-five percent of it is oxidized, mostly in the liver, to form water and carbon dioxide (a gas that dissolves in the blood, goes to your lungs, and is exhaled). The rate of its oxidation is pretty much the same over time but varies depending on how well a person's liver functions. People who drink regularly burn alcohol faster than casual drinkers. Chronic alcoholics burn it even faster. The remaining 5% to 10% of the alcohol is eliminated unchanged by perspiration, in urine by way of the kidneys and bladder, and in the breath by way of the blood as it reaches the lungs.

Calculating Approximate Blood Alcohol Levels

Since driving with a 0.08% BAC is illegal, or at least a basis for being presumed under the influence, it can be helpful for you to be able to estimate your own blood alcohol level at any given time, based on the number of drinks you had and the time you had them. Although a person's exact blood alcohol level depends on a number of factors, there's a simple, reasonably accurate way you can figure what your highest possible blood alcohol level could be (for example, if you drank very fast on an empty stomach).

If you divide the number 3.8 by your body weight in pounds, you should obtain a number between 0.015 and 0.040. Call this your own personal "blood-alcohol-maximum-per-drink" number. This is the maximum percentage alcohol that will be added to your blood with each "drink" you take. For the purposes of this calculation, a "drink" is a 12-ounce, 4% alcohol, bottle of beer, or a 4-ounce glass (a small wine glass) of 12% alcohol wine, or a one-ounce shot glass of 100 proof liquor (most bars's mixed drinks have this amount of alcohol). (Micro-brewery beer, malt liquor, pint bottles of beer, large (6 oz.) wine glasses, 20% alcohol ("fortified") wines, and very stiff or large mixed drinks should be counted as "1½" drinks.) For each such "drink," your blood alcohol concentration will be increased by about the percentages in the chart below.

EXAMPLE:

Linda Light, weighing a petite 100 pounds, could possibly have had a blood alcohol level of up to 0.038% from just one drink and up to 0.076% from two drinks. Three drinks could put her over the 0.08% blood alcohol level, especially if she drank them quickly on an empty stomach. Hans Heavy, on the other hand, weighs in at 240 pounds, and his maximum blood alcohol increase per drink is only 0.016%. He's barely feeling the effects of the first one. To get past 0.08% blood alcohol, he'd have to down at least six drinks in an hour.

Likely Maximum Blood Alcohol Level (%)

Your Weight in Pounds	Drinks Consumed in One Hour				
	1	2	3	4	5
100	0.038	0.076	0.114	0.152	0.190
120	0.032	0.064	0.096	0.128	0.160
140	0.027	0.054	0.081	0.108	0.135
160	0.024	0.048	0.072	0.096	0.120
180	0.021	0.042	0.063	0.084	0.105
200	0.019	0.038	0.057	0.076	0.095
220	0.017	0.034	0.051	0.068	0.085
240	0.016	0.032	0.048	0.064	0.080

Legend:

☐ over 0.05%; subject to prosecution for driving under influence

☐ over 0.08%; guilty of misdemeanor if you drive a vehicle

$$\text{Approx. blood alcohol level (\%) over time} = \frac{3.8 \times \# \text{ of drinks}}{\text{body weight}} - \frac{.01 \times \# \text{ of minutes} - 40}{40}$$

Note: The numbers in the chart above may vary depending on the sex and physical condition of the person drinking. Numbers may be higher for females and people in poor physical condition.

Now let's look at how long the alcohol-elimination process takes. After about 40 minutes have passed, your body will begin eliminating alcohol from the bloodstream at the rate of about 0.01% for each additional 40 minutes. So, once you multiply the number of drinks you've had by your blood alcohol maximum per drink, subtract 0.01% from that number for each 40 minutes that have passed since you began drinking—but don't count the first 40 minutes.

Note: If you are so addled by alcohol that you cannot do the math, you are probably too drunk to drive.

For those of you who like mathematical shorthand:

EXAMPLE:

100-pound Linda Light's blood alcohol level after two drinks gulped down rather quickly could be as high as 0.076%. But if she drank them over a period of an hour and 20 minutes (or 40 minutes beyond the first 40 minutes) her blood alcohol would be about 0.010% less, or 0.066%. Forty minutes later, it would be down to about 0.056% and so on. (Keep in mind that these are only approximate calculations.)

Finally, for those of you who prefer bar graphs over numbers and formulas, a reproduction of a set of graphs printed by the California Department of Motor Vehicles is provided below.

Effects of Alcohol

Alcohol affects you because of its presence in the brain cells. It reaches your brain within seconds after it has been absorbed into your bloodstream.

The three serious types of impairment resulting from the "depressant" effects of alcohol on the brain are:

- less efficient vision and hearing
- lack of muscular coordination (clumsiness), and
- deterioration of judgment and self-control (euphoria and loss of inhibitions).

Again, the extent of impairment will vary from person to person, and the above figures represent only a range of averages. Some people, particularly regular drinkers, will have a sort of built-up immunity to alcohol. Still, their BAC may be 0.08% or more. At the other extreme, people who normally abstain from alcohol begin to suffer slight impairment at a blood alcohol level as low as 0.02%! Moderate drinkers begin to show mild symptoms at 0.04% to 0.07%, while some heavy drinkers require 0.07% to 0.09% to suffer any impairment at all.

Some persons, who over long periods of time consume large amounts of alcohol on a daily basis, may never be seriously affected in terms of muscular coordination—although alcohol can still cloud their judgment. (Of course, claiming that your 0.27% blood alcohol had no effect on your driving because you've been an alcoholic for years is not a

---

ALCOHOL IMPAIRMENT CHART
DRIVING UNDER THE INFLUENCE OF ALCOHOL AND/OR DRUGS IS ILLEGAL*

There is no safe way to drive while under the influence. Even one drink can make you an unsafe driver.

Drinking alcohol affects your **Blood Alcohol Concentration (BAC).** It is illegal to drive with a **BAC** that is .08% or more (.04% or more if you drive commercial vehicles; .01% or more if under 21). However, a **BAC** below .08% does not mean that it is safe or legal to drive. The charts below show the **BAC** zones for various numbers of drinks and time periods. **Remember:** "One drink" is a 1 1/2-ounce shot of 80-proof liquor (even if mixed with non-alcoholic drinks), a 5-ounce glass of 12% wine, or a 12-ounce glass of 5% beer. These "one drink" equivalents

change if you are drinking ale, malt liquors, fortified wines, port, brandy, different proof liquor, **or** if you are drinking on an empty stomach, are tired, sick, upset, or have taken medicines or drugs.

How to use these charts: Find your weight chart. Then, look for the total number of drinks you have had and compare that to the time shown. If your **BAC** level is in the grey zone, your chances of having an accident are 5 times higher than if you had no drinks, and 25 times higher if your **BAC** level falls in the black zone.

BAC Zones:	90 to 109 lbs.	110 to 129 lbs.	130 to 149 lbs.	150 to 169 lbs.	170 to 189 lbs.	190 to 209 lbs.	210 lbs. & Up
TIME FROM 1st DRINK	TOTAL DRINKS 1 2 3 4 5 6 7 8	TOTAL DRINKS 1 2 3 4 5 6 7 8	TOTAL DRINKS 1 2 3 4 5 6 7 8	TOTAL DRINKS 1 2 3 4 5 6 7 8	TOTAL DRINKS 1 2 3 4 5 6 7 8	TOTAL DRINKS 1 2 3 4 5 6 7 8	TOTAL DRINKS 1 2 3 4 5 6 7 8
1 hr							
2 hrs							
3 hrs							
4 hrs							

Technical note: These charts are not legal evidence of actual BAC. Although it is possible for anyone to exceed the designated limits, the charts have been constructed so that fewer than 5 persons in 100 will exceed these limits when drinking the stated amounts on an empty stomach. Actual values can vary by body type, sex, health status, and other factors.

Legend: ☐ (.01%–.04%) Possible DUI—*Definitely unlawful if under 21 years old* ▨ (.05%–.07%) Likely DUI—*Definitely unlawful if under 21 years old* ■ (.08% Up) Definitely DUI

* VC §§23152, 23153, 23136, 23140 DUI=Driving under the influence of alcohol and/or other drugs.

DL 606MO (REV. 10/2004)

recommended line of defense, since you must be found guilty if the jury believes your blood alcohol was 0.08% or more while you were driving.)

Effects of Blood Alcohol		
% Blood Alcohol	State	Symptoms
0.01–0.05	relaxation	mild feeling of relaxation, very little effect
0.05–0.12	mild euphoria	slower reflexes, less coordination, lowered inhibitions, and increased self-confidence
0.08–0.25	impairment	memory and muscular coordination greatly reduced
0.15–0.30	great impairment	dizziness, disorientation, confusion
0.27–0.40	drunken stupor	inability to stand or walk; vomiting likely
0.35–0.50	coma/near death	body temperature fails and death from respiratory paralysis may result

What does "under the influence" really mean? Do you wonder why the exact figure of 0.08% blood alcohol is used to define an offense? Is it because everyone is drunk at that level, or is it just a nice convenient round figure having little to do with reality?

The truth lies somewhere in between. Here's the story.

In 1939, the American Medical Association had a "Committee to Study Problems of Motor Vehicle Accidents" look into the blood alcohol level at which a person is "under the influence" as far as driving is concerned. As a result of the study, the AMA and the National Safety Council concluded that:

- A person whose blood alcohol was 0.05% or less is definitely not under the influence.
- A person whose blood alcohol was between 0.05% and 0.15% might be under the influence, depending on the individual and the circumstances.
- A person with over 0.15% blood alcohol was definitely under the influence.

Many states use only the first of the above conclusions in the form of a presumption that a person with less than 0.05% blood alcohol is not under the influence. But the range of alcohol levels between which a person legally may or may not be under the influence is conservatively set at 0.05% to 0.08% in most states, rather than at the range suggested by the AMA study, namely 0.05% to 0.15%. For years, the law defined 0.10% and above as under the influence, even though many experts believe that this cutoff level should be 0.15%. However, as of July 2004 every state and the District of Columbia had lowered the 0.10% cutoff to 0.08%.

Blood, Breath, and Urine Tests for Alcohol

Most drunk-driving arrests result in the arrested person taking a "chemical test" for the presence of alcohol in her blood, breath, or urine. This section briefly explains the law that requires this, as well as the tests themselves.

The "Implied Consent" Law

Almost every state has a so-called implied consent law. Such laws require any person lawfully arrested for driving under the influence to give a blood, breath, or urine sample when taken to the jail or police station. ("Lawfully arrested" means the officer had a "reasonable suspicion" to pull you over, and then "probable cause" to arrest you. An officer has a reasonable suspicion to stop you if he sees you commit a violation or drive erratically. If, after he pulls you over, he notices the obvious symptoms of intoxication, he will then have "probable cause" to physically arrest you and charge you with driving under the influence.) If you refuse, your driver's license will be suspended by your state's motor vehicles department for anywhere between three to 12 months, depending on the state. This is true even if you're eventually found not guilty of the current drunk driving charge.

Your Right to a Choice of Tests

Even though you must submit to some kind of test, you usually have the right to choose between a blood, breath, or urine test, though some states have eliminated the urine test as a choice in recent years. If one of the tests is unavailable, you are required to take another of the available tests. For example, if the police department's breath tester is broken, you will be required to take a blood or urine test.

Which test should you choose? It depends on the circumstances. If you had only one beer, glass of wine, or mild drink, your blood alcohol will be under 0.05%, a level so low that no sane prosecutor would try the case. Because results from a breath test (unlike those from a blood test) can be directly displayed on the measuring device right away, it will become clear that you're sober, and the police might therefore let you go. On the other hand, if it's been less than an hour since you've finished your last drink (more, if you've eaten food), your body is still absorbing alcohol. When your body is absorbing alcohol, a breath test will give an erroneously high value. I once observed a test in which a person drank a few ounces of tequila, and half an hour later she took a blood and a breath test. The blood test showed 0.05% alcohol, but the breath test read "0.10%."

The reason for this result is that while your body is absorbing alcohol, your arterial blood alcohol level is higher than your venous blood alcohol level, and a breath test measures the higher arterial blood alcohol. So, if you last drank less than an hour before you're tested, don't take the breath test. Choose the blood test if you're sure you're below 0.08%.

Of the three tests, the urine test is probably the least accurate. This is because the percent of alcohol in the urine is not necessarily the same as in a person's blood. It's about 1.33 times the BAC level. So, to convert a urine test result into an equivalent blood alcohol level requires division of the urine alcohol level by 1.33. However, this number is an average, and you can argue at trial that this average figure didn't apply to you. For this reason, if you're in the unfortunate position of knowing you had way too much to drink and are offered a choice, the urine test is the one to pick.

Other Rights

The rule is that you do not have the right to have your attorney present for the test. After the results are in on your blood, breath, or urine test, you have the right to a copy of the results, and many states also recognize the right to have part of a preserved blood or urine sample collected by the police tested by an independent laboratory.

The Chemical Tests: How They Work, How They Fail

In this section, we introduce you to how the different tests work and some of the ways they go wrong.

Blood Tests

Other than directly measuring the alcohol content of your brain cells (which can be dangerous), the most accurate test to determine the possibility of alcohol affecting

your driving is the blood sample test. Challenging the accuracy of this test is not as easy as challenging the accuracy of the breath or urine tests. Also, a blood sample is a very good indicator of whether you had taken any drugs.

However, if you have submitted to (or were coerced into taking) a blood test, there are several ways you may be able to challenge its accuracy.

The most common modern method for analyzing alcohol in a blood sample utilizes a "gas chromatograph," a device that vaporizes a liquid sample and passes the vapor through a "column" of dry chemicals that separate the vapor. Different vapors come out of the other end of the column at different times, and when the alcohol vapor comes off, its amount is measured by a detector whose output is displayed on a graph or digital readout. This method also relies on the use of standard solutions containing known amounts of alcohol to "calibrate" the gas chromatograph. Still other tests involve reaction of the alcohol with an enzyme.

A much older (and rarely used) procedure for the chemical analysis of blood samples for alcohol involves distilling the alcohol out of the blood and reacting it with a chemical called an "oxidizing agent." The more alcohol there is, the more oxidizing agent is used, allowing the analyst to calculate the alcohol from the amount of chemical required to oxidize all the alcohol. This oxidizing agent is really a solution of potassium dichromate ($K_2Cr_2O_7$) in distilled water. Its concentration has to be known with great precision in order for the result to be accurate.

In challenging any type of chemical analysis, a good defense lawyer should know how to cross-examine the analysts to shed doubt on the accuracy of the result. Did the analyst prepare the "standard" solution herself, or just take someone else's word for its content? Does the analyst periodically check the solution concentration to make sure it hasn't changed? Are tests periodically performed on samples of known alcohol concentration?

Also, most laboratories that analyze blood or urine samples run numerous samples every day, making some errors on some samples (maybe yours!)—more probable than if an analyst were carefully concentrating on just one. Proper record keeping and laboratory organization are necessary to guard against sample mixups, as different parts of the analyses are carried out in different bottles and beakers. You may be able to cast some doubt on the test readings by raising questions about their record keeping.

Finally, blood samples that aren't properly preserved and sit around a long time before being analyzed have a tendency to either coagulate or decompose. If the sample coagulates, so that the red blood cells separate out from the liquid blood portion, the alcohol is further concentrated in the remaining liquid portion—contributing to a false high reading. If the sample decomposes, a false high reading will also be obtained, because one of the chemical products of this decomposition is alcohol. Therefore, it is important that the analysis be done shortly after the sample is taken, and that the sample be properly preserved to minimize decomposition.

These are only remote possibilities, however. More than likely, the analysis of a blood sample will be correct, and a very good indicator of the blood alcohol in your system, at least at the time the sample was taken.

Breath Tests

Usually, you should take the breath test only if you finished your last drink at least an hour before the test. However, if you've had very little to drink, and it's been at least an hour since you stopped drinking, you may want to opt for the breath test. With this test, the police will know your approximate blood alcohol level immediately, and if the reading indicates less than 0.05% blood alcohol, they may release you right away. But don't count on it. They may simply keep you in custody until someone bails you out. Also, after seeing the low alcohol reading and still being convinced your driving ability truly was impaired, they may think you're on drugs instead, and insist on a blood sample after that.

An analysis of breath gas gives only an indirectly determined value for blood alcohol. A breath test determines how much alcohol is in some portion of exhaled air, not how much alcohol is in the blood. To calculate content of blood alcohol from that of exhaled air, the content of alcohol in the air is normally multiplied by the number 2,100. This number, known as a "partition coefficient" or "partition ratio," is used because the lung air exhaled by an "average" person usually has 1/2100th the amount of alcohol of an equal volume of blood. Using this "average" figure amounts to little more than scientific guesswork. For example, one study showed some people have lung air alcohol concentrations 1,500 times smaller than their blood alcohol values, while other people have lung air alcohol concentrations 3,000 times smaller. Also, the value varies for the same person over time and depends on body temperature and even respiration rate. As with results from a urine alcohol analysis, the calculated blood alcohol level (already printed or displayed on a readout on the machine) may be erroneous.

EXAMPLE:

Based on an "average" for all persons studied, the law assumes your blood alcohol content to be 2,100 times the content of alcohol in your breath. (Actually, this calculation is already done inside the breath-analyzing device.) So, if your breath contains 0.00004% alcohol, this number multiplied by the "partition coefficient" of 2,100 will give a calculated percentage of 0.08. But if your own "blood-to-breath" ratio is really 1,500 to 1, the 0.00004% breath alcohol content really means a blood alcohol level of 0.06%. Thus, the results could "prove" your blood alcohol was an illegal 0.08%, when in fact it was less than that.

Formerly, a person with a "borderline" breath alcohol level was allowed to use the "erroneous partition coefficient" defense to show a breath test inaccurate. However, many states now define the offense in terms of grams of alcohol per 210 liters of breath (a value consistent with a 2100:1 partition coefficient), as well as grams of alcohol per 100 milliliters of blood. Thus, any evidence tending to show a partition coefficient other than 2100:1 will have no bearing on the concentration of alcohol in the breath gas itself, and will be disallowed. On the other hand, such evidence should be allowed in those states that have not defined the offense in terms of a certain amount of alcohol in a certain volume of breath gas.

Alcohol-containing substances in your mouth can also produce falsely high readings, since the amount of alcohol vapor given off by anything in your mouth is much greater than any amount you exhale from your lungs. This includes stomach fluid vomited or regurgitated up within 20 minutes of taking the test, some toothache medicines, mouthwashes, and breath fresheners. Even a burp just before or while you blow into the breathalyzer tube may cause a falsely high reading. For this reason, the person administering the test is supposed to watch you for at least 20 minutes prior to taking the test to make sure you don't burp, belch, regurgitate, vomit, or put anything into your mouth.

There is also the possibility of a malfunction in the breath-testing devices. To assure accuracy, the device must be frequently calibrated with air containing known amounts of alcohol. The police department's records should indicate how often the device has been calibrated, serviced, and used. A lapse in record keeping and/or police memory as to calibration and preparation of sample solutions can help your attorney establish reasonable doubt about the accuracy of the instrument. Other errors may result from the particular type of breath gas analyzer used.

Finally, because breath gas analysis is often inaccurate, you may be asked to take the tests two, or even three, times to produce a consistent result. Your failure to give them all the breath samples they want will result in your license being suspended by the DMV.

Breath Gas Analyzers: The most common device uses a beam from an infrared heat source. When the beam encounters alcohol vapor, some of its energy is absorbed by the alcohol molecules. The more infrared energy absorbed, the higher the blood alcohol.

This method measures alcohol to the exclusion of other organic materials (like acetone on the breath of diabetics) better than some older devices, but it is easily subject to the same interferences from alcohol-containing substances in your mouth. Also, the measuring devices have to be periodically maintained and standardized.

Urine Tests

The urine test is less accurate than the blood or breath tests, which is why the trend is now to allow use of the test only when the blood and breath tests are unavailable.

The urine test is the least accurate primarily because urine isn't blood, which actually contains the alcohol. So assumptions have to be made from a urine test about how much alcohol was ingested. Thus, the urine alcohol level has to be "correlated" to an "equivalent" blood alcohol level. An "average" 1.33:1 ratio of urine alcohol to blood alcohol is generally used. However, studies have shown that some people have alcohol levels only 40% as high in their urine as in their blood, while others have twice the alcohol content in their urine as in their blood. The urine test will give an erroneously high result if your urine has a higher concentration of alcohol than usual. Your urine may have a higher concentration of alcohol even if it's been a few hours since you last drank and your body is eliminating alcohol that is still in your system. This means that the blood alcohol level the prosecution infers from a urine alcohol analysis might be incorrect in some cases.

EXAMPLE:

The prosecutor assumes your urine alcohol to be an "average" 1.33 multiple of your blood alcohol. If a sample of your urine is found to contain, say, 0.133% alcohol, the prosecutor would divide this value by 1.33 to calculate a blood alcohol value of 0.10%. But if your kidneys actually pump out urine with an alcohol content twice that of your blood, a 0.133% urine alcohol content, divided by two, corresponds to only a 0.066% blood alcohol value. Thus the prosecutor would try to "prove" your blood alcohol level was 0.10% when, in fact, it was under 0.07%.

Also, a specimen of bladder urine represents only a composite of a continuously changing blood alcohol content. The pool of urine in the bladder at any given time is an accumulation of secreted urine since the last emptying of the bladder. It therefore tells much less about a person's blood alcohol at a particular moment than does a blood sample. This can work for or against you. If you had a lot to drink several hours beforehand and haven't urinated since that time, the urine test result may be misleadingly high. If your drinking was relatively recent, though, say within an hour of the time you gave the sample, and especially if you'd had any nonalcoholic liquids before that, the urine test would give a misleadingly low result. Because of this, the only way to properly test a person's urine is to have him or her void the bladder and then produce a second urine sample. The police know this, and will insist that you also produce a second sample 20 minutes later. If you can't, you'll have to take the more accurate blood test or the breath test, under penalty of license suspension if you refuse.

Urine samples are analyzed for alcohol in almost the same way as blood samples. The results are therefore also subject to some of the same laboratory errors.

If you do take the urine test, the police are required to give you the right to some privacy, but you can't insist on going alone into a bathroom where you might be able to secretly dilute the sample with tap or toilet water. At the very least, though, they have to exclude all persons of the opposite sex from the room in which you give the sample.

In sum, then, most chemical analyses of your breath, blood, or urine will give an accurate indication of your actual blood alcohol level. However, the tests are not infallible, and an experienced criminal defense attorney may be able to cast enough doubt on borderline test results to convince a jury that you might not be guilty.

License Suspension Penalties and Procedures

Years ago, a person convicted of driving under the influence did not necessarily face a driver's license suspension for one conviction. The DMV would suspend a person's driver's license only if the person's driving record showed other violations as well.

Then, in response to changing attitudes toward drunk driving, license suspensions became automatic for a first offense. Typically the court had discretion not to suspend a driver's license on a first offense.

Now, however, almost all states have enacted procedures under which your license is suspended before any conviction, and your suspension is handed to you by a police officer. Suspension is then automatic, unless you request a hearing from the DMV within a certain time period. If you can't convince the DMV to overturn your suspension, your license is suspended—even if the court dismisses or reduces the charges.

After arresting you for driving under the influence, a police officer will take away your driver's license and present you with both a notice that your license is suspended effective at a later date and a temporary license to allow you to drive within that period.

The request for hearing then must be made to the DMV within the time allowed, or the suspension will go into effect, even if the charges are later reduced or dismissed in court.

Whether you default or show up at the hearing and lose, your driver's license will be suspended for a period of time that depends on a number of factors, including:

- whether you refused a chemical test, or, if you submitted to one, whether it showed your blood alcohol was 0.08% or more, and
- the total number of prior convictions of driving under the influence, or suspensions received for it in the past.

Dealing With a DUI Charge

The following is only a very brief summary of what you need to consider if faced with a drunk-driving charge.

Evaluating Your Case

After you've been arrested for driving under the influence and have been released from jail, you should try to objectively evaluate your case. Your alternatives include:

- simply pleading guilty as charged

- trying to plea bargain down to a reduced charge like reckless driving
- asking for a trial before a judge, or
- demanding a jury trial.

The general rule is that if you choose to fight the charge, you should usually insist on a jury trial—you'll have a better chance than with a case-worn and possibly cynical judge who has seen a lot of guilty people. The only exception to this general rule is when your defense is fairly unusual or technical. For example, if you staggered out of a bar and into your car and fell asleep—but you didn't drive—a judge might be more receptive to your defense than a jury.

The U.S. Supreme Court has ruled that a person accused of drunk driving punishable by up to six months in jail isn't entitled, under the U.S. Constitution, to a jury trial. (*Blanton v. City of North Las Vegas* (1989) 489 U.S. 538). However, most states allow for a jury trial anyway, though Hawaii, Louisiana, and Nevada do not. A few other states (Alaska, New Hampshire, and Virginia) allow a jury trial only after an appeal following a trial by a judge alone. In most states, the prosecutor must convince all twelve jurors of your guilt, as opposed to just one judge in a nonjury trial.

Still, even jury trial conviction rates for driving under the influence are high, though they vary in different parts of the country. (Sadly, this is partly because special interest groups have, over the years, fostered a public attitude to the effect that eradicating the drunk-driving problem is more important than having fair trials.) Part of the money you're paying your lawyer is for the value of his or her experience in knowing what a local jury is likely to do in a given situation.

Generally, the more a jury is likely to find you guilty of driving under the influence (or with an over-0.08% blood alcohol level), the more you will want to plea bargain, or negotiate a settlement, with the prosecutor. Since drunk driving juries unfortunately put a lot of faith in the blood test results (and the prosecutor's scientific mumbo-jumbo that goes along with it), it is these results that are most likely to affect your choice of options.

As a general rule, a person whose blood alcohol test results are higher than 0.12% will have a very low chance of winning at trial. This is especially true in the many states where an over-0.08% blood alcohol level is sufficient to convict you—whether you were drunk or not. The only way you can be acquitted of such a charge in those states is to shed doubt on the validity of the test results so that the jury either entirely disbelieves them or thinks that after adjusting for possible errors in your favor, your blood alcohol might have been less than 0.08%. It is very difficult for even a trained and experienced lawyer to do this. Therefore, a confident prosecutor is not likely to enter into a plea bargain where you agree to plead guilty to a reduced charge like reckless driving.

If your blood alcohol tested out at between 0.08 and 0.11%, your chances of winning in a trial are slightly better. You still have to convince a jury that the test results are at least inaccurate enough to raise a reasonable doubt as to whether your

blood alcohol was 0.08% or higher at the time you were driving.

Whether you have a decent chance of convincing a jury you weren't under the influence will depend largely on the type of testimony your lawyer can elicit from anyone who was with you either before or while you were driving.

If your blood alcohol was measured at less than the legal limit of 0.08% that applies in most states, your chances of beating a drunk-driving charge are better. First, you won't be convicted of having a blood alcohol of 0.08% or more, and the prosecutor will have to establish that you were under the influence at the below-0.08% level. However, if your blood alcohol level was found to be slightly under 0.08%—say, 0.06% or 0.07%—measured about an hour after you were driving, the prosecutor would then claim that it was higher—namely 0.08%—when you were driving, and fell below that level before the blood or breath sample was taken. A skilled attorney should be able to properly cross-examine the prosecutor's expert witnesses to show that the likelihood of one's driving ability being affected at a blood alcohol level of less than 0.08% is small. Naturally, the further below 0.08% your blood alcohol was, the better your chances are of being acquitted and the more likely the prosecutor will be willing to plea bargain.

What if you refused to submit to a blood or breath test? Your chances of beating the drunk-driving charge at trial might be slightly better than if you have submitted to the test and the results showed a very high blood alcohol level. (However, your refusal to take the test can be used against you, and jurors may consider this to be a damning admission on your part.) The prosecutor may be unable to convict you for having a blood alcohol level of 0.08% or more, but she still may be able to convict you of having been under the influence. This will depend almost entirely on how much weight the jury gives to the testimony of the police officer and prosecution witnesses, compared to how much the jurors will believe any testimony you can present. And, of course, your refusal to take the test will result in a license suspension.

Getting a Lawyer

As mentioned earlier, defending yourself against a drunk-driving charge in a jury trial is not recommended. Once you've been released from jail and have had a chance to evaluate your case, you should think about getting an attorney to represent you, in addition to putting in a hearing request to your state's DMV. If you're unable to afford an attorney, you should ask the judge to appoint a lawyer for you when you first appear in court. Even if your case seems hopeless, you have nothing to lose by taking advantage of free legal representation. If you aren't poor enough to qualify for a court-appointed lawyer, and believe that your case falls in the narrow range where you may be able to win a jury trial, begin by making an appointment with an attorney experienced in criminal defense work. Even though you may be unable to afford to pay her to defend you in a jury

trial (the fee for this could be as high as several thousand dollars), you should be able to afford the fee for one or two office visits. At the very least, you can hire her for the limited purpose of fully explaining your options to you, or perhaps to try to work out a plea bargain with the prosecutor. Defense attorneys' statistics show that the chances of beating a drunk-driving charge by going to trial are low. If your case is rife with hopeless circumstances (for example, blood alcohol over 0.15%, dismal failure on coordination tests, and so on), you should be wary of an overly optimistic lawyer who tells you your chances are excellent while demanding more and more money as the case drags on.

Plea Bargaining

Plea bargaining (sometimes also referred to as "sentence bargaining") is a process where a criminal defendant (or his or her lawyer) and the prosecutor reach a compromise, then the defendant enters a guilty plea to a reduced charge or, sometimes, in exchange for the promise of a reduced fine or jail sentence. Plea bargaining generally takes place over the phone or at the prosecutor's office, and often at a "pretrial conference" in the judge's chambers before trial. As part of the process, the judge informally tells you— or your lawyer—the sentence that he or she will impose if you plead guilty.

The "bargain" of a plea bargain is that the prosecutor avoids having to try a questionable case but still gets to rack up a conviction, while the person accused of drunk driving receives the minimum sentence or, perhaps, only a less-serious conviction for reckless driving.

Plea bargains in drunk-driving cases, however, are no longer as common as they were many years ago. In light of the fact that all states but one have reduced the 0.10% limit to 0.08%, and many have flatly outlawed driving with a blood alcohol level of 0.08% or more—regardless of whether the driver is under the influence—it is common for prosecutors to obtain convictions in the formerly borderline cases (0.08% to 0.12% alcohol levels).

Despite the attempts of "law and order" types to forbid plea bargaining, it will always be with us. Without it, defense attorneys would have nothing to lose by pleading each and every one of their clients not guilty and demanding a jury trial all the time. When you consider that only about 10% of all serious criminal cases ever go to trial, and that nearly all the remaining cases are plea bargained, an end to plea bargaining would increase fivefold the number of trials in the criminal courts. This would require more courts, judges, court personnel, and taxes.

Although you may wish to conduct your own plea bargaining negotiations, it may be a good idea to hire a lawyer to do it for you. A prosecutor may not be as willing to enter into a plea bargain with an inexperienced defendant who might well do a poor job of representing herself. Also, an experienced lawyer who regularly handles drunk-driving cases will be more familiar with local practices, prosecutors, and judges than you can ever hope to be. Nevertheless,

many defendants who have taken the time to educate themselves both as to the law and to the nuances of bargaining have done every bit as well as, and sometimes better than, lawyers and have saved themselves a big fee.

Pretrial Court Proceedings

Because drunk driving cases are more complex and should generally be handled by an attorney, this section is designed to give you information you'll need to intelligently participate in your attorney's defense of your drunk driving case.

Arraignment

Some time after you're arrested, you will appear before a judge for arraignment. You will be asked to plead to the charge, either guilty or not guilty. Arrangements will also be made regarding your right to counsel and bail. If you tell the judge you can't afford to hire a lawyer, she will probably ask you to fill out a financial disclosure form and refer you to the public defender's office. In more rural areas, the judge may appoint a private defense lawyer to represent you. Most defendants charged with misdemeanors who have not already posted bail are released on their own recognizance at arraignment. Having an attorney represent you at arraignment is normally unnecessary. At this stage, you are only entering a plea, and you can plead not guilty and insist on a jury trial. You do not have to specifically request a jury trial; it is assumed you want one unless you expressly waive that right.

You can always change your plea to guilty or nolo contendere, or drop the demand for a jury trial later. If you're also charged with having suffered prior under-the-influence convictions, you should deny them so that you or your attorney can challenge their validity later. At arraignment, the case will also be set for a "pretrial conference."

Motions to Suppress Evidence

If the police illegally arrested you and/or obtained any evidence against you in an illegal manner, your attorney may be able to schedule a special pretrial hearing to suppress certain evidence. The prosecution is then prevented from using it at trial. For example, if you consented to give a blood sample only after the police beat you into submission, your attorney may want to make a "motion to suppress" the test results, thereby keeping them from being introduced into evidence at trial.

A motion to suppress is heard several weeks (sometimes months) before the trial actually takes place. It is heard only before a judge, perhaps one who will not be presiding at your trial. This type of motion is fairly technical and complicated, and will probably involve cross-examining the officer who arrested you. You're advised not to try to handle it yourself.

Motions to "Strike a Prior"

A person who pleads guilty to, or is convicted of, a second or third offense of driving under the influence can suffer a far heavier penalty than a first offender. To obtain the heavier penalty, the prosecution must "charge" the prior conviction against you. When you initially plead "not guilty" to the offense, never admit any priors charged against you. Simply "deny" them. This is perfectly legal. If you "admit" them, you destroy any chance of challenging their validity on technical grounds.

By having a prior conviction "stricken," you face a less-severe penalty if convicted on the current charge. The procedure to strike a prior is based on whether you were properly informed of and/or intelligently waived (gave up) certain rights at any hearings related to the prior offenses. Again, this type of motion is extremely technical and better left to your attorney.

The Pretrial or Settlement Conference

In most places, a "pretrial conference" or "settlement conference" is scheduled some time before a jury trial. This conference usually occurs inside a judge's chambers and is where most plea bargaining (and sentence bargaining) occurs. The prosecutor usually begins by emphasizing the blood alcohol test results and summarizing what the police officer and any other witnesses will testify to. This is to establish that he or she has a very strong case, implying that the defendant might as well plead guilty, or at least accept any offer of a plea bargain. To sweeten this prospect, the prosecutor might also offer to recommend a minimum sentence to the judge in exchange for a guilty plea. The judge might indicate whether or not he or she will accept such a recommendation; if the judge says he'll accept it, this will tell you or your lawyer what your sentence will be if you plead guilty to the original or a reduced charge.

If the prosecutor refuses to consider offering you the prospect of pleading guilty to a lesser charge and/or recommends more than the minimum sentence if you plead guilty, this is the time for you or your lawyer to briefly summarize your defense to the judge and prosecutor. You should emphasize the proposed testimony of any witnesses you may have regarding how sober you were just before you were driving. Also, if the blood alcohol test results are not much above 0.08%, indicate that you're prepared to cross-examine the chemist or breath gas analyzer operator regarding the scientific validity of the results. (This is especially important where a urine or breath test is involved.)

Then, depending on the judge's personality, he or she may try to convince you, your lawyer, or the prosecutor to compromise. (Some judges are very forceful in this regard and even take pride in insisting on compromise, so as not to have to do as many jury trials.) If a compromise is worked out, a time will be scheduled (possibly right then and there) for you to plead guilty to the original or a reduced charge in the courtroom. If not, a trial date will be set if one hasn't been already.

The Trial

The trial of drunk-driving cases is similar to the trial of any other misdemeanor offense. (The jury trial procedure is explained in Chapter 13.)

State-by-State DUI/DWI Comparison Chart

Below is a state-by-state listing of the following features of DUI/DWI laws.

BAC Limit/Absolute?: The blood alcohol concentration (0.08% or 0.10%) at which a person is presumed guilty of driving under the influence, or the limit at which driving is illegal. States that absolutely prohibit driving at or over the 0.08% or 0.10% limit, regardless of whether the driver is under the influence or not, are indicated with a "yes" under the "Absolute" column.

Administrative Suspension (Admin Suspension): We indicate "yes" or "no" to note whether the state has a system allowing the motor vehicles department to suspend the driver's license of a person arrested for driving at or over the legal limit.

Refusal Suspension: In this column we indicate the license suspension penalty for refusing an officer's request to take a blood, breath, or urine test for alcohol.

Jury Trial: States that deny a jury trial on a first-offense DUI/DWI are indicated, as are states that allow it only after a "de novo" trial following an appeal from a trial in front of a judge without a jury. All other states allow jury trials for DUI/DWI in the first instance.

State	BAC Limit	Absolute?	Admin. Suspension	Refusal Suspension	Jury Trial
Alabama	.08%	yes	yes	3 months[1]	on appeal
Alaska	.08	yes	yes	criminal[1]	
Arizona	.08	yes	yes	12 months	
Arkansas	.08	yes	yes	6 months	on appeal
California	.08	yes	yes	12 months	
Colorado	.08	no	yes	12 months	
Connecticut	.08	no	yes	6 months	
Delaware	.08	yes	yes	12 months	
D.C.	.08	no	yes	12 months	
Florida	.08	yes	yes	12 months	
Georgia	.08	yes	yes	12 months	
Hawaii	.08	no	yes	12 months	no jury trial

[1]Refusal is a separate criminal offense with the same penalties as DUI itself.

State	BAC Limit	Absolute?	Admin. Suspension	Refusal Suspension	Jury Trial
State-by-State DUI/DWI Comparison Chart (continued)					
Idaho	.08	no	yes	6 months	
Illinois	.08	yes	yes	6 months	
Indiana	.08	yes[2]	yes	12 months	
Iowa	.08	no	yes	8 months	
Kansas	.08	no	yes	12 months	
Kentucky	.08	no	yes	6 months	
Louisiana	.08	no	yes	6 months	no jury trial
Maine	.08	no	yes	275 days	
Massachusetts	.08	no	yes	4 months	
Michigan	.08	no	yes	6 months	
Minnesota	.08	no	yes	12 months	
Mississippi	.08	no	yes	3 months	
Missouri	.08	no	yes	12 months	
Montana	.08	no	no	6 months	
Nebraska	.08	no	yes	12 months	
Nevada	.08	no	yes	cannot be refused[2]	no jury trial
New Hampshire	.08	no	yes	6 months	on appeal
New Jersey	.08	yes	no	6 months	
New Mexico	.08	no	yes	12 months	
New York	.08	no	no	6 months	
North Carolina	.08	yes	yes	12 months	
North Dakota	.08	no	yes	12 months	
Ohio	.08	yes	yes	12 months	

[2]Police have authority to insist on forced blood test in the event of refusal.

State-by-State DUI/DWI Comparison Chart (continued)					
State	BAC Limit	Absolute?	Admin. Suspension	Refusal Suspension	Jury Trial
Oregon	.08	yes	yes	12 months	
Oklahoma	.08	no	yes	6 months	
Pennsylvania	.08	yes	yes	12 months	
Rhode Island	.08	no	no	3–6 months	
South Carolina	.08	no	no	3 months	
South Dakota	.08	yes	yes	criminal	
Tennessee	.08	no	no	12 months	
Texas	.08	yes	yes	3 months	
Utah	.08	yes	yes	12 months	
Vermont	.08	no	yes	6 months	
Virginia	.08	no	yes	6 months	on appeal
Washington	.08	yes	yes	12 months	
West Virginia	.08	no	yes	12 months	
Wisconsin	.08	yes	yes	12 months	
Wyoming	.08	no	yes	6 months	

First Steps to Fight Your Ticket

So You've Decided to Fight 124

Taking the First Steps 124

    Contacting the Court for Information 124

    Deciding How to Plead 125

    Should You Insist on an Arraignment? 127

    What Happens at Arraignment.. 127

    Trial by Declaration or Affidavit... 130

Using "Discovery" to Build Your Case 134

    If Your Discovery Request Is Ignored 134

    What to Do With the Officer's Notes.. 137

So You've Decided to Fight

If you are reading this chapter, it should mean you have already:

1. Looked up and studied your ticket and the law you are charged with violating (Chapter 2)

2. If you are eligible, at least considered the possibility of wiping out the ticket by attending traffic school (Chapter 3)

3. Considered the consequences of pleading guilty on your driving record and insurance premiums (Chapter 3), and

4. Found what you think is a defense with a reasonable chance of success (Chapters 5, 6, and 7).

There is no question that a determined person with a good defense can achieve great success in traffic court. And with the information you'll find here, your chances of prevailing should greatly increase.

Taking the First Steps

Before you show up in traffic court for your trial, there are some things you *must* do, and more you *should* do. In this chapter, we will review how basic traffic court procedure works and coach you on how to increase your chances of success.

Contacting the Court for Information

The date by which you must pay the fine or ask to appear in court should be printed on your ticket. For obvious reasons, paying up is usually made very easy. But if you want to fight, you may need to call the court to find out exactly what you need to do. Be prepared for frustration. Many courts have automatic phone systems from hell (that is, designed not to answer even one of your sensible questions). Persevere—or stop by the court clerk's office before the drop-dead date—and you should find a live person who can help.

Court Websites

More and more state and local courts are setting up websites. The websites vary widely in quality and usefulness. Some local court websites contain nothing but the court's address, while the most sophisticated sites have detailed FAQs (answers to frequently asked questions) explaining how traffic violations are handled in that jurisdiction, and others even have online systems for paying parking and traffic tickets.

You can look for your local court's website by entering the name of that court in an Internet search engine, such as www.google.com. Also, be sure to check the appendix in the back of this book, which lists a number of state and local court websites.

If you do speak to a live clerk, either by phone or by trekking to the courthouse, you'll want to have your ticket in hand to ask for the following information:

- Does the date on my ticket indicate my court date, or just the date by which I have to say whether I plan to contest my ticket?

- What additional steps must I take to fight my ticket?
- Is it possible to obtain an extension of time in which to decide whether I want to contest the ticket or schedule a trial date?
- Am I eligible for traffic school?

Deciding How to Plead

After you get basic information about your ticket and your options, you'll have to decide on a course of action. In most states, if for any reason you won't go to traffic school, you'll normally have four options:

- **Pay the fine** (called "forfeiting bail" in many places, the equivalent of pleading guilty).
- Plead **guilty with an explanation**.
- Plead **nolo contendere**.
- Plead **not guilty** (often this can be done at the clerk's office without entering a formal plea).

TIP

Do your homework. Before going to the court clerk's office or a court kiosk, you'll want to do the research necessary to decide whether you'll contest your ticket. Often this will save you a return trip to the courthouse.

Now let's look at each of these options in more detail.

Paying the Fine (Forfeiting Bail)

If you decide to pay the fine (equivalent to entering a guilty plea), this fact will appear on your driving record. If your record is otherwise spotless, a single violation should not affect your driving privileges or insurance premiums. But it's also true that you never know if you'll get another moving violation a week after (unless, of course, you switch to public transit, your bike, feet, or stay at home). Then, of course, you would be in greater jeopardy of an insurance premium increase and—if you get several more tickets—a possible license suspension. That's why we believe, if you aren't eligible for traffic school (see Chapter 3) but have a decent defense, it often makes sense to assert it.

Courts make it easy to pay the fine in most cases. They almost universally allow you to do so by mail or through the court clerk's office. Rarely will you be required to appear in court and admit your guilt. Traffic offenses where a formal guilty plea may be required in some states include driving more than 20 mph over the speed limit, reckless driving, and alcohol-related violations, like driving with an open alcoholic beverage container. If you have been in an accident related to the ticket, read the sidebar "If You Were Involved in an Accident," in this section.

If You Were Involved in an Accident

In most states, if you pay the ticket to the court clerk without appearing before a judge (most courts allow this except for the most serious violations), you do not subject yourself to civil liability as you would if you entered a guilty plea in court. But check with your insurance company or a lawyer to make sure.

If for any reason you are required to appear in court to enter a plea and have absolutely no defense, plead "nolo contendere." This special plea, available in most states, is equivalent to a guilty plea as far as your ticket is concerned, but can't be used against you if you are later slapped with a civil damage lawsuit from someone else involved in the accident.

However, if you are found guilty after trial in some states, this may result in the other party winning any lawsuit against you based on the accident. This is a legally complex issue, so you should seek a lawyer's advice before going to trial for a ticket arising out of an accident.

Plead Guilty With an Explanation

If you did it and have no decent defense, there is no need to go to court and plead guilty, as was common in times past. Just pay the fine (forfeit bail) and the deed is done. But one exception to this rule occurs in areas where you are allowed to enter a "guilty with an explanation" plea. As the name suggests, this involves pleading guilty but telling the judge a good enough story that she may reduce or even suspend the fine. Even where allowed, this is rarely a good approach. Even if a sympathetic judge reduces or "suspends" the fine, the offense still goes on your driving record and your insurance rates may rise. People who do not want to go to the trouble of preparing a good defense but who want to take a shot at tugging at the judge's heartstrings sometimes try this approach. It's far better to plead not guilty and take your best shot at trying to convince the judge you are not guilty. Also, the officer may not show up in court, which often results in the case against you being dismissed.

Plead Nolo Contendere

A plea of nolo contendere (pronounced "no-lo con-tend-er-ray") literally means: "I do not choose to contest the charge." While rarely necessary, this plea makes sense if you have been in an accident and, for some reason, you must enter a formal plea in court (can't just forfeit bail at the clerk's office). Because a nolo contendere plea admits only that you are not contesting the facts stated in the criminal charge (in this case, the ticket), it cannot be used as an admission of guilt in other cases. By contrast, a guilty plea can often be used against you in another lawsuit. All of this can be critical if you face the possibility of a civil lawsuit for damages because of a claim that you damaged property or caused injury or death to another person.

TIP

What if a judge balks at your nolo plea? Some judges hate nolo contendere pleas. They figure you are either guilty or not guilty. If your judge resists allowing you to enter a nolo contendere plea, tell her that there was an auto accident—if true, of course. This should change her mind. If the judge still says no, plead not guilty. This will give you a chance to discuss strategy with your insurance company and, if the situation is serious, a lawyer.

The Not Guilty Plea

Under our legal system, it is always your legal right to plead not guilty. This is true whether you think you are guilty or not. In many places, you can plead not guilty by mail or telephone, or by using a traffic court kiosk. In almost all others, this can be done at the court clerk's window. In either case, you may be required to post a fee—often called bail—which you get returned if you win. In a very few rural areas, to enter a not guilty plea you must appear before a judge at a brief court proceeding called an arraignment (see discussion below).

Should You Insist on an Arraignment?

Many courts have completely abolished the arraignment procedure by which you enter your plea in front of a judge. But in other courts, you do have the right to insist on entering your plea in court (although you may not be told about it unless you ask).

Here are a few reasons why you might want to do this:

- At arraignment you can ask about your right to obtain—or "discover," in legal jargon—the evidence the officer will present against you at trial. (See below for other ways to discover evidence.)
- This is often when and where you can ask for a jury trial, if your state is one that allows it for ordinary traffic violations. (If you are not allowed arraignment in your state, be sure to ask the court clerk how to ask for a jury trial, if you are allowed one. See the appendix.)
- This is where you can plead nolo contendere to a violation arising out of an accident. (Normally this is necessary only if the accident makes you ineligible to forfeit bail. See sidebar above).

What Happens at Arraignment

SKIP AHEAD

If you have decided not to be arraigned, you may skip to the next section, "Using 'Discovery' to Build Your Case."

Arraignments are used by the court to inform you of what you are charged with, as well as outlining your basic legal rights—including the right to an attorney, to cross-examine the officer, to call witnesses to testify for you, and, in some states, to request a jury trial. (See the appendix for whether your state allows trial by jury.)

At an arraignment, the judge will usually address traffic defendants in a group, informing them of their rights, which include:

- The right to a trial at which the state has the burden of proving you guilty beyond a reasonable doubt. (If you are charged with exceeding a "presumed" speed limit, the state must show "beyond a reasonable doubt" that you exceeded the speed limit. After that, you have the burden of proving that your speed was safe.)
- The right to see, hear, and cross-examine the prosecution's witnesses (usually just the ticketing officer)
- The right to call or "subpoena" witnesses to testify for you
- If the offense is punishable by a jail sentence—as with drunk or reckless driving—the right to a court-appointed lawyer, and
- The right to a jury trial if your state allows one for traffic offenses (see the appendix).

If you plead guilty or no contest, the judge will probably ask whether you understand your rights. If you say you do, you will not be able to complain later.

CAUTION

Insist on a jury. To save court time a judge may tell you, "I recommend that you choose (or accept) a court trial." In the parlance of lawyers and judges, "court trial" or "bench trial" means a trial before a judge, not a jury. So if a judge tries to push for a court trial in a state where you have

a right to a jury, insist you want a jury trial by saying, *"No, Your Honor, I want a jury trial."*

Entering a Not Guilty Plea at Arraignment

If you request an arraignment, the judge will ask you how you plead. Answer "not guilty." At the same time, you should specifically request the officer's presence at your trial (in some states you may waive this right without knowing it unless you insist on it to the clerk or at arraignment) and demand a jury trial. (Check the appendix to see if your state allows jury trials, and read Chapter 3 to see if it is the best choice for your case.)

 TIP

Don't be talked out of your right to a jury trial. Assuming you do the homework necessary to cope with a far more complicated courtroom situation, your chances of winning are almost always better in front of a jury than before a judge, often because jurors feel they have been treated unfairly in traffic court and may side with you.

Another reason to press for a jury trial is that it may cause the prosecutor to dismiss it (especially likely if the prosecution's case really is weak). Another possibility is that the prosecutor may offer you an opportunity to plead to a reduced charge or attend traffic school, if it is otherwise not an option. In short, even if the judge tries to dissuade you from trying your case in front of a jury, there can be good reasons to insist on it.

In some states you may be asked at your arraignment whether you have been convicted previously of any traffic offenses.

Occasionally, higher fines are imposed on repeat traffic law offenders. Never lie. If you do have prior offenses (sometimes shortened to the term "priors"), it is best to fess up or, if they are in other states or might be hard to find, say, "I deny the validity of any prior convictions." This is acceptable language in the court system even if, in fact, you have forfeited bail or been convicted of one or more prior traffic offenses. All you are saying is that it is up to the prosecution to find and present evidence of any prior traffic offenses.

Understand Speedy Trial Rules

The Sixth Amendment to the United States Constitution guarantees "a speedy and public trial" in all criminal cases but fails to say exactly what "speedy" means. Many states have laws defining that last term. For example, California requires that a case be dismissed if not brought to trial within 45 days of entering a not guilty plea before a judge.

Especially where your state's speedy-trial deadline is short, harried traffic court judges are likely to ask you to waive your right to a speedy trial. Often this is done at an arraignment or if you make a motion to discover the officer's notes. Typically, the judge will say something like, *"Do you waive time for trial?"* or even just *"Do you waive time?"*

If you enter a not guilty plea at a clerk's office in California and some other states, he will insist that you sign a form giving up your right to a speedy trial in exchange for the convenience of skipping a formal arraignment (where you would go to court and plead not guilty). In other places, you may have a choice as to whether you wish to waive time. So if you are asked to "waive time," politely ask the clerk if you have the option of refusing without having to go through with an arraignment. If so, you will almost always want to say "no." Here's why. In busy courthouses, your trial will probably be scheduled towards the end of the time allowed by the law. This means if the officer does not appear for the trial and the judge does not dismiss the ticket (something she may, but is not required, to do), she will have to reschedule your trial with the officer present before the "speedy trial" deadline. This may be impossible. In that case, you win.

Consider Delaying the Arraignment and/or Trial

Be prepared to negotiate for a convenient trial date. If the judge proposes a date on which you have a conflict, speak right up and tell him why it is inconvenient. He will very likely set a later date. But be careful not to accept a date that is past the number of days allowed in your state to conduct a speedy trial, because by doing so you would probably give up ("waive") your right to a speedy trial.

TIP

Sometimes it pays to delay. Instead of proceeding right to trial—or even entering a guilty plea, if that's what you eventually plan to do—you may want to put things off for several weeks or months. For example, you may be able to delay the trial date until after a time when any new points from a conviction would cause the state to suspend your license. This would be a good idea if you have points on your record that would expire during the delay. Often it's possible to get a delay by going to the court clerk a few days before the appearance deadline listed on your ticket and asking for an extension. In many courts, the clerk will give you at least one delay without much coaxing.

Trial by Declaration or Affidavit

In nine states (most notably California and Florida—see the appendix for the others), you have the option of presenting your defense in writing, rather than personally appearing at a trial. Typically, you make your testimony in a "declaration," which is a written statement you type up and sign, swearing you are telling the truth. You do this by adding this phrase at the end of your signed statement: "I declare under penalty of perjury that the foregoing is true and correct. Executed on [date] at [city and state])." Some courts may require you to have your statement notarized instead of, or in addition to, swearing it is true (precise rules will be available from the court clerk).

This procedure is called "trial by declaration" or "trial by affidavit." Even in states that don't have laws allowing this procedure, some courts will permit it anyway. Check with your court clerk, if you think you might want to use this option.

One obvious advantage of opting for a trial by declaration is that you don't have to appear in court for a trial—a big help if you got your ticket far from home and don't relish driving a hundred or more miles to testify. Another advantage is that you can take time to draft a convincing, well-thought-out defense, which may convince a judge better than the oral testimony of an inexperienced, nervous defendant.

But there is a big downside of not appearing in front of the judge: You give up your right to present your defense in person, to get the case dismissed if the officer doesn't show at trial, and to cross-examine the officer if he does show up. For example, you'll never hear what the officer says and won't have a chance to poke holes in a weak presentation. Many courts also require the officer to present specific written testimony when you opt for this procedure—without giving you the opportunity to see the officer's statement before you prepare yours. But in some states you do have a right to request a copy of the officer's notes before you submit your written statement to the court.

If trial by declaration is available (see the appendix), and you think you might want to opt for it, contact the court clerk to ask about the procedure. Some courts require that you use their forms to print or type your statement. Courts may also require you to pay the fine in advance, in the event you're convicted. Every court has a policy

October 1, 20xx
5227 Anza Street
San Francisco, California 94121

Traffic Court Clerk
Superior Court of Alameda County
Oakland-Piedmont-Emeryville District
661 Washington Street, Second Floor
Oakland, CA 94607

CERTIFIED MAIL, RETURN RECEIPT REQUESTED

Re: People v. Lenny D. Leadfoot, Municipal Court No. A036912-B
    Traffic Citation - Oakland Police Dept. No. 99-O-12345
    Declaration of Defendant Lenny D. Leadfoot in Support of Trial by Written
    Declaration

Dear Clerk:

As allowed under state law/local practice, I enclose a check for $123 bail, plead not
guilty to the above-referenced charge, and submit the following declaration:

On September 20, 20xx, at approximately 10:30 a.m., I was driving my 1996 Honda
Civic, License No. 3JXS505, west on Breezy Boulevard, a four-lane divided highway,
between Drag Boulevard and Zoom Street. I was in the right-hand lane. The weather
was clear and dry. There was no traffic in my direction other than a large panel
truck (visible in my side view mirror) in the left lane, several car lengths behind me.
The truck overtook and passed my vehicle shortly before I crossed the Zoom Street
intersection. As that occurred, I wondered whether I was driving too slowly, and
noticed that my speedometer indicated I was going 34 mph. The posted speed limit
was 35 mph.

Officer Stickler of the Oakland Police Department stopped me approximately two
blocks past Zoom Street. He informed me that he had determined my speed on his
hand-held radar unit to be 49 mph. He said that he had read my speed at the Breezy
Boulevard–Drag Boulevard intersection from the intersection at Zoom Street,
which a street map will show is 500 feet away. Officer Stickler responded to several
of my questions by stating that the radar beam width was "about six degrees," and
that his unit had been "calibrated recently with this little knob," pointing to the

"calibrate" position on the controls of the unit. He said he hadn't used a tuning fork, and that he didn't have one in his possession. He also indicated that his unit was capable of reading speeds of both oncoming and receding traffic. Traffic was heavy in the opposite direction at the time, but not in my direction.

I believe that there exists a reasonable doubt as to the accuracy of Officer Stickler's radar reading. As can be seen from the diagram below, a six-degree beam width at 500 feet will indiscriminately read speeds of vehicles across a width of 55 feet, all four lanes of traffic.

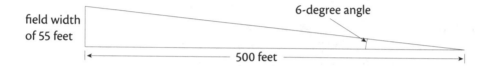

field width of 55 feet

6-degree angle

500 feet

The radar unit may therefore have been reading both speeds of traffic in my direction (including a truck target much larger and more likely to reflect radar beams than my small Honda Civic) and the heavy traffic in the other direction. This being so, it is doubtful that the speed he recorded was mine.

Also enclosed is the declaration of Wilhelmina D. Witness.

I declare under penalty of perjury that the foregoing is true and correct. Executed on October 2, 20xx, at Rough and Ready, California.

Lenny D. Leadfoot

Lenny D. Leadfoot

Attached Declaration of Wilhelmina Witness

Re: People v. Lenny D. Leadfoot,
        Superior Court No. A036912-B
        Dept. No. 99-O-12345
        Declaration of Wilhelmina D. Witness for Trial by Written Declaration

I, Wilhelmina Witness, declare:

On September 20, 20xx, at approximately 10:30 a.m., I was riding as a passenger in an automobile driven by Lenny D. Leadfoot. Mr. Leadfoot was relaxed and not driving very fast for conditions. There were no other cars on the road in our direction of travel that I could see, other than a large truck that passed us on the left shortly before we crossed the Zoom Street intersection. We were talking as we drove westbound on Breezy Boulevard in Oakland. As we drove past Zoom Street, Mr. Leadfoot said that a police officer was pulling us over. I was surprised because I didn't know why we were being pulled over. We drove to the side of the road and waited for the officer. I asked Mr. Leadfoot why we were being pulled over, and he said he did not know.

The officer approached the driver side of the car and spoke to Mr. Leadfoot. He told Mr. Leadfoot he was driving 49 mph in a 35-mph zone. I was surprised because I didn't think that we were going that fast. I think this because, when Mr. Leadfoot suddenly said, "Looks like an officer's behind me with his red lights on, I better pull over to let him pass," I looked over at the speedometer, just before he slowed to pull over, and it read about 35 mph.

I declare under penalty of perjury that the foregoing is true and correct. Executed on October 2, 20xx, at Rough and Ready, California.

Wilhelmina D. Witness
Wilhelmina D. Witness

that your statement be submitted within a certain time period.

Before submitting your defense, be sure to read Chapters 5 and 6, or Chapter 7 on traffic violations, as well as Chapter 10 on preparing your case for trial, to get an idea of the types of defenses that can work and that won't work. Keep in mind that if you have any witnesses whose testimony you think may be helpful, you can also present their declarations or affidavits, in addition to yours. Above is a sample declaration.

Within a few weeks after submitting your written declaration (or affidavit, if required), you should receive a notice in the mail with the judge's verdict. If the notice says you were found not guilty, any fine ("bail") that you prepaid should be refunded to you.

Using "Discovery" to Build Your Case

In any fight, it is best to know your opponent's strategy. Fortunately, you often have the legal right to do this (called "discovery"). In many states you have the right to demand access to the officer's notes made at or soon after your ticket was issued. You also have the right to demand access to other information, like instruction manuals on the use of equipment that was used to clock your speed. (See Chapters 5 and 6 for information on what types of equipment are used to catch speeders and Chapter 10 on how to challenge the use of the equipment. You must check with your local court clerk to confirm you have the right to demand discovery in your state.)

This information can be a huge help when cross-examining the officer and presenting your own case at trial.

To discover the officer's notes, you must make a specific written request for the disclosure of all notes or documents relevant to your case. If you have an arraignment, you may be able to do this there. But if, as is far more common, you plead not guilty and post bail without an arraignment, you'll need to make your request promptly by mail. Send your discovery request to both the police agency that ticketed you and to the local prosecuting agency. The request should be printed or typed on 8½" by 11" paper and look like the one shown below.

If Your Discovery Request Is Ignored

Because so few defendants ask to see the evidence against them, many police, prosecutors, and even some judges believe this right to discovery is not available in traffic court. Accordingly, even though your discovery request is probably proper in your state, you may find it's ignored. If so, you'll need to persist in making this request, reiterating that you believe access to the officer's notes is critical to presenting your defense.

If you get no response to your discovery request within three weeks, you will need to go to court and make a "pretrial motion" to ask the judge to order the police to release the notes to you. Lawyers call this a "motion to compel discovery," or dismiss the case. Your best bet is to call or visit the court clerk to schedule this motion before

IN THE SUPERIOR COURT OF CALIFORNIA
COUNTY OF LOS ANGELES
VAN NUYS BRANCH

THE PEOPLE/STATE OF CALIFORNIA,
Plaintiff,
vs.
DANIELLE DEFENDANT,
Defendant.

REQUEST FOR DISCOVERY
Court Docket No. A-1234567
Citation Number: 99-HK-1234
Date Issued: 4/15/2003
Police Agency: Los Angeles Police Dept.
Citing Officer: Smith   Badge No. LA-1234
Prosecuting Agency: Los Angeles City Attorney

TO THE ABOVE-NAMED POLICE AND PROSECUTING AGENCY:

1. The above-named defendant hereby requests that you provide, to the defendant whose address is indicated below, copies of any and all relevant written or recorded statements of witnesses, including any statements, diagrams, or drawings made by the citing officer on any piece of paper—including the reverse of his/her copy of the citation—or other medium of information storage.

2. The following are names and addresses of defense witnesses, other than defendant, who will testify at trial:

   ( )   None.

   (X)The following: Jane Doe, 345 Main St., Van Nuys, CA 90012 (818) 555-5678

3. The following copies of notes made by defendant immediately after the ticket was issued and recorded statements of witnesses are attached:

   ( )   None.

   (X)   See attached.

DATED: May 17, 20xx

Danielle Defendant

DANIELLE DEFENDANT
12345 Market Street
Los Angeles, CA 90010
Tel: (213) 555-1234

your scheduled trial date. Failing this, it may be possible to have your motion to compel discovery considered on the day of your trial. (See the next section for how to do this.)

Assuming a pretrial hearing to consider your discovery request is scheduled, be prepared to show the judge a copy of your written discovery request. Then ask him to formally order the prosecution or police agency to provide a copy of the officer's notes. Be sure to ask the judge to order that this be done prior to any scheduled trial date, so you have enough time to use them to prepare.

If your discovery request has still been ignored when your trial date rolls around, you may want to ask the judge to dismiss your case. Here is sample language that, of course, will need to be adjusted to fit your facts:

> *"Your Honor, the prosecution has failed to provide the discovery I properly requested (and, if true, "that you ordered"). I move to dismiss the case on account of the prosecution's failure to provide discovery. Here is a copy of the written request I made a month ago for the officer's notes. I sent them to the prosecutor and police agency, and they both ignored me. I have not waived my right to a speedy trial, and I shouldn't have to. I can't properly prepare for trial even if the notes are produced now. As a result, I request that the charges against me be dismissed."*

The Reason Cops Have Perfect Memories

Have you ever wondered what the officer who just ticketed you is doing, sitting in his patrol car after writing you up? He is probably writing notes—something on the back of your ticket—with details of why he ticketed you and what the conditions were at the time. Just before trial, he will typically review his notes, and sometimes refer to them while testifying. With courtroom experience, an officer can often glance down at his notes every few seconds, rattling off a narrative that sounds like he was recounting something that happened yesterday. But because the officer probably won't remember much about what happened and doesn't want to be tripped up fabricating a detail, most officers will depart very little from their notes. In short, if you can discover the officer's notes, you can expect his testimony will stick pretty close to this script.

If the following requirements are met, you may get your case dismissed at this point:

- You are entitled to discovery under state law.
- Your state has a speedy-trial law entitling you to trial within a certain period, and you haven't given up the right to a speedy trial.
- Postponing the trial to allow the prosecution to get the notes for you would require you to give up your

right to a trial within the "speedy trial" time allowed.

- You made your request for "discovery" promptly (and within any time limit).

If the judge won't dismiss your case, renew your request right then that you be given a chance to examine the officer's notes. The judge should at least be willing to give you a few minutes to do this.

What to Do With the Officer's Notes

If you receive a copy of the officer's notes, you'll want to study them carefully. It's possible that these notes may cause you to reevaluate your defense strategy, when you know what the officer is going to say at trial. Here are some things to look for:

- **Detail.** If the officer's notes don't say much, she probably won't have much to say at trial, unless you gave her a reason to remember your specific case (another big reason why it's never wise to behave like an idiot when you are pulled over). On the other hand, the more detailed her notes (such as a fact-specific statement convincingly laying out what you did), the better she'll probably sound at trial.
- **What the notes don't say.** If the notes lack key details, you may be able to challenge the officer's memory. Look to see if the notes:
  1. Mention which lane you were in.
  2. Say exactly how the officer recorded your speed, if you were cited for speeding. (For example, if pacing

was used, how far the officer paced you before stopping your vehicle.)
  3. Have detailed specific information about road and weather conditions and other nearby vehicles. For example, if you were cited for an unsafe turn across traffic, the notes should detail the exact traffic situation justifying the officer's judgment call. (See Chapter 7 for a variety of situations.)
  4. Report where the officer was when she observed you.

- **Diagrams.** Police will often make a diagram on the ticket, especially with violations that occur at intersections, like running a stop sign or stoplight, unsafe turns, or failure to yield. If the officer does a careful job of including significant details, she will probably look well prepared in court. If not, you have a better chance to raise a reasonable doubt as to your guilt by demonstrating through cross-examination that the officer can't honestly remember what happened.
- **Driver statements.** Most officers will note any admissions made by the driver on pulling him or her over ("Said she was going 70, asked for a break"), sometimes quoting them directly ("Yes, I ran the stop sign, but my daughter's pet iguana was sick and I had to get her to the vet"). Of course, you are far better off if there are no such admissions written down.

> ### 💡 TIP
>
> **Deciphering police notes.** Some officers write their notes in easy-to-read narrative detail; others use abbreviations, which are sometimes hard to decipher. Here are hints that may help you decipher police slang:
>
> - S/V = "subject vehicle" (your car, truck, or motorcycle)
> - D or (△) = "defendant" (you)
> - Est. = Police officer visually estimated your speed
> - R or r = "radar" unit, sometimes also followed by the radar unit serial number
> - Cops usually list how far they paced you or measured your speed using a VASCAR system in tenths of a mile (e.g., "0.3" means one-third of a mile and "1.5" means a mile and a half). (See Chapter 6.)
> - BUMP = "bumper pace." The officer is recording how long he kept a constant distance between your rear bumper and his front bumper to read your speed on his speedometer.
> - Traffic lanes are often abbreviated. For example, "lane No. 1" might appear as "Ln. 1" or "L 1" or just "#1." Lanes are counted from the center of the road (median), with lane No. 1 being the first lane and the lane to its immediate right being lane 2.

Preparing for Trial—Your Case

Asking for a "Continuance" (Postponement) 140

Gathering Your Notes and Research 142

Diagrams, Maps, and Pictures 142

    How to Use Your Diagram and Maps in Court 144

    How to Use Your Photographs in Court 145

Preparing Your Testimony 146

    Exceeding Maximum Speed Limits 147

    Exceeding "Presumed" Speed Limits 148

    Running a Stoplight 149

Preparing Your Witnesses 150

    Organizing Witness Testimony 150

    Subpoenaing Witnesses 151

Preparing for the Prosecution's Cross-Examination 151

n this chapter we tell you how to prepare for your day in court, including:

- Preparing your evidence
- Outlining and practicing your testimony, and
- Helping your witnesses prepare their testimony.

Some people think they can beat a ticket by simply showing up in court and telling a terrific story to the judge or jury. They couldn't be more wrong. In theory, you are innocent until proven guilty. In truth, unless your presentation includes evidence or testimony that convinces the judge that you are not guilty, he will usually side with the police officer. Juries—in the states where they are allowed—tend to be more friendly towards the driver, but convincing one that there is a reasonable doubt as to your guilt can be an uphill battle.

This chapter will show you how to prepare your case so that you have a decent chance of walking out of the courtroom as a winner. We do this by explaining how to best organize and present your testimony and your evidence. And we also focus on how to prepare and present any eyewitnesses to your best advantage. But first, let's focus on what you must do if you need more time to prepare.

Asking for a "Continuance" (Postponement)

Here are some reasons why you may want to delay your day in court:

- You need more time to prepare.
- You or a key witness will be out of town.

What Is Reasonable Doubt?

To be convicted of a traffic violation in most states, you must be found guilty beyond a "reasonable doubt." The legal definition goes like this: "Reasonable doubt is not a mere possible or imaginary doubt, but that state of the evidence where you do not have an abiding conviction, to a certainty, of the truth of the charge."

Now that's as clear as mud, isn't it? Here is a real-life example of reasonable doubt that may help: John is tried for murder, and all the jurors vote "guilty" except Jake, who holds out for a not guilty verdict. The jury is hung. A local citizen later confronts Jake, saying, "How could you say John didn't do it?" "I didn't say John didn't do it, I'm just not sure that he did," Jake replies.

- You need to delay the time of your possible conviction in order to keep from accumulating too many "points" on your driving record over a specific period.

To delay your trial, make your written request for continuance at least a week (more if possible) in advance of the trial date. Send copies of your request to the police officer's department and any prosecuting official. Most continuances made on the day of trial will be denied, but usually at least one delay will be granted if it is made several weeks before the trial date. Be aware, though, that by asking for a continuance beyond the last day allowed for trial under any speedy-trial law, you give up that right. You can't later complain that you were denied a speedy trial because you yourself asked for a trial date after the speedy-trial law deadline.

Here is an example of a request for a postponement:

---

123 Parker St.
Berkeley, CA 94710

Jan. 1, 20xx

Clerk, Superior Court
Berkeley-Albany Judicial District
2120 Martin Luther King Jr. Street
Berkeley, California

Re: People vs. Safespeed, #A-123456

Trial Date: Jan. 15, 20xx

Dear Sir or Madam:

I am scheduled to appear for trial in the above matter on Jan. 15, 20xx. Unfortunately, I will be out of town on that date due to my employer's insistence that I attend a two-week seminar in New York between Jan. 1 and Jan. 20, 20xx. I therefore request that trial be continued to Jan. 25, 20xx. Please inform me as to whether the continuance will be granted and when my trial will occur.

Sincerely,

Sam Safespeed
Sam Safespeed

cc: Officer G. Growlski
      Berkeley Police Department

If you don't receive a reply before the scheduled trial date (or before you leave town), call or visit the court clerk. If the continuance hasn't been granted (or if dealing with the clerks proves fruitless), it is best, if possible, to appear in person on the trial date to see if your request has been granted. Be as prepared as you can to go to trial that day, even though you plan to ask again for a continuance. If you have a good reason and you show proof that you tried to contact the police and prosecutor in advance of the trial, your request should be granted. If you are really going to be out of town, write the judge directly, by priority mail or fax. Refer to your earlier request and ask for an urgent postponement.

Occasionally, because of an officer's scheduled vacation or other anticipated absence, the prosecutor or officer will ask the court to postpone your trial date, notifying you by mail or phone. Be sure to check if the court has actually granted the request. If not, your best approach is to show up in court on the trial date and object to the delay. This allows you to argue that you have gone through considerable trouble to come to court for trial, and it is unfair to make you return at a later date.

If it appears that the court is going to delay your trial, you should check out your state speedy-trial rules. (See Chapter 2 on researching the law.) If the court has postponed the trial until after that date, you should bring this up at the new trial date and ask that the case be dismissed. You can say, *"Your Honor, I move to dismiss under the speedy-trial rule, because the case was continued beyond the last date allowed for trial, without my consent."*

Gathering Your Notes and Research

Start your trial preparation by writing down everything you can remember about your traffic violation. It's best to do this as soon as possible after the incident, while your memory is still fresh. You may also want to go back and photograph or diagram the scene from different angles and locations, if explaining to the judge or jury the exact location of vehicles, signals, or other physical objects will be relevant to your case.

Remember, as discussed in Chapter 2, it's important to compare the facts of what happened to you to all legal elements of the traffic violation you are charged with. Or put another way, as you recollect the details of what happened, do so with an eye to convincing the judge that the prosecution has failed to prove you committed one or more of the necessary elements. As part of doing this, it may be helpful to write down each element of the violation on one column on a page and compare it with the actual circumstances of your violation to see if your actions failed to meet every aspect of the charge against you.

Here is an example:

Elements of Violation	My Actions
1. Driving a vehicle	1. Yes, I was
2 On a highway	2. Yes
3. Made a U-turn	3. Yes
4. In a residence district	4. No. There were only two district residences on the block, which was just outside of town. "Residence district" is defined as 15 or more residences over a quarter of a mile. Went back and counted. Only seven residences one-half-mile back from U-turn, only 10 residences one-half-mile ahead.
5. Traffic approaching within 200 feet, either direction	5. No. My rearview mirror showed no traffic behind. Approaching car was 15 to 20 car lengths (225 to 300 feet) ahead.

Diagrams, Maps, and Pictures

Diagrams or enlarged maps of the place where you got the ticket are often useful to help the judge understand what happened. That's why so many officers include them in their notes and show them to the judge at trial. And that's also why you'll be better equipped to illustrate inaccuracies in the officer's testimony by preparing a diagram of your own.

Here are some common situations where diagrams are a big help:

- In radar or laser speed cases, they can help illustrate how the radar or laser beam might have intercepted targets other than your vehicle.

- Where pacing was used to give you a speeding ticket, a diagram may illustrate where the officer was when she first saw you and where you both were when she stopped your car. This can show that the officer was closing in on you and thus could never have accurately measured your speed.

- In defending against traffic-signal and stop-sign violations you may be able to show the officer would have been unable to accurately see the charged violation from the location where he was watching.

- For turning violations, you can show how far away oncoming or cross traffic was from your vehicle when you made your turn.

- With tickets stemming from an accident, you want to show how your driving was safe under the circumstances and that the accident was caused by the other driver. (See Chapter 7 for a variety of "moving violation" defenses and Chapter 5 for details on accidents caused by speeding.)

A good diagram should be reasonably detailed but not too cluttered. Thus for an intersection, it should normally include the location of stop signs or signals, dividers or traffic islands, crosswalks, limit lines, and the location of parked vehicles. In addition, it should indicate the approximate widths of the streets and traffic lanes. With speeding violations, where the officer paced you over a long stretch, the diagram should show any intersections, nearby buildings, and other principle landmarks and, of course, it should indicate the distance between where you first saw the officer and where she stopped you.

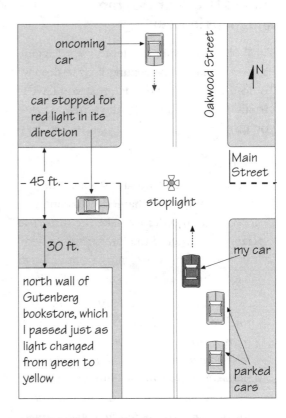

TIP

How to prepare a diagram. Never try to draw your diagram in court. The result is sure to be time-consuming and klutzy. Instead, carefully prepare it beforehand. Use a large piece of thick white paper, cardboard, or foamboard, and several thick felt-tip pens. Use black or dark blue to denote roadways and intersections, and other colors for vehicles and traffic signals. If you are artistically challenged, have a more talented friend help.

How to Use Your Diagram and Maps in Court

You'll obviously want to refer to your diagram in court as part of presenting your testimony. To do this, inform the judge that you have a visual aid that you would like to use when you testify.

EXAMPLE:

You made a left turn at a stoplight and were stopped and charged with running a red light in order to make the turn. You claim you entered the intersection when the arrow light was turning from green to yellow. In court, you testify as follows:

"As I approached the intersection and got into the left-turn lane, I saw a green-arrow signal, which changed to yellow just as I crossed the final line of the crosswalk at the entrance to the intersection. As I made the turn, I saw the officer's car behind two other cars. I proceeded because the light was yellow in my direction and because a car was right on my tail, making a quick stop unsafe. I have a diagram of the intersection. I made it last week just after I went back to the intersection. May I please show it to the court?"

At this point, if a prosecutor is present, you show it to her (otherwise to the cop). Then hand it to the court clerk (who may mark it Exhibit #1 before handing it to the judge). If the courtroom has an easel or blackboard, place your diagram there, facing the judge or jury. If not, find a place to prop it up so that it can be seen clearly. (The judge or clerk will probably help by telling you how to do this.)

Your testimony should continue something like this:

"Your Honor, my car is shown on this diagram in green. The dotted green arrow shows my path as I completed the turn. The officer's vehicle is indicated in red. The roadway is outlined in black, and its curvature is shown, indicating that if the officer had been 100 feet behind me as he testified, he would not have been able to see my vehicle around the curve. The road is marked to scale, as I've confirmed with a photocopy of that portion of a city map, which I'd like to have marked as Exhibit #2 and present to the court. At this time, I ask that evidence...."

How to Use Your Photographs in Court

In addition to diagrams, you may want to use photographs. Photos are best used to show conditions like:

- Obscured traffic signs or signals
- The view from where the cop was sitting when she claimed to have seen your vehicle
- Road obstructions such as curves and hills, or buildings that restrict visibility, and
- Road width and straightness to show that an over-the-limit speed was safe, if you're charged with violating a "presumed" speed limit (see Chapter 5).

TIP

Have key photos enlarged. It's hard to look at 3x5 photos, especially in a courtroom where you are trying to explain why the photo helps establish your case. It's far better to present 8x10 enlargements that the judge can see without a magnifying glass.

There are some things photos don't show well, including situations where road and traffic conditions rapidly change, so that what happened when you were ticketed can't really be replicated. It also rarely helps to show the judge photos of an accident scene taken after the vehicles have been moved. You must personally take any photograph that you intend to use in traffic court or, if someone else is the photographer, have that person come to court with you. This is because you—or the photographer—must testify where and when the picture was taken.

To refer to a photo and show it to the judge, formal trial court rules require you to have it marked as an exhibit and formally introduced into evidence. But in most traffic courts, judges will simply look at your photo without the need for a lot of legal formalities. Here's an example of what to say (if the judge is not a stickler for formality, leave out the part about marking it for identification):

"Your Honor, I would ask that this photograph be marked for identification as Exhibit #1." Show it to the prosecutor or officer, then hand it to the clerk, who will mark the exhibit. *"I took this picture along Main Street, at the same place where the officer indicated in his notes—and just now testified to—that he was parked when he says he saw me fail to stop at the stop sign on Market Street at its intersection with Main. I took it just two weeks after he issued me the citation, at the same time, 4:45 p.m., during the same rush-hour conditions. I believe it accurately shows the impaired visibility the officer had of traffic coming in my direction, and it shows why he couldn't have had a very clear view of where he claims I ran the stop sign. I request that this Exhibit #1 be introduced into evidence."*

Preparing Your Testimony

Defendants who know what to say and when to say it are far more likely to win than are defendants who stand up and hope to come up with a convincing story. In short, if you've come this far, you want to be well prepared. One big key to doing this is to carefully practice your presentation.

Why You Should Always Testify

Although you're not required to testify, it's almost always a good idea. Judges won't admit it, but they generally assume that a defendant who tries to claim that the prosecutor hasn't proven her case—while at the same time asserting the Fifth Amendment right to silence—must be guilty. You'll almost always do better by explaining your version of what happened as clearly, honestly, and forcefully as you can than you would by declining to testify.

 TIP

How to practice your testimony. After you have practiced making your presentation enough times that you are getting pretty good, have a tough-minded friend or family member play the part of the judge. Ask them to try to poke holes in your case by occasionally interrupting your presentation with questions (many judges do this). Do this several times until you feel comfortable answering questions about your version of what happened and the evidence you present to back it up. When you are done, ask your skeptical friend for a verdict. If your friend convicts you, the judge is likely to do so. Keep practicing until you convince your volunteer judge that you are innocent.

One good approach to presenting traffic court testimony is to outline the key points you want to make on an index card well in advance of your court date (leave space between entries for later additions). Be sure your testimony establishes an adequate defense to the violation (for example, it clearly demonstrates you didn't commit at least one key element of the violation). Use your notes as you practice making your presentation. (It's fine to glance at your outline, but it is a mistake to simply read it.) Then in court, after you cross-examine the officer and learn new facts, quickly add to or edit your outline This way, when it's finally your turn to testify, you should be prepared to tell a smooth and well-thought-out story.

For those who have never previously appeared in traffic court, it is a great idea to drop by and watch a few cases. Sure, this takes a couple of hours, but you are almost sure to learn more than enough to make this a wise use of the time. There is not enough space to provide sample testimony for every possible violation, but the following examples provide a road map to preparing your testimony, no matter what charge you face.

Exceeding Maximum Speed Limits

In states with an "absolute" speed limit, you should focus your testimony preparation on arguing that you were not speeding *at all*. If you simply say you were going 38 mph and the officer testifies it was really 48 mph, the judge will almost always choose to believe the cop's version. However, there are some good defenses you can mount that could even the odds a little. In preparing your testimony, consider if any of the following approaches fit your case:

- *"The officer didn't keep a constant distance between our vehicles when he 'paced' me. I could see him in my rearview mirror bearing down on me fast. It took him just a few seconds to close from about half a mile back to being right behind me, which is when he activated his lights. In fact, after glancing at my speedometer and seeing that I was going at the speed limit, I was convinced the officer was speeding to an emergency farther down the road. When I realized he was after me, I was genuinely surprised."*
- *"There was other traffic in my direction in front (or back) of me. The officer's wide radar beam could have hit the other traffic at the distance he was from me. Some of this other traffic was going faster."*
- *"The road wasn't straight. Visibility was poor due to curves and hills. He could not have seen me for the time necessary to determine if I was speeding, which I was not."*
- *"There were other vehicles similar to mine on the road at the time. One, the same make and color as mine, passed me. After the officer rounded the curve, he pulled me over by mistake."*

Here is an example of testimony in an "absolute" speeding case:

"When the officer stopped me for speeding, it was 5:15 p.m. I had just left work to go home. I wasn't in a hurry. I drive Highway 123 home every day, and I know the speed limit's 55 mph. Just before Officer Kwota pulled me over, I had slowed going around a curve because I needed to move from the left to right lane to prepare to turn right on Market Street. I had to pause for a moment because another red 1995 Chevy Blazer, almost identical to mine, passed me in the right lane at a high rate of speed and exited at Market Street. By this time, I had slowed to about 35 mph because I was still trying to move over to the right. At this point, I saw Officer Kwota's car come around the curve in the right lane. I was going to wait to allow him to proceed past me before getting in the right lane, but, to my surprise, he got into the left lane behind me and turned on his emergency lights. After I pulled over, the officer asked me if I knew why he had stopped me, and I said, 'No, I think you stopped the wrong car.' I told him that a similar-looking car had sped past me just after coming around a curve. He then asked me if I knew how fast I was going, and, not knowing where and when he was referring to, I said, 'somewhere between 35 and 50 mph.'"

> **TIP**
>
> **Notice how the testimony in these sections is specific and detailed.** The more detail and specifics, the more convincing your testimony—a lot more convincing than simply saying, "I wasn't speeding, man. I was doing 50. I was cool."

Exceeding "Presumed" Speed Limits

When you're charged with violating a "presumed" speed, you have a much better shot at winning. (See Chapter 5 and the appendix for states that use this system.) Here you should focus your testimony preparation on arguing that you were not speeding, but, even if you were, it was only a few miles over the limit in a situation where this was safe. But always start by understanding that unless it was obvious you were over the limit, your best approach is to admit nothing and make the prosecution prove it. (Assuming it's true, you can simply testify that you were going at or below the limit.)

If you really were going slightly over the limit, you should consider making as many of the following points as fit your situation:

"Even if I was going slightly faster than 30 mph, it was safe to do so because:

- *"There was very little vehicle or pedestrian traffic on the road."* This is a particularly good argument if you can truthfully tell the judge you were ticketed at 6:00 a.m. or some other

time when traffic is known to be light.

- *"There was little or no other traffic in my lane, in my direction (or in both directions) for at least a half mile."*
- *"There was no cross traffic or uncontrolled intersections."*
- *"There were several lanes in each direction, and there was no one else even in my lane."*
- *"Even if I did exceed the speed limit, it was by less than 5 mph."*
- *"The road in question has an artificially low speed limit."* Here, a picture of a wide, straight two-lane road with no traffic but a 25-mph limit might be convincing.
- *"The weather was clear (no rain, fog, hail, etc.)."*
- *"The road was dry."*
- *"The road was well lighted by regularly spaced street lamps."*
- *"There were no sharp curves, hills, dips, or other such 'natural' road defect requiring a slower speed."*

Here is one example of testimony against charges of speeding with a "presumed" speeding violation:

"I'm sure I didn't exceed the speed limit, but even if I did, it must have been by a small amount. Certainly by the time I saw Officer Ticketem and checked my speedometer, I was going right at the 35 mph limit. But even assuming I was going a little faster a few minutes before, it was very safe to do so. Please let me explain. I was in the left of two lanes in my direction, there was no traffic ahead

in my direction—except for one vehicle that suddenly passed me on the right. The road is a four-lane divided highway, two lanes in each direction, and it was straight, and slightly downhill in my direction, so that I could see ahead for about a half mile. The next intersection, with Market Street, was about a quarter of a mile ahead, I could see the green light, and there was no cross traffic waiting at the intersection. There were no pedestrians either. It was 6:45 p.m. in July, and most people were home eating dinner. It was still daylight, the weather was clear, and the road was dry. In fact, it was the kind of situation where even going 45 or 50 mph would have been safe, even though I wasn't going nearly that fast.

Running a Stoplight

When you're accused of running a red light, the issue is usually whether your vehicle entered the intersection after the light changed from yellow to red. To be guilty, the front bumper of your vehicle must have passed into the cross street after the light changed (see Chapter 7). If either of the following is true in your case, you should assert the defense:

- *"I was driving at (or below) the speed limit."*
- *"I was only several car lengths from the intersection when the green light turned yellow."*

Both of these defenses are based on the idea that the yellow light must last long enough for a car traveling at the speed limit to make it through the intersection before the light turns red. If you testify you were a few car-lengths from the signal when the light turned yellow, you are, in effect, saying that you must have entered the intersection when the light was yellow, since you were so close.

- *"I looked up at the light and noted that it hadn't yet changed to red as my car entered the intersection."* (A diagram might be very useful.)
- *"I didn't think I could safely stop the car because I feared being rear-ended by someone tailgating me."*
- *"I proceeded through the yellow light cautiously."*

Here is one example of testimony against charges of running a stoplight:

"I was driving at the speed limit, 35 mph, on Warren Street. I know this because I looked down at my speedometer just as I began slowing to prepare to turn at the intersection with Maple Street. The green light changed to yellow as I was only about two car lengths in front of the entrance to the intersection. So I continued, and the light was still yellow as my car crossed over the crosswalk and entered the intersection. As is my habit, I glanced up at the traffic signal overhead—which continued to stay yellow until it passed out of sight over the top of my windshield. At all times the cross traffic heading in both directions on Maple Street was stopped, so my turn did not create a dangerous situation.

TIP

Be as specific as possible. Go back to the scene and attempt to determine the exact distance you were from the light when it changed from green to yellow (for example, maybe the car in front of you just turned into a gas station), the duration of the yellow light, and your car's speed. With the help of a diagram, based on the facts you present, you could argue that you only could have entered the intersection while the light was still yellow. If you show you were 100 feet away from the intersection at a gas station entrance— going 35 mph when the light turned from green to yellow—you can figure out how many feet per second you were traveling and prove you were well into the intersection before the light turned yellow.

Preparing Your Witnesses

You have the right to present witnesses who were present and observed the situation that caused you to be ticketed. This will usually be someone who was in the car with you, but it could be a pedestrian or the driver of another vehicle. But before you ask a potential witness to testify for you, you'll obviously want to be sure he agrees with your version of what happened.

Organizing Witness Testimony

If you have more than one witness, write down all their names. Then write a description of what each will say and how their testimony will help your case. Decide in what order they should testify to present a logical sequence of events.

CAUTION

Don't let a witness bend the truth. Occasionally a friendly witness will volunteer to stretch the truth on your behalf. Lying in court (perjury) is a felony and can result in jail time. In addition, a skilled prosecutor can expose even one small lie, and it will usually destroy the credibility of everything else your witness says, even if much of it is true.

Witnesses who are organized and prepared are far more convincing than those who are neither. Start by acquainting your witness with the various legal elements of the case and the strategy of your defense. Her testimony should support one or more key aspects of it. Just as you did when you prepared your own testimony, have someone pretend to be the judge, and have your witness practice her testimony several times. Helping your witness prepare in this way is completely legal and routine. Every lawyer rehearses witnesses. In case the prosecutor asks your witness whether she has discussed her testimony with you, she should simply be prepared to say something like this: "Yes, I was a little nervous and wanted to do a good job of telling the truth."

It is also wise to put yourself in the role of the prosecutor and ask the witness some tough cross-examining questions. We discuss how to cope with cross-examination below. Have your witness read that section.

Explain to your witness that there's a possibility she will be asked to step outside the courtroom when you testify, in order to prevent her from adjusting her testimony to be consistent with yours. This is not a punishment, just a routine court procedure. (You also have the right to insist that the state's witnesses be similarly excluded, should two or more prosecution witnesses testify against you.)

Subpoenaing Witnesses

A "subpoena" is a document that requires a witness to appear at the time and place of your trial. Failure to appear can result in arrest and jail or fine for contempt of court. If the witness was a friend or family member riding in your car, she will often agree to appear without a subpoena. But if the witness was unknown to you—like a pedestrian or another driver—you'll want to serve him with a subpoena telling him to show up at your trial. There are three common situations where you will want to subpoena an essential witness:

- A witness wants to testify on your behalf but needs to be excused from work or school.
- A witness whose testimony is essential to your case doesn't want to appear in court for some reason, but you are pretty sure he will testify in your favor if required to appear.
- A witness has volunteered to testify but is unreliable, and you believe he may forget to show up if not subpoenaed.

At your request, the court clerk must issue a subpoena in a traffic case. Rules and procedures as to how this is done and who may serve the subpoena vary from place to place. Be sure to ask the court clerk how a subpoena is to be prepared and served.

CAUTION

It's usually a mistake to subpoena a hostile witness. As a general rule, it's a mistake to subpoena a person who is totally opposed to the idea of appearing in court. A person who is dragged to court against his will is likely to be so mad he could mold his testimony in such a way as to hurt your case. There is a big exception to this rule: Where you can't win without the person's testimony and you believe there is some chance he'll tell the truth under oath, it makes sense to risk serving a subpoena on a hostile witness who won't show up voluntarily.

CAUTION

Be aware of distance rules. A witness can't be required to attend court if he lives out of state. In some areas, even a witness who lives in the state can't be compelled to travel over a certain distance to the courthouse, usually 50 to 100 miles.

Preparing for the Prosecution's Cross-Examination

A prosecutor gets a chance to cross-examine you and any other person who testifies on your behalf. If a prosecutor is not present, sometimes the judge will ask the officer if he wants to cross-examine. Most officers will decline. In this situation, the judge may ask a few questions on her own.

As you probably know, the purpose of cross-examination is to poke holes in your story and the testimony of your witnesses. In case you or your witnesses have to respond to cross-examination, keep the following things in mind:

- Keep your cool: Don't respond in an evasive, hostile, or argumentative manner.

- Keep your answers short and focused on the specifics of the question asked of you. That way you won't end up unnecessarily volunteering information that turns out to hurt your case.

- Although you can be told to answer only "yes" or "no" to a question, you have the right to fully explain any answer you give. It can be a good idea to do this if the prosecutor asks you a seemingly damaging question. For example, if you are asked how fast you were going and you truthfully reply 30 mph in a "presumed speed" area where the speed limit was 25 mph, you would want to add that because no cars were on the road, it was safe to do so. If the prosecution tries to cut you off in the middle of your explanation, turn to the judge and say, *"I believe I have the right to explain as part of my answer. May I continue?"*

- Tell the truth. Obvious as this may sound, many people think they can get away with "stretching the truth." The last thing you'll want is for a skilled prosecutor to expose a lie (or even get you to retract a minor point). This is likely to happen when you are less than truthful in response to a question to which the prosecutor already knows—and can prove—the answer.

- If you don't know, say so. Many people are so afraid to admit ignorance they trip themselves up, often needlessly. If your witness was talking and didn't notice whether two cars turned ahead of you on a yellow light (but can say you crossed the limit line when it was still yellow), make sure she knows it's okay to respond "I don't know" when she does not.

Preparing for Trial—The Officer's Testimony and Cross-Examination

When and How to Object to Testimony 154

Officer Reading From Notes 154

Assuming Facts Not in Evidence 155

Hearsay Evidence 156

How to Cross-Examine the Officer 157

Coping With an Officer's Nonresponsive Answer 159

Testing the Officer's Power of Observation 160

Sample Questions 160

Cross-Examination Questions for Specific Violations 162

Usually the prosecution's case consists solely of the testimony of the ticketing police officer. That testimony will usually sound, in part, something like this:

> *"I was parked observing traffic, when I observed the defendant enter the intersection at Maple and Pearl Streets, heading south on Maple after the light had turned red. There was heavy traffic at the time and several cars had to apply their brakes to avoid an accident. The road was also wet from a rainstorm earlier in the day."*

You should listen closely to what the officer says and focus on ways to challenge her testimony. Depending on what the officer says, you may be able to:

- Make a legal objection that results in the officer's testimony being excluded from your trial, or
- Successfully ask the officer questions (called cross-examination) to cast doubt on the officer's version of the facts.

When and How to Object to Testimony

Few people have the legal knowledge to raise picky technical objections. Fortunately, in most traffic trials, you don't need it. In fact, raising lots of objections in traffic court can quickly become counterproductive, because it's more likely to raise the hackles of the judge than to help you win your case.

Objecting to testimony is a tactical decision. Always ask yourself: "How likely am I to succeed?" As part of doing this, you should also consider how damaging the testimony is to your case. For example, if the officer is providing background detail about the weather or road conditions that has little to do with whether you committed a particular violation, you gain little by objecting, even if your objection is technically correct.

But a few well-placed objections can serve a major purpose. That's because the testifying police officer probably expects you to be unprepared and nervous, and she is likely to be overconfident. (After all, she has probably testified many times before.) If you are able to surprise her with even a few valid objections, you may well throw her off balance and weaken her testimony.

Here are three valid tactical objections that might help you disconcert the officer.

Officer Reading From Notes

Immediately after issuing your citation, most police officers will note what happened on the back of their copy. They do this so that later, if there is a trial, they can remember what happened. But in most states it is technically improper for the officer to simply read directly from her notes (or from any other document) while testifying in court, unless she first follows several important procedural steps (lawyers call this "laying a proper foundation.") The officer must first testify that she:

- can't remember all the details of the violation
- recorded them shortly after issuing the citation, and
- needs to refer to them to refresh her memory.

Because most people who get tickets never object to note reading, most officers don't know how to follow these technical procedural steps (called "laying the proper evidentiary foundation"). This gives you a golden opportunity to toss a stick into the cop's spokes by saying: *"Objection, Your Honor. The witness is clearly reading from notes, which are hearsay and should be excluded from the trial."* In all likelihood the judge will simply tell the officer to lay the proper foundation as outlined above and, if she succeeds (sometimes with coaching from the judge), proceed with her testimony, using the notes.

In addition to asking the officer to follow proper procedures to admit this type of hearsay into evidence, the judge should direct the officer to let you read the notes. (You may have to politely ask.) Sit down and carefully do just that. But when you finish, don't hand them back if the officer still hasn't created the proper legal foundation for using them along the lines set out above. Then when the judge asks you to return them, politely renew your "hearsay" objection and ask that the officer testify based on her "independent recollection"—that is, without looking at her notes. Even if the judge rules that the officer can use her notes, you have won two important things:

- You have gotten to read the officer's notes, if you had been denied that right before trial.
- You can claim in your closing argument that the officer has a poor memory for events and can't really contradict any evidence you present, which should, of course, raise a reasonable doubt as to your guilt.

TIP

Object if the judge "coaches" the officer. Sometimes a judge will try to help a befuddled officer lay a proper foundation for getting around the hearsay rule and using the notes. If so, you may want to politely renew your objection by saying, *"Objection, Your Honor. With all due respect, it appears as though the court is helping the officer testify by asking leading questions. I again ask the court to simply instruct the witness to testify from memory or lay a proper foundation for the use of this written material."*

At this point, the judge will either allow your objection (require that the officer lay a proper foundation or not use her notes) or overrule it. Either way, you have made your point, and it's time to move on.

Assuming Facts Not in Evidence

Another common improper ploy that officers use while testifying is to say something like: "I saw the defendant's vehicle go through the stop sign [or commit other dastardly acts]...." Here the officer is basically tying you (the "defendant") to what she observed by looking at a vehicle, which may or may not have been yours. This type of objection would be important if your defense rested on the officer identifying the wrong vehicle.

The proper way for the officer to testify is for her to say that she observed "a vehicle" (rather than "the defendant's vehicle") commit a violation, and that she then pulled over that vehicle and identified you as the driver, usually by asking you to produce your driver's license. When, however, you allow the officer to shortcut the process by testifying that she observed "the defendant's" vehicle, you've allowed her to improperly establish that you were the driver of the wayward vehicle that she says she saw.

Making an objection in this situation is sensible only if there is some reasonable question as to whether the vehicle the officer initially saw was really the one you were driving.

In objecting to the officer's "assuming facts not in evidence" or "lack of personal knowledge," you say something like this:

> *"Objection, Your Honor. This testimony assumes facts the officer hasn't testified to. There is no evidence before this court as to who owned or was driving the vehicle that this officer claims to have seen. The officer could not possibly have personal knowledge of the identity of the owner of a vehicle she merely sees traveling on the road. I move that her testimony not be considered."* (Lawyers would ask that it be "stricken," but you may be better off sticking to plain English.)

Here the judge will probably do one of two things: "Sustain" (grant) your objection and then "strike" (disregard) the officer's testimony (by often saying something like, *"So stricken. Continue, Officer Jones"*). Or the judge will ask the officer to "rephrase" her testimony (sometimes coaching her to say that she first saw the offending vehicle and then identified you).

Hearsay Evidence

In most states when an officer, or any witness, testifies to something she didn't personally observe, the law calls this "hearsay." (Reading from notes is one type of hearsay.) Such testimony is generally not allowed, provided you make an objection. If a prosecutor's question calls for hearsay (*"And what did Officer Smith tell you, Officer Jones?"*), you should quickly interject with, *"Objection, Your Honor, the question calls for hearsay."* If the officer blurts out hearsay to a proper question before you have a chance to register your objection (Q: *"How fast was the defendant driving?"* A: *"Officer Smith told me it was 75 miles an hour."*), your objection should be, *"Objection, Your Honor, that's hearsay, which I move be eliminated (stricken) from the record."*

Unfortunately, there are a number of exceptions to the hearsay rule, which allow certain types of hearsay to be considered by a judge or jury. Probably the most common in traffic court allows an officer to testify to any statements you made, which would tend to prove your guilt. (Q: *"Do you know why I stopped you?"* A: *"Because I was going 80."*)

Although it doesn't make sense to engage in an in-depth study of the rules of evidence just to go to traffic court, it can be a good idea to be prepared to object to two of the most common situations in which hearsay crops us:

- **When an accident occurs.** Here you should object if the officer—who probably didn't witness the accident—attempts to testify to what another person involved in the accident, or an eyewitness, told him. Again, the rule is the officer can testify only to what she saw, not what she heard from other people.

- **For speeding citations involving a plane.** You'll definitely want to object if the officer in the patrol car attempts to testify as to what an officer in an aircraft said your speed was. The ground officer must testify as to what she did and saw, not what the airplane officer told her. (See Chapter 6 for more on how to fight tickets involving airplanes.)

EXAMPLE:

Your vehicle collides with another at an intersection controlled by stop signs at all four entrances. You tell the officer you entered the intersection first, and that the other driver ignored the stop sign. But based on the statements of the other driver and a bystander, the officer concludes you were at fault for failing to yield to the vehicle to your right. You contest the ticket and go to trial. In court, the officer appears, but neither the other driver nor passenger is present. When the officer testifies what the driver and passenger said about the accident, you should immediately say, *"Objection, Your Honor, that's hearsay. It should not be considered."* The judge should agree with your objection by saying, *"sustained,"* which means the testimony is disallowed. Of course, a prosecutor can subpoena the people who witnessed the accident, allowing them to testify directly. But busy prosecutors often neglect to do this for traffic court cases, or the witnesses don't appear.

How to Cross-Examine the Officer

Preparation is the key to successfully questioning (cross-examining) the officer—with an eye towards raising a reasonable doubt as to your guilt. You can ask almost anything you want, so long as the answer you're seeking is in some way relevant to your effort to prove you didn't commit a particular element of the violation or to some other valid defense. Develop your cross-examination step by step, beginning with the least important background questions and ending with the ones that go to the heart of your defense.

TIP

Don't go fishing. If you don't have a specific reason to ask a particular question, don't ask it. Unfocused questions rarely result in answers that will help your case, and they commonly give the officer a chance to repeat damaging facts likely to convict you. Also, be sure your questions do not include an admission of guilt, such as, *"Where were you when I ran the stop sign?"* Instead, they should always be non-committal, such as, *"Where were you when you claim I ran the stop sign?"*

Below are the types of questions you'll want to ask in trials involving common traffic violations. If your situation is not covered, use what you learn here to develop a set of your own questions designed to show how the officer could have been mistaken in her observations.

Make a double-spaced list of questions you intend to use, and take it with you to trial. Then, depending on the officer's testimony earlier in your trial, pencil in necessary additions and changes. But remember, even after you ask a question, you'll want to retain as much mental flexibility as possible. That's because your next question should often be keyed to the officer's response. For example, if the officer's answer is evasive, be prepared to bear down with more specific questions until you either get the answer you want or force the officer to lie.

The best way to cross-examine is to ask specific—not open-ended—questions. For example, avoid questions such as, *"What happened then?"* or *"Why did you stop me, anyway?"* The officer could seriously tarnish your defense by replying, *"Because you broke the law."* Far better to ask questions such as, *"Isn't it true that there was a large hedge between your location and mine?"* and *"Isn't it true you stopped me because of a radio report from an aircraft, and you didn't determine my car's speed yourself?"*

Your goal in cross-examination is to show the judge or jury:

- The officer's powers of observation were not perfect.
- One or more legal elements of the particular offense are missing. (See Chapter 2 for more on elements of the offense.)
- The existence of a defense, such as mistake of fact, where you didn't know the stop sign was there until too late because the sign was obscured by trees (see Chapter 3).
- The officer was doing several things at once.
- The officer may have lost sight of your car between the time she observed the offense and the time she pulled you over.

Of course, you may occasionally get an unexpected answer. If you do, you'll have to rely on your broad understanding of the facts to decide whether to ask more detailed questions or quickly switch to the next line of questions.

 TIP

Never argue with the officer. It is almost always a mistake to adopt an antagonistic stance towards the officer. And it never makes sense to try to argue with him. Even if the cop answers a question untruthfully, or gives a ridiculous answer, it's your job to try to expose his fabrication by politely asking more direct questions, not by saying, *"That's just not true"* or *"How could you tell such a whopper?"*

EXAMPLE:

Your Question: *"Officer, how far were you from my vehicle when you initially took your radar reading?"*

Officer's Answer: *"500 feet."*

Your Bad Response: *"Officer, you know darn well that the radar beam width at that distance can't differentiate between vehicles in adjacent lanes. This whole deal is a sham."* (This is an argument, and isn't allowed during the cross-examination phase.)

Your Good Response: (in the form of a second question): *"Officer, you previously testified that your radar unit has a beam width of six degrees. Isn't it true that at 500 feet from your radar unit this means the beam will be over 100 feet across?"*

Your Good Follow Up: *"On the road where I was ticketed, aren't the individual lanes much narrower than 50 feet?"*

Coping With an Officer's Nonresponsive Answer

If you succeed in asking the officer a good, pointed question—one to which a truthful answer might prove damaging to the prosecution—there is a good chance she'll try to avoid answering by either changing the subject or saying she can't remember. This is where you need to bear down by asking more specific questions—if the officer is truly putting road blocks in your way, ask the judge to order her to answer your question.

Where and How to Cross-Examine

Courts differ somewhat as to how you are expected to conduct your cross-examination, especially in traffic cases. If there is a lectern podium in the courtroom, you may be asked to pose your questions from there. Or you may be expected to ask them from your place at the counsel table where you have been sitting. It makes little difference as long as you stand up (the best way to keep you on your toes). But never walk up to where the officer is sitting unless you want to ask him to refer to a diagram, chart, or notes. If so, some judges will expect you to first ask, *"Your Honor, may I approach the witness?"*

EXAMPLE:

You are challenging a motorcycle officer's ability to see what happened by attempting to show that because he was not wearing any goggles or other eye protection while "pacing" your vehicle at a high rate of speed, the wind blowing into his unprotected eyes obscured his vision. Later you'll make the point in final argument that he may have lost sight of the vehicle committing the offense, before pulling over your similar-looking car.

EXAMPLE:

Your Question: *"Isn't it true, officer, that you were not wearing any eye protection while you were riding your motorcycle on the day in question?"*

The Officer's Nonresponsive Answer:
"Well, I could see very well, and the windshield on my motorcycle...."
At This Point, Interrupt and Say: *"Objection, Your Honor; Officer Growlski's answer is not responsive to my question. I ask that the witness be instructed to answer the question I asked."*

Another frequent annoyance occurs when, after an officer answers your question, she starts to give an unrelated speech about how bad your driving was. This can be unnerving, and damaging to your case. Fortunately, it is also highly improper. You may say, *"Your Honor, I ask the court to instruct the witness to confine her answers to my questions."*

Testing the Officer's Power of Observation

The basis for nearly every traffic prosecution lies in the officer's perceptions. Put bluntly, if you can establish both that the officer can't see more than 100 feet and that your vehicle was 200 feet from where she was sitting when the "violation" occurred, you should win without breaking a sweat. But it's not just the officer's hearing or eyesight that are issues. Because she is probably testifying many months after ticketing you (and has likely handed out hundreds of tickets in the intervening time), her memory of what happened—or lack thereof—can often be a big issue at trial. The more you can establish she doesn't remember where, why, and how she stopped you, the more doubt you raise as to the accuracy of her testimony, and the

more likely it is that the judge or jury will find a reasonable doubt as to your guilt.

Following is a list of some of the types of general questions you might want to ask in order to test the officer's knowledge of the location and conditions where she observed you. Review these sample questions before trial, and leave out those that would be irrelevant in your case. Also, be prepared to leave out any questions that the officer answered in her initial testimony.

TIP

Keep it interesting or you'll put the judge to sleep. Your questions should always be designed to quickly get at key issues. If you seem to be getting nowhere with a particular line of questioning, move on to better questions before the judge or jurors nod off.

Sample Questions

Your first questions should often be designed to get the officer to admit she was doing a number of other things besides observing you (starting her car, driving her car, talking on the radio, and so on). The more tasks the cop admits to performing, the more doubt you may be able to cast in your final argument as to how clearly she was able to see what you were doing.

1. *"Where were you located when you first saw my vehicle?"*
2. *"Where was my vehicle when you first saw it?"*
3. *"Was your car (or motorcycle) parked or moving at the time?"*

If parked:

4. *"Was your engine idling, or was it off?"* (If idling, you can later argue that she was already intent on stopping someone regardless of whether she saw a violation or not.)

If the engine was off:

5. *"What did you do to start your vehicle?"*
6. *"Did you turn on your lights?"*
7. *"Did you use your two-way radio?"* (These questions are aimed at showing the police officer was too busy doing other things to watch you for more than a second before deciding you were speeding.)
8. *"Did you start your engine just before you saw the alleged violation, or while it was occurring?"* (If just before, you can argue in your closing statement that she made up her mind to stop you before she saw any violation. If during, she might have been too busy starting the engine to observe things very well.)

If moving:

9. *"In which lane were you traveling?"*
10. *"In which direction were you going?"*
11. *"How fast were you driving?"* (Leave this one out for speeding violations. You don't want the cop to say she had to go 90 mph to catch you.)
12. *"Did you have a clear view of the traffic on the road when you claim you observed the violation?"*
13. *"Was there any other traffic on the road other than your vehicle and mine?"*

If other traffic: (Your goal here is to ask questions regarding the number and types of other vehicles on the road and their movements. The less she remembers, the better your later argument will be that she can't remember much of what happened that day. On the other hand, if she describes other vehicles in great detail, you may be able to later claim that she may not have observed your car accurately, because she was so busy watching everything else.)

14. *"Could you describe the vehicles in front of your vehicle?"*
15. *"Could you describe the vehicles on either side of you?"*
16. *"How fast was the flow of traffic?"*

If slower than your vehicle, ask:

17. *"Did you see my vehicle passing any others?"*

TIP

Use the cop's answers to frame further questions. Here is an example of how you should use the cop's answers to frame subsequent questions. If she says you passed other vehicles, ask her for specifics (type of vehicle, color, make). She probably won't remember. If she says other traffic was slower than you, but also has said you weren't passing other vehicles, she's contradicting herself, and you'll want to point this out in your closing argument. If she says she was traveling at the same speed as or faster than your vehicle, your over-the-limit (but under-65) speed might have been safe, and therefore legal in "presumed" speed law states. Follow up with questions on this point, such as those listed below. If she says there was no other traffic, again, your over-the-limit speed might be considered safe under the circumstances in presumed speed law states. (See the appendix for the laws in your state.)

If you're charged with violating a presumed speed limit or, in an absolute speed limit state, driving under the limit but too fast for conditions, you can ask:

18. *"Do you consider yourself to have fairly well-developed powers of observation and memory for details concerning weather and road conditions?"*

Then, ask the officer about every possible detail and hazard on the road, leaving out all hazards that were really there. This way her answers will make it seem like the roadway was pretty safe, or that she can't remember all the details. Road conditions you'll want to ask about can include:

- **Highway width.** *"Officer, isn't it true that there were two lanes in each direction?"*

- **Divider strips or islands.** *"Isn't it also true that there were divider islands present, so as to separate opposite directions of traffic? Isn't it true that this island minimizes the possibility of a collision with traffic in the opposite direction?"*

- **Sharp curves.** *"Isn't it true there were no sharp curves over the area you say you determined my speed?"*

- **Dips or hills.** *"Isn't it true there were no dips or hills over the area you say you determined my speed?"*

- **Railroad crossings.** *"There were no railroad crossings either, were there?"*

- **Road repairs in progress.** *"There were no road repairs in progress, were there?"*

- **Obstructions on the road.** *"There weren't any other obstructions in the road, were there?"*

- **Soft shoulders.**

- **Spilled liquids.**

- **Pedestrians, bicyclists, or animals in the road.** *"There were no pedestrians present, were there?"* (If she answers *"yes,"* ask her to describe where they were and what they looked like. If it's not in her notes, she likely won't recall.)

TIP

If the officer repeatedly says he can't remember. The more the officer says he can't remember, the better, since you can later use his poor memory to cast doubt on the accuracy of his testimony about your violation when you make your final argument. In this connection it is often a good idea to ask questions you know the officer won't be able to answer. The best way to prepare to do this is to look at his notes beforehand. (See Chapter 9 on "discovery.")

Cross-Examination Questions for Specific Violations

The remainder of your cross-examination of the officer should be directed at undermining her testimony on the specific elements of the offense you are charged with, or getting her to admit circumstances justifying your violation. (See Chapter 3 for a review of the principal legal theories to beat a ticket.)

It follows that these cross-examination questions depend greatly on the violation charged. For example, in radar speeding cases, you might want to bring out the officer's lack of familiarity with her radar unit. But where you were cited for speeding after an officer paced your vehicle with hers, it would make no sense to make this inquiry.

Speed Violations in General

The following questions deal with how the officer measured your speed. (See Chapter 6 for more on measuring speeds.) The officer will undoubtedly testify as to the method she used. It will then be up to you to cast doubt on the accuracy of her claims through cross-examination.

Visual Speed Estimation

If the officer estimated your speed only through visual observation, without pacing your vehicle using radar, laser, or VASCAR, ask questions like these:

1. *"Over what distance did you see my vehicle travel?"* (If the officer says it was short—or you can introduce evidence such as the location of a hill, curve, or traffic lights proving it was short—you can later argue she couldn't have arrived at an accurate speed estimate.)

2. *"Did my speed change after you observed me?"* (If she says you slowed down after you apparently saw her car, you can later argue that the original high estimate was good only over a tiny distance and, therefore, inherently unreliable. If she says your speed suddenly went up or down, ask her to explain exactly where. Few officers have that good a memory, a fact you may be able to use in your final argument to cast doubt on the accuracy of

the officer's other observations. See Chapters 12 and 13 for more on how to make a closing argument.)

3. *"Was my vehicle traveling toward you, away from you, or across your line of vision?"* (If accurate, you can say in closing argument that it is more difficult for the officer to estimate the speed of vehicles moving in a more or less direct line toward or away from her than if vehicles are traveling across her field of vision. Of course, before you cross-examine on this issue, you should introduce evidence during the presentation of your case on this point.)

4. *"Have you ever participated in controlled tests where you were asked to estimate vehicle speeds?"* (Most officers will say no—a point you can bring up in your closing argument. If the officer says she has participated in such tests, ask whether she always guessed the exact speed correctly. If she says "yes," she's obviously lying—no one is that good; if she says "no," you can later point out that she admitted how difficult it is to estimate correctly.)

Speed Estimated by Pacing Your Car

If the officer's estimate of your speed was based on her looking at her own speedometer while following or "pacing" you, the following questions are usually helpful. (Also see Chapter 6, where we discuss possible defenses to tickets based on pacing.)

1. *"Over what distance did you follow my vehicle at a steady rate of speed?"* (The shorter the distance, the better your argument that she made an inaccurate reading.)

2. *"Was the distance between your car and mine always constant?"* (If she says "yes," she's obviously mistaken, since eventually she almost surely had to close in on you to pull you over. What she wants to say is that the distance was the same over the entire time you were being paced, at which point she sped up to stop you.)

If she seems to deny that at some point she sped up, follow up with questions like these:

3. *"Did you observe your speedometer while you were following me?"*

4. *"How many times did you observe it?"*

If she says she was watching it almost constantly, follow up with questions like these:

"When pacing at a constant speed, is it important that you watch the subject vehicle continuously?"

If she says "no," you can follow up with a question like this:

5. *"If you don't watch a vehicle continuously during pacing, isn't it possible to lose track of the car you are pacing and focus on a similar-looking vehicle?"* (If the officer continues to deny the need to look at the vehicle continuously, move on and attack her methods in your closing statement. See Chapter 6 on

"pacing" for more on how pacing works.)

6. *"Was there other traffic?"* (Ask only if there was.)

7. *"Which lanes were the other vehicles in?"*

8. *"Can you describe any of the other vehicles?"*

9. *"Were you paying attention to the other traffic in order to drive safely?"*

10. *"How often did you observe my vehicle?"*

If she testifies that she was watching her speedometer carefully and testifies in detail to other traffic on the road (she may do this to try to impress the judge), follow up with:

11. *"So you were watching my vehicle, other traffic, and your speedometer all at the same time?"* (If she says "no," she was mostly watching your vehicle, ask, *"And you were watching other traffic too, correct?"* Then, during your closing argument, you can argue that she was mostly watching your car and others, without much time to glance down at her speedometer.)

12. *"How far behind my vehicle were you while you were pacing it?"*

If she was pacing from more than a few hundred feet back, ask:

13. *"Do you agree that the ability to pace depends on good depth perception, so that you can follow at a constant distance?"*

14. *"Do you also agree that the farther away an object is, the more difficult it is to pace it?"* (If she says "no," ask

her which is more accurate—a pace at 100 feet, or a mile behind.)

15. *"Have you recently participated in controlled tests where you paced a vehicle a known speed from (whatever distance she claims to have paced you)?"* (The answer will almost always be "no.")

If at night:

16. *"Officer, you paced my vehicle at night [or dusk], correct?"*

17. *"Would you agree it's harder to keep a constant distance, in order to conduct an accurate pace, at night than in the daytime?"*

She should agree. If not, continue with questions like this:

18. *"Isn't it harder to accurately pace at night when you can see only two taillights, as opposed to driving in the day when you can see the whole car body?"*

In attacking the accuracy of her speedometer, you can ask:

19. *"How long before you cited me was the speedometer in your patrol car (or motorcycle) last calibrated?"* (If the officer tries to simply say, "it was accurate," she's bluffing, and you'll want to ask her to please answer your question. If a speedometer hasn't been calibrated recently, this is definitely a fact you'll want to use as part of your final argument; see Chapter 6.)

20. *"Did you bring a record of the most recent speedometer calibration with you today?"* (She almost never will.)

21. *"Are you aware that speedometer accuracy is affected by tire circumference?"* (She will probably say "yes.")

22. *"Are you also aware that tire circumference is affected by tire pressure and wear?"* (Again, she will probably agree.)

23. *"Then isn't it fair to say that speedometer accuracy is affected by tire pressure and wear?"* (She may try to hem and haw, but eventually should concede the point if you repeat the question.)

If she just doesn't seem to get it, ask this next question:

24. *"If you had worn or low pressure tires on your car, the odometer would erroneously read high, correct?"*

25. *"Were your tires' pressures checked when your speedometer was calibrated?"* (Probably not.)

26. *"Were they checked on the day you cited me?"* (Probably not.)

27. *"Are you aware that a tire's air pressure depends on its temperature?"*

28. *"Have the tires on your patrol car been rotated, or have any of them been changed since the last speedometer calibration?"* (See Chapter 6 for more on tire-wear and pressure problems.)

Speed Estimated From Aircraft

CROSS REFERENCE

Airplane tickets and your possible defenses to them are discussed in Chapter 6.

As discussed in more detail in Chapter 6, there are two ways for the officer to determine your speed from an aircraft:

- By timing the passage of the vehicle between two markers on the roadway, or
- By using ground markers and a stopwatch to determine how fast the aircraft is going and then using the aircraft to "pace" the vehicle below.

Depending on which method is used, your cross-examination should normally attempt to cast doubt on:

- The accuracy of the timing method the aircraft officer used to time the passage of your vehicle—or the aircraft—across two highway markings. (See Chapter 6.)
- The ground officer's knowledge of the distance between highway markings. Remember, if this is based on what she was told by the airplane officer, it is "hearsay" evidence to which you should object.
- The accurate identification of your vehicle by the aircraft officer.
- The ground officer's proper identification of your vehicle from the aircraft officer's description.
- The accuracy of the timing of passage of either the vehicle (method 1 above) or the aircraft (method 2 above) across the two highway markings.

These questions for the aircraft officer apply regardless of which method was used to measure your speed:

1. *"Officer Aircop, you used a stopwatch or other timing device to time the passage of the aircraft or vehicle between the two highway markings, correct?"*

2. *"Isn't it true that you timed the passage of the aircraft/vehicle [depending on which method was used] over a fixed distance?"* (The answer will always be "yes.")

3. *"Did you actually measure the distance between the highway markings on the ground?"* (The answer will be "no," at which point you should ask the judge to "strike" the officer's previous testimony. Simply say, *"Your Honor, I move to strike the officer's testimony as to the speed of the vehicle, since it was based on a distance divided by time that was not within this officer's personal knowledge."* If the judge strikes the testimony, you have won your case, because there is no other evidence of your speeding. If the judge refuses, you must, regretfully, move on.

4. *"Did you watch my vehicle that whole time without looking away?"*

If she says "yes," ask:

5. *"Did you have a stopwatch and a log to read my speed?"*

If she answers "yes," ask:

6. *"Didn't you look down at them and write log entries?"*

If "yes," ask: (The point you want to make in the next two questions is that the officer is doing many things, including looking at a stopwatch and log, and watching many cars, so she can easily lose sight of a particular car.)

7. *"Did you report other vehicles for speeding at or near that time?"*

8. *"How many cars were you monitoring?"*

9. *"Over what distance did you time my vehicle?"* If she says she timed your vehicle over a short distance, like 0.1 or 0.2 mile, ask:

10. *"Officer Aircop, could you state again the time it took my vehicle to travel between the two markings?"* (Be prepared to use the formula in the sidebar "Converting Miles Per Hour to Feet Per Second" (in Chapter 6) to calculate the speed you would have been going, based on the answer to this question. For example, if the officer says the two markings were an eighth of a mile apart (one eighth of 5,280 feet, or 660 feet), the time to cross the marks would be 660 feet divided by 110 feet per second, or 6.0 seconds.)

Then ask:

11. *"If because of normal reaction time, you didn't start the stopwatch until half a second after my vehicle passed over the first mark, the true time my car passed between the two points would have been* [example—6.5] *seconds, correct? Incidentally, I have a calculator if you would like to check the calculation."*

    "And at [example—one eighth of a mile or 660 feet] and [example—6.5] seconds, the true speed would have been [example—660 feet/6.5 seconds = 102 feet per second or 69] mph, correct?"

Ask this question only where the officer determined the aircraft speed by using the markings, then "paced" your vehicle with the aircraft.

 TIP

Use the officer's notes before trial to help you do the math. If you have been able to obtain the officer's notes before you go to trial (see Chapter 9), you'll know the distance between the road markings and can do the math in advance. Simply do the calculation: speed (feet per second) = distance (feet)/time (seconds), then divide that result (in feet per second) by 1.47 to calculate what the officer should say the elapsed time was. Then, see if you can use a slightly longer time based on the officer's likely reaction time to compute a substantially slower speed.

12. *"And isn't it true that you determined your aircraft's speed this way before you finally determined my vehicle's speed?"*

13. *"How much time passed between the time you calibrated the speed of the aircraft and the time you paced my vehicle?"*

14. *"If a headwind had slowed the aircraft after you timed its passage between the highway markings, wouldn't you have had to again fly between the markers to determine your slower speed relative to the ground?"*

15. *"Did you do that?"*

16. *"Are you certain the wind speed did not change during this time?"*

17. *"To determine the aircraft speed, what reference point on the aircraft did you use to check the aircraft passage over each line?"* (Usually it will be a wing or wing strut.)

18. *"How far was that object from you?"* (Usually a few feet.)

19. *"If you had moved your head forward or backward while observing your reference point passing the first or second marker, the elapsed time on your stopwatch would be incorrect, isn't that so?"* (If she denies this, ask her to hold up a pencil at arm's length against a distant object in the courtroom about 20 to 30 feet away. Then ask her to move her head one foot forward or back while holding the pen steady. Finally, ask if the pen doesn't seem to line up a few feet off. The shorter the distance between the two reference points on the highway, the more significant this type of error is—over long distances it won't affect the reading of your speed enough to matter.)

Additional questions to ask the air officer, which can be used with either speed measuring method:

20. *"When you identified what you say was my vehicle, you didn't read a license plate, did you?"* (This can't be done from 500 feet in the air.)

21. *"You didn't radio down the make or model of the vehicle did you?"* (Only ask this if the air officer's log doesn't mention this. It often won't, since they often can't tell this from 500 feet up either.)

If there was other traffic:

22. *"Were there other vehicles on the highway?"*

If she answers "yes," ask:

23. *"Could you describe the other vehicles by make or color?"* (If she can't describe the make and model of your vehicle or other vehicles, you can question her memory in your final argument and raise the possibility that she stopped the wrong one.)

24. *"Did you report other vehicles for speeding, along with mine?"* (If the officer answers "yes," you can argue that her attention was divided among several vehicles, opening up the possibility that she was confused and mixed up your safe speed with another car's speeding).

Questions for the Ground Officer (Can Be Used With Either Speed Measuring Method):

Ask these questions only if Officer Aircop says she radioed Officer Groundcop.

25. *"Officer Groundcop, isn't it true you were first alerted to my vehicle only because of the radio report from Officer Aircop?"*

If she says "yes," and the ground officer in the patrol car didn't testify she paced you after hearing the report from the air officer, ask:

26. *"So, then, your knowledge of the vehicle's speed was based solely on the radio report, correct?"* (If she says "yes," you should ask the judge to "strike" her testimony because it is based on "hearsay," what the air

patrol officer told her through the radio. Even if the judge denies your request, you should argue in your closing statement that the officer who actually ticketed you was acting on secondhand information, which is inherently unreliable.)

Speed Estimated by VASCAR

CROSS REFERENCE

VASCAR tickets and your possible defense to them are discussed in Chapter 6.

If the officer used VASCAR to determine your speed, your goal in asking questions is to show:

- She may have had reaction time error after your car passed the first point, clocking too short a time and thus too high a speed.
- She may have had difficulty seeing the stop or start point, thereby mistiming when you passed one or both.
- There may have been an odometer error due to low tire pressure or tire tread wear, which can produce a false reading. (The VASCAR unit is calibrated to the vehicle's odometer.)
- In the moving mode, the officer might have operated the unit incorrectly when faced with the necessity of pressing the buttons four different times while monitoring traffic. (Again, see Chapter 6 for an explanation of how an officer uses VASCAR in a moving vehicle.)

All VASCAR Modes

Ask these questions to cast doubt on whether the officer pushed the buttons at precisely the right times.

1. *"How far apart were the two points between which you measured my vehicle's passage?"*

2. *"How many seconds did you clock my vehicle passing between the two points?"* (If the two points were fewer than 500 feet apart, the time should be 5 to 10 seconds, depending on the speed and exact distance, and a reaction time error can be significant.)

If the officer's answer is in this range, ask the next questions. If the time is 10 seconds or longer, skip to question 11.

3. *"Could the length of time it took you to press the time or distance switches have been a factor in measuring my speed?"* (The officer will probably say "no," explaining that she didn't react to your car passing points as she pressed the switches, but instead correctly anticipated when it passed the markers, thereby getting your speed correct.)

If so, ask:

4. *"But if, when I passed the first reference point, you hadn't anticipated perfectly but instead reacted after my car passed the point, the time you measured would actually be a little too short, correct?"* (The answer should be "yes.")

If she won't admit this is true, follow up with:

5. *"Well, assume that if, when I passed the first point, you reacted and then pushed the 'time' switch half a second later. Wouldn't my time be erroneously low?"* (If she finally concedes the point, follow up with:)

6. *"And this would mean the speed you recorded would be erroneously high, right?"*

💡 **TIP**

Run the numbers. Use your calculator to do some quick math. For example, if the distance between the markers was 200 feet and the time the officer measured was 3 seconds, that would work out to 200 feet/3 seconds = 67 feet per second. Divide this by 1.47 to get 45.4 mph. It follows that if the officer reacted half (0.5) a second late, your true time of passage between the reference points was really 3.5 seconds, and your speed 200/3.5 = 57 feet per second. Again, divided by 1.47, your real speed was 38.8 mph. Assuming the speed limit is 40, you can plausibly argue you weren't speeding.

7. *"Assume you had reacted rather than anticipating, and your reaction time when I passed the first point took half a second. Now you testified that you measured my time between the two points as [example—3.0] seconds. So isn't it true that the true time of passage would have been closer to [example—3.5] seconds?"*

8. *"At [example—200 feet] and [example—3.5] seconds, that's an average speed of [example —57.1] feet per second, correct?"* (If she says she

can't do the math in her head, offer to let her use your calculator).

9. *"And you divide feet per second by 1.47 to get miles per hour, correct?"* (If she admits this, ask the next question. If not, skip to a new line of questions exploring how this number is derived in your final argument.)

10. *"And 57.1 feet per second, divided by 1.47, works out to 38.9 mph, doesn't it?"* (Obviously, this should be adjusted to your situation.)

Stationary VASCAR

Here your prime goal is to question the officer's ability to accurately observe when your vehicle passed a distant point.

11. *"Officer, how far from the two reference points were you located?"* (She'll almost surely say she was closer to one point than to the other.)

If she admits to being more than several hundred feet from one of the points but much closer to the other, ask:

12. *"So, isn't it true that it was easier for you to hit the 'time' switch when my vehicle passed over the nearer point?"*

If she refuses to give you a clear answer, follow up with:

13. *"Is it easier for you to hit the 'time' switch at the proper second when a car is 50 feet away than when one is half a mile away?"* (Assuming she says 50 feet away, ask question 12 again.)

14. *"Have you recently taken part in controlled tests of your ability to*

judge when a car has passed over a point hundreds of feet away?" (Most likely not.)

15. *"Isn't it also true that if you misjudged when my car passed the distant point, that would result in your time measurement being incorrect?"*

16. *"And that, in turn, would mean that the speed your VASCAR device recorded was incorrect, right?"*

CAUTION

Quit while you're ahead. If the officer surprises you by conceding a big favorable point, it's often best to quit this line of questions. Later you can refer to the officer's admission as part of your final statement to argue that there is reasonable doubt as to your guilt. If instead you follow up with more questions on the point you've already won, the officer may qualify or withdraw his admission. For example, he might say that while the VASCAR speed reading may have been wrong, it would make no real difference since you were going so much faster than the limit.

Moving VASCAR—Officer Coming From the Same Direction

Here you want to focus on the fact the officer must execute four time/distance switch clicks in a short time, something that isn't easy to do.

17. *"Officer, to use VASCAR while your vehicle is moving, you have to press the 'time' switch twice, and the 'distance' switch twice, correct?"* (She should say "yes.")

18. *"And that's a total of four operations, correct?"*

19. *"And if you had improperly pressed the 'distance' switch at exactly the point where your car passed beginning and end points, that would result in an error, correct?"*

20. *"And the same is true with respect to judging my vehicle passing the two points when you had to push the 'time' switch twice, correct?"*

21. *"And if you did these four operations in the wrong order, wouldn't that also result in a major error?"*

22. *"And you had to do all four things accurately, over a period of just how many seconds?"* (This is a little bit of a trick question. You hope she'll refer to the time it took you to pass between two points, rather than the longer time it took her to click the time switch twice as you passed the two points, then pause and hit the distance switch as she passed over each point.)

If she falls into your trap, follow up with any of the applicable questions below.

Moving VASCAR—Officer Coming From the Opposite Direction

The use of VASCAR in these circumstances is particularly tricky. Study Chapter 6 on VASCAR to understand why this is true before setting out to cross-examine the officer. The point is that the big possibility for operator error opens great opportunities for your cross-examination. Here are some questions designed to show the judge how difficult it is for an officer to properly use VASCAR in this way. This will definitely be a point you'll want to hit hard in final argument.

23. *"Now you say you saw my car coming from the opposite direction, picked out a reference point, and clicked 'time,' correct?"*

If "yes," ask:

24. *"Had you had experience using that reference point before?"* (Probably not, since she picked it quickly because it was near you as she was coming from the opposite direction.)

25. *"And when our cars were opposite, you clicked 'time' again as you simultaneously clicked 'distance?"*

26. *"Did you do this with one hand down, while also looking at my car? Or did you look at the VASCAR machine?"*

27. *"And then you clicked 'distance' again when you reached the second marker?"*

28. *"Again, did you do this with one hand down, while also looking at my car, or did you look at the VASCAR machine?"*

29. *"Between the time you saw my car pass the reference point from the other direction and the time you passed it, did you take your eyes off that reference point?"* (If the officer gets a little confused with all this, it's fine.) If she admits she did take her eyes off the mark, you may be able to argue in your closing statement that her distance determination could be incorrect because she refocused on a wrong reference point after looking away from the first point.

VASCAR—Moving Mode and Stationary Mode— Odometer Used to Measure Distance

30. *"Now, officer, you measured the distance between the two reference points by clicking your 'distance' switch twice as you drove between them, correct?"*

31. *"And your VASCAR unit is connected to your car's odometer cable to allow for you to do this?"*

32. *"Then the accuracy of the measured distance, and hence speed, depends on your odometer's accuracy, correct?"*

33. *"If you switched to smaller tires after your odometer was calibrated, there would be more revolutions of the odometer cable for the same distance, and hence an erroneously high distance and speed, correct?"*

34. *"Isn't it true that to be accurate the VASCAR unit's odometer module must be calibrated every so often against a premeasured distance?"*

35. *"When was this VASCAR unit last calibrated in this way?"* (If it's been a long time since the VASCAR unit was calibrated for odometer accuracy, you should argue in your closing statement that the "distance" reading, and hence the calculated speed, is suspect.)

36. *"Isn't it also true that if your tires were very worn, or if your tire pressure was too low, your tire circumference would be slightly smaller?"*

37. *"And that would result in your recording an erroneously high distance and speed, correct?"*

38. *"When did you last check the tire pressure in your vehicle?"* (Again, if she doesn't know or it's been a considerable time, you can later argue the VASCAR reading may have been wrong.)

Speed Estimated by Radar

If the officer used radar to measure your speed, use some or all of these questions. Your goal is to show:

- She doesn't really know how radar works.
- She was not careful about maintaining her unit's accuracy.
- The speed she measured may not have been your vehicle's.

Ask these questions only if the officer did not show you the radar readout at the time you were stopped.

1. *"Does your radar unit have a control that allows you to 'lock in' the targeted vehicle's speed onto the readout?"*

If "yes":

2. *"Did you show your unit's speed to me when you stopped me?"* (Assuming the answer is "no," claim in your final argument that because she could easily have shown you your speed, there must be some reason she chose not to.)

3. *"Could you please describe briefly how speed-determining radar works?"* (If she can't do this—or gets it wrong—consider using this admission as part of your final argument.)

4. *"Isn't it true that delicate and sensitive electronic measurement instruments*

such as radar units must be calibrated often to make sure they're accurate?"

5. *"Did you calibrate your unit immediately before and after you measured my claimed speed?"*

If "no," use this point in your final argument. If "yes," ask:

6. *"How exactly did you calibrate the unit?"*

If she says she turned on the unit's "calibrate" switch:

7. *"You mean, you didn't use a tuning fork?"*

8. *"Doesn't the radar unit's manufacturer recommend calibration with a tuning fork?"*

9. *"Isn't a tuning fork certified as accurate by a testing laboratory a better way to check the unit's accuracy than using the unit's own internal electronics, which may be faulty?"*

If she says she used a tuning fork:

10. *"What was the certified speed for the tuning fork you used?"*

If it's much different from the speed she says she clocked you at—for example, 25 mph, but your car was clocked at 60 mph—follow up with:

11. *"Isn't it true that checking radar accuracy with a tuning fork at one speed is not a guarantee of accuracy at a different speed?"*

12. *"When was the tuning fork itself last calibrated by an independent testing laboratory?"*

13. *"Do you have a certificate of accuracy for this particular tuning fork?"*

No matter what calibration method was used:

14. *"Has your radar unit ever malfunctioned in any way?"*

If she says "no," ask:

15. *"Then it's never been repaired, or taken to the shop, as far as you know?"*

If she says it hasn't, ask:

16. *"You mean, not even for routine maintenance?"*

17. *"What's the maximum range, in thousands of feet, of your radar unit?"*

18. *"What is the beam width of your radar unit in degrees?"* (Don't settle for an answer in "lanes." As discussed in detail in Chapter 6, the beam width will get wider the farther the unit is from your vehicle, and you want to emphasize this point. If she doesn't know the beam width in degrees, ask her how much wider the beam gets for each thousand feet distance from the radar unit. Be prepared to quickly calculate the beam width at the maximum range, so you can follow up with the next question.

19. *"So then, at the maximum range, where you can still determine a target's speed, the width of the beam is about* [calculate here] *feet, isn't it?"*

20. *"Isn't that much wider than one lane of traffic?"*

21. *"Isn't this wide enough to reflect beams from other nearby vehicles or even a low-flying aircraft or nearby trains?"* (Obviously, use this last part only if you were cited near railroad tracks or an airport.)

22. *"When you aim your radar unit at a nearby object, your unit's antenna will pick up signals reflected from other more distant sources, won't it?"* (She may say "yes," but that the unit is made to track the strongest reflected signal.)

If so, follow up with:

23. *"Did you know that a more distant, but larger, vehicle may reflect a stronger signal than a smaller nearby vehicle?"*

Ask the next four questions only if it was windy the day when you were cited:

24. *"Have you ever obtained what turned out to be a false speed reading by incorrectly aiming a radar unit, for example, at another vehicle or a tree blown by the wind?"*

25. *"And if those surfaces are in motion, they can cause a false reading on a radar unit, can't they?"*

26. *"Isn't it true that windblown tree limbs or even leaves can sometimes reflect radar signals to generate a false reading?"*

27. *"Even blowing dust or rain can sometimes do this, can't it?"*

28. *"Do you know what a harmonic frequency is?"*

29. *"Are you aware that harmonic frequencies of nearby radio transmissions, for example from CB sets, can cause false radar readings?"*

30. *"Did you know that electrical interference from nearby power lines*

or transformers or even high-voltage neon lights can generate false radar readings?"

31. *"When you estimated my vehicle's speed, were you first observing my vehicle with your eyes or using your radar unit?"*

If the officer was looking at your vehicle:

32. *"So, then, you had already assumed I was exceeding the speed limit before you took a radar reading?"*

If the officer was looking at the radar unit:

33. *"So, you had already formed an opinion of my speed before looking up at my vehicle?"*

34. *"Could a completely untrained person use your radar unit accurately?"* (The answer should always be "no.")

35. *"Could you please describe the training you've had in the use of radar?"* (Most officers will try to pretend the salesman's two-hour pep talk they probably received on how to use a particular radar unit was an intense "seminar.")

36. *"How long ago were you given this training?"*

37. *"How long did the training last?"*

38. *"Was this training conducted by a salesperson for the radar-device company?"*

39. *"Did you have supervised 'hands-on' instruction out on the road?"*

40. *"Have you participated in any tests where you used radar to measure a vehicle's speed, then were told the correct speed?"* (Almost never; if

she says "yes," try to get her to give precise details.)

Speed Estimated Using Laser

In your cross-examination of an officer who used a laser gun to estimate your speed, you want to bring out the following points:

- The officer doesn't really know how laser works.
- The laser unit might not have been aimed and used correctly.

1. *"Officer, how does laser work?"* (This is harder to describe than radar, and the officer may not do a good job.)

2. *"Isn't it true that the laser unit works by measuring distances, using the speed of light and the time it takes a reflected beam to return, between the laser unit and the target vehicle?"* (The officer will probably agree that it sounds right.)

3. *"How many distance measurements does it make in a second?"* (She probably won't know.)

4. *"Isn't it true that the laser unit emits three separate light beams? And that each beam hits a different spot on the target vehicle?"*

5. *"And isn't it also true that when you aim the laser unit to get an accurate reading, you must aim it at the same part of the target vehicle during the entire time of the measurement?"*

6. *"Isn't it also true that if, over the measurement period, you first aim it at the passenger area, then move the gun slightly so the beams hit the hood, that at least part of your measurement will take into account*

the five or so feet difference between those two points?" (If she admits this, you can later argue in your closing statement that this caused an error. See Chapters 11 and 12 on closing arguments.)

7. *"Have you read the instruction manual for this unit?"*

If "yes," ask:

8. *"Doesn't it refer to this type of possible error?"*

If the cop seems confused, follow up with:

9. *"Was it possible you made this type of error?"*

10. *"Was there other traffic in my direction?"* (Ask only if there was—a point you can make in your testimony if she doesn't admit it.)

11. *"Isn't it also true that if one of the three beams reflected off a vehicle near mine, going at a different speed, and another beam reflected off my vehicle, your laser gun would have produced an incorrect result?"*

12. *"And isn't it possible, if you were, say, a quarter of a mile away, and an adjacent car going in my direction passed me, that one of the three beams might have hit my car, with the others hitting the second car?"*

Especially if she says this is unlikely, follow up with:

13. *"But isn't it true that the possibility of this type of error is also mentioned in your instruction manual?"*

"Presumed" Speed Limit Questions

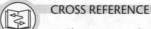 **CROSS REFERENCE**

In Chapter 5 we discuss "presumed" speed limits in detail. Look at your state's information in the appendix to see if your state uses the presumed speed limit system.

In preparing your cross-examination questions, start by thinking of the actual road, traffic, and weather conditions when you were cited. Then use this information to edit and fine-tune the following questions. For example, if it was raining or foggy, the less said about the weather, the better. Also, don't ask about traffic conditions if traffic was fairly heavy (unless you believe you can use this information to cast doubt on whether the cop stopped the right car). Similarly, it usually makes sense to ask next about highway conditions if you were ticketed on a two-lane winding, hilly road.

Here are some sample questions.

If the traffic was light:

1. *"Was there a lot of traffic in my direction?"*

2. *"How many vehicles were there in my lane?"*

3. *"How many were behind me?"*

4. *"How many were in front of me?"*

5. *"What was the average distance between vehicles?"*

The point of many of the following questions is to establish, in a presumed speed area, that it was safer to exceed the limit in order to keep up with the flow of traffic around you.

6. *"Was I ticketed at rush hour?"*

7. *"Was most of the traffic going at about the same speed you say I was going?"*

8. *"Did you see my vehicle pass any others?"* (Don't ask if you did pass other vehicles.)

If she says "yes," follow up with:

9. *"Could you describe the vehicles I passed?"* (She probably can't—a fact you may be able to use later in your final argument to cast doubts on the accuracy of her testimony.)

Then, only if she says you weren't passing other cars, ask:

10. *"So, then, it's true that I was going slower, or at least at the same speed as the other traffic?"*

Ask all the following questions that fit in an effort to show that even if you did slightly exceed the speed limit, it was safe to do so.

If there was no rain:

11. *"Was the road pavement dry?"*

If there was no fog or rain:

12. *"Was the visibility good?"*

If it was a clear day:

13. *"Was the sun shining? Were clouds obscuring it?"*

If you were cited at night but visibility was good:

14. *"Are there street lights along this stretch of road?"*

15. *"Were the lights on?"*

If the road had at least two lanes in your direction:

16. *"How many lanes did the road have in my direction?"*

If the road was divided by a median or barrier:

17. *"Did the road have a divider or barrier down the middle?"*

If there were no intersections near where you were cited:

18. *"Were there any intersections nearby?"*

If there were intersections, but all were controlled by stoplights:

19. *"Were there any uncontrolled intersections nearby?"*

If there were no blind curves:

20. *"Were there any sharp turns in the roadway?"*

If the road was flat:

21. *"Were there any hills obscuring the view from the roadway?"*

If there were no pedestrians:

22. *"How many pedestrians were in the area?"*

23. *"Were any pedestrians crossing the road? Trying to cross?"*

 TIP

Don't forget to make these points in your testimony. If the road, traffic, and weather conditions really were good, the above line of cross-examination questions should help your case. But remember, the best time to convince the judge that you really were driving safely is when you present your testimony along these lines. (See Chapter 10.) But if you can get the officer to agree that traffic was light and road conditions were good, you'll certainly want to refer to her statements in your final argument as part of your claim that the officer agreed with your description of conditions.

Running a Stoplight

The defense to this one is usually fairly straightforward. Since it's legal to enter an intersection on a yellow light, the main job of cross-examination is to cast doubt on whether the officer accurately observed that the traffic light was red when the front of your car drove across the "limit line" or cross street.

1. *"Did you see my vehicle at the time the green light first turned to yellow?"* (If she says she didn't, then she could have seen you only a few seconds before she says you ran the red light, creating at least doubt as to her ability to see something happen so fast.)

2. *"For how many seconds does the yellow light stay on?"*

If she says she doesn't know how long the yellow light was lit, follow up with:

3. *"Can you estimate how long the yellow light was lit?"* (If she still won't volunteer an answer, you can contend in your final argument that her powers of observation weren't that good.)

Questions related to your speed:

Ask only if you weren't speeding, and if the ticket itself and the officer's notes are silent about this point. The point here is to show that if you were going the speed limit, the duration of the yellow light was too short to allow you to come to a complete stop before the yellow light turned to red. Believe it or not, traffic signals are not all timed to allow

a proper stop given the speed limit (see sidebar below).

4. *"In your opinion, was I traveling at or near the speed limit?"*
5. *"What was that speed limit?"*
6. *"How many feet from the intersection was my vehicle when the green light turned yellow?"*
7. *"What is the normal stopping distance at that speed limit?"*

Speed and Distance: How to Do the Math

Once the officer testifies as to your speed and location when the light turned yellow, you will want to make a quick calculation with a pocket calculator. Multiply the speed in miles per hour by the number 1.47, giving your speed in feet per second. Next, divide this number into the number of feet she said you were from the intersection when the light turned yellow. This will give you the number of seconds you had to enter the intersection before the light turned red. If this number is less than the number of seconds the yellow light was on (based on your timing or the officer's estimate), then you would have entered the intersection while the light was still yellow. You can introduce your timing test during your own testimony and refer to it in closing arguments.

If the officer was on the cross street (at right angles to the one you were on), she probably assumed that when she saw the red light change to green, the yellow light had changed to red in your direction. If this seems to be the case, ask:

8. *"Could you see the color of the light facing me from your location?"* (If she says "yes," stop here.)

But if she says "no," ask:

9. *"Why do you say I entered the intersection on a red light if you couldn't see my light?"* (She will undoubtedly say because her light went green.)

10. *"You mean you assumed my light turned from yellow to red at exactly that time?"* (She will most likely answer "yes.")

11. *"Did you promptly examine the signal to determine whether the light in my direction was properly synchronized so as to turn red when the one in your direction turned green?"* (Very few officers check the lights for synchronization. If the officer did not, you can contend in your final argument that it sheds doubt as to whether the light was really red when you entered the intersection. This argument is helped if you also establish that the officer was not in a good position to see exactly when you entered the intersection. If you have established this, you should hit this point hard in your closing arguments. See Chapter 7 on strategies for beating red light tickets.)

If the officer was at an angle that would have made it difficult to observe, you might ask this:

12. *"Isn't it true that you couldn't see the color of the signal facing me from where you were?"*

Running a Stop Sign

Defending this type of case almost always comes down to a choice between your claim that you stopped and the officer's assertion that you didn't. Here there are commonly only two defenses aimed at raising reasonable doubt:

- Whether you came to a complete stop behind the "limit line" or the imaginary line at the corner where a painted line would go, or
- Whether there was a regulation stop sign controlling traffic in your direction.

Your questions of the officer will depend on where she observed you. If she testified she was on a cross street, or on the other side of the intersection, not at the entrance to the intersection, ask:

1. *"When you observed my vehicle, were there other vehicles in front of you?"*
2. *"How many?"*
3. *"Can you describe them?"* (Unless her notes indicate, she probably won't remember the number of vehicles in front, or their descriptions.)
4. *"How far down the street could you see?"*

 CAUTION

Don't cross-examine when a stop sign is hidden. As noted in Chapter 7, you can sometimes defend a stop-sign charge by claiming the sign was obscured. If that is your claim, it's probably best not to cross-examine the officer. That's because she will probably say she saw the sign clearly. Better to simply tell your story—backed up by a diagram and, if possible, a witness—when it's your turn.

Illegal Turns

Here we look at a few questions you might ask when ticketed for an unsafe turn. Whether a particular driver is really guilty beyond a reasonable doubt of making an unsafe turn is usually a subjective judgment, unless there is a clearly visible sign absolutely prohibiting the turn. Therefore, you should ask the same sorts of questions you would ask for speeding in a presumed speed law area in order to show that under real-world conditions your turn was done safely. The following questions should be helpful.

If the turn was at an intersection:

1. *"Was the intersection controlled by a traffic signal?"*

2. *"Did you see the color of the signal when I entered the intersection?"* (Unless the officer was directly behind you, she could not have seen the signal.)

3. *"Did I come to a complete stop in the intersection before turning?"* (Ask only if you did—it tends to show you were being careful.)

4. *"How many feet was the oncoming vehicle from me when I made the left turn?"*

5. *"How fast was the oncoming traffic moving?"*

Based on the answers to questions 4 and 5, the time you had, in seconds, to make the turn before being hit by the oncoming traffic is equal to the distance of the oncoming vehicle from yours in feet divided by 1.47 multiplied by the speed of oncoming traffic in miles per hour. If this works out to five seconds or more, you can later argue that there was plenty of time for you to turn safely.

6. *"Was my turn signal flashing?"* (Ask only if it was.)

7. *"For how long?"*

8. *"Did any vehicle blow its horn in response to my turn?"* (Ask only if none did.)

9. *"Did the oncoming vehicle slow down, in your opinion, because of my turn?"* (She will almost always answer "yes.")

10. *"Did that vehicle screech its tires?"* (Ask only if it didn't.)

If the cop says "no," you should ask:

11. *"Could the oncoming vehicle have slowed down because the driver was waving me to turn?"*

12. *"Isn't it true that many safe drivers slow down at intersections out of general caution, whether or not someone up ahead is turning?"*

Trial Before a Judge (No Jury)

Introduction 182

    Understanding the Courtroom 182

    Traffic Trials Without a Prosecutor 185

    Trials Handled by a Prosecutor 186

Trial Procedure 186

    Clerk Calls the Case 186

    Last-Minute Motions 186

    Opening Statements 188

    The Prosecution's Testimony 189

    Your Cross-Examination 192

    Redirect Examination 192

    Reserved Opening Statements 192

    Your Testimony 193

    Witness Testimony 194

    Closing Statements 194

    The Verdict 199

    The Sentence 200

Appealing for a New Trial 200

Introduction

In most of the 50 states, you do not have the right to a jury trial in a traffic ticket case, which means a judge alone decides whether or not you are guilty. In the others, you can insist on a jury trial. (See the appendix for the jury trial rules in your state.) When only a judge is present, traffic violation trials tend to be fairly informal—certainly more so than the trials for serious crimes portrayed in movies or on TV. Informality is particularly likely when the only witness for the state is the police officer and no prosecutor is present. (This is common in many states.) Here we provide you an overview of what is likely to happen with and without a prosecutor.

Understanding the Courtroom

Traffic court trials are generally conducted in courtrooms that look much like those on television. In addition to the judge, a clerk and a bailiff will normally be present. The clerk sits at a table immediately in front of the judge's elevated bench, or slightly off to the side. Her job is to keep the judge supplied with necessary files and papers and to make sure that proceedings flow smoothly. Depending on the state, there may also be a court reporter present who keeps a word-by-word record of proceedings.

Be a little early for your trial (it can take a few minutes to find the right courtroom, which in some states is called a "department"). Once you arrive, tell the court clerk or bailiff you are present, then take a seat in the spectator section.

Courtrooms are divided about two-thirds of the way toward the front by a sort of wooden fence known as "the bar." The judge, court personnel, lawyers, and you (after your case is called) use the area in front of the bar. The public, including you and other people waiting for their cases to be heard, are seated in the main body of the room. When the judge or clerk reads (calls) the name of your case, you may cross through the bar into the area where the judge sits. When you come forward, you sit at one of two long tables, known as the counsel tables, facing the judge.

In courtrooms that follow an informal approach, your witnesses should accompany you to the counsel table. At more formal trials, they remain behind the bar (as does the police officer) and testify at the witness stand only when their names are called. If you watch a few cases before yours, you'll quickly see how things are being handled. In some courtrooms, you and any witnesses will be asked to raise your right hand and swear to tell the truth before the judge arrives. In a few, you or your witnesses will be sworn in only just before testifying.

TIP

Be polite and respectful. Be polite (but not obsequious) to all court personnel—most especially the judge. This may be tough to do if you have a genuine beef with the legal system and feel truculent or angry. But realize that if you express your anger or hostility, the judge is very likely to hold it against you. Judges want

A Typical Courtroom

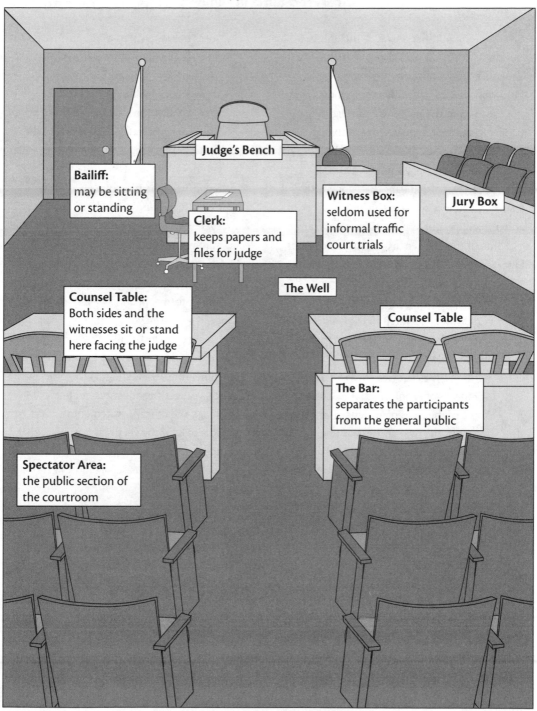

Judge's Bench

Bailiff: may be sitting or standing

Clerk: keeps papers and files for judge

Witness Box: seldom used for informal traffic court trials

Jury Box

The Well

Counsel Table: Both sides and the witnesses sit or stand here facing the judge

Counsel Table

The Bar: separates the participants from the general public

Spectator Area: the public section of the courtroom

Informal Procedures in Some States

An increasing number of states (including Florida, Massachusetts, Michigan, Rhode Island, Oregon, and Washington) have completely "decriminalized" traffic offenses. In most cases, this means that the procedures for fighting traffic tickets are much less formal than in states where traffic cases are decided in criminal court. Though this may sound reassuring, unfortunately it also means that along with formality you lose some of the important rights and procedures guaranteed in criminal court.

Some of the differences you may encounter in states with a civil traffic system include:

- A lower burden of proof. The standard the government must meet is often—but not always—lowered to the preponderance or clear and convincing standard, which makes it harder for the person fighting the ticket (see the "Different Standards of Proof" sidebar in Chapter 3).
- Some of the rules of evidence (for example, the hearsay rule) or rules of criminal procedure (for example, rules permitting discovery of the officer's notes before trial) may not apply. Again, the suspension of these rules makes it harder to win your case.
- Some states, including Florida and Rhode Island, have set up administrative agencies completely separate from the courts for hearing traffic violations, so you never see a courtroom or a real judge, just a hearing officer. In some cases (for example, Washington, D.C.), even your first appeal is heard within the administrative agency.

In some of the states with civil traffic systems, you have the choice between a formal and informal hearing. Given the choice, you should almost never opt for an informal hearing, especially if the rules in your state say that an officer doesn't have to be present at an informal hearing. By insisting on the officer's presence, you get the advantage of being able to challenge the officer's statement in court. And you also gain the very real possibility that the officer will not show up to testify against you, which means the case will most likely be dismissed.

you to be able to separate your emotion from the facts of the case. And remember: No matter how informal a courtroom, all judges, when spoken to, expect to be called "Your Honor."

Traffic Trials Without a Prosecutor

In many states, it's common for traffic court trials to be handled without the presence of an assistant district attorney or other prosecuting attorney. After the clerk calls the case, the police officer simply presents his testimony as to why he thinks you are guilty. Then you have a chance to cross-examine before presenting your defense.

With no prosecutor present, the judge normally will allow the officer to tell his side of the story in narrative form, perhaps interrupting to ask a few questions. You should then have an opportunity to ask the officer relevant questions—called cross-examination. As discussed in Chapter 10, you should be prepared to cross-examine the officer.

 CAUTION

What to do if the judge tries to get you to waive cross-examination. Some judges may not tell you that you have the right to cross-examine, or recommend that you just skip this stage and present your defense. But as discussed in Chapter 11, in most states they must let you cross-examine if you insist. It is usually wise to do so, since getting the officer to appear unsure of what happened or to admit he can't remember key facts is one important way to create a reasonable doubt as to your guilt.

After you question the officer, you get to present your side of the dispute and present the testimony of any of your witnesses. At any time during either presentation or after you are both done, the judge may ask questions. Finally, the judge will announce her verdict of guilty or not guilty. If she finds you guilty, she will usually pronounce sentence (the fine) right away.

 TIP

The judge is boss: Be prepared for anything. While this chapter outlines the usual ways a traffic case works, understand that judges have a great deal of leeway in running their own courtroom. Some judges won't listen patiently to your well-prepared and practiced presentation. Instead, they will insist on questioning you, the officer, and all witnesses. And, as noted above, a judge may even try to rebuff your attempts to cross-examine the officer, ask questions of your own witnesses, or make a final statement.

It will greatly help you understand what is expected (and modify your presentation accordingly) if you can watch a few cases in the courtroom of the judge who will hear your case. And it should also help if, in advance, you make a concise list of the points of your defense that you feel must be made during the trial. Then, if the judge derails your presentation, you can glance at your list and say something like this: *"Your Honor, I have prepared a few brief points that I think are crucial to my case and would like to be allowed to present them to you."* Most judges will slow down and grant you this polite request.

Trials Handled by a Prosecutor

In some courts, a prosecutor (normally a lawyer from the district, county, or city attorney's office) will present the state's case. As mentioned, this is likely to result in a more formal courtroom proceeding. In addition to each side presenting its own testimony and having a chance to cross-examine witnesses, each party may also make a formal opening and closing statement. In theory, you have the right to make an opening statement before the officer testifies, and a closing statement after all evidence is presented, but if no jury or prosecutor are present, many judges will try to save time by pressuring you to waive these procedures. To find out in advance if a prosecutor will be handling the case, you can try to ask court personnel or actually go to the courtroom where traffic cases are held and see what the standard procedure is.

Trial Procedure

This section takes you step by step through a traffic court trial, with information on your options at the various stages of the proceedings. For simplicity's sake, through-out this section the term "prosecutor" and "the prosecution" will be used to refer to whomever is doing the prosecuting against you, whether it is the police officer, an assistant district attorney, or other prosecuting attorney.

Clerk Calls the Case

Your trial begins when the clerk calls your case, usually by saying, "State [or "People"] vs. [your name]." Assuming you and your witnesses have already been sworn in, you should now come to the front of the courtroom and sit at one of two tables (usually the one farthest away from the jury box). Whether you stand or sit when making your presentation (and often where you do so) depends largely on the courtroom's architecture and the preference of the judge. Most courtrooms have a traditional witness box next to the judge's bench where you and any witnesses—including the officer—may be asked to testify. However, many traffic court judges prefer that you and your witnesses tell your story from behind your table, while the officer does the same from the adjacent table. To ask questions during cross-examination, you simply turn slightly to face each other (but do not leave your table).

To start the proceeding, the clerk (or the judge) may then recite the bare facts of the case. He may say something like, *"Mr. Loo, you are charged with a violation of Section 1180 of the Vehicle and Traffic Law of the State of New York, by driving 48 mph in a 35-mph zone on the 400 block of Main Street in Sun City."*

Last-Minute Motions

Before the prosecution begins its case, you may want to make one or more requests of the judge. These are called "motions" and, depending on the facts of your case, might include:

- Requesting a continuance if you need more time
- Requesting dismissal of the charges for failure of the prosecution to disclose the officer's notes as per your written request
- Requesting the judge to order the prosecution to provide you a copy of the officer's notes so you can better prepare for trial, or
- Requesting dismissal, if the prosecution has taken too long to bring the case to trial.

To make a motion, stand up as soon as the judge stops speaking and say, *"Your Honor, I would like to make the following motion."* Then, depending on the motion, you continue along these lines: *"I move to dismiss this case based on the fact that the prosecution has completely ignored my written request to discover the officer's notes. I have here a copy of that request made on January 15, 20xx."*

Below we cover other situations where you may wish to make a motion.

If Officer Fails to Show Up (Lack of Prosecution)

One of the cornerstones of the American legal system is that you have the right to confront your accusers and cross-examine them when you are charged with a criminal offense, even if it is minor. If the officer fails to show, you should point out to the judge that this right has been denied and your

case should be dismissed. (Lawyers call this a "dismissal for lack of prosecution.") Make sure the judge knows how inconvenienced you have been by the officer's failure to show up.

Here is an example of what you can say (adjusting the facts to fit your circumstances, of course):

> *"Your Honor, I move that this case be dismissed. I am ready to proceed to trial. I've subpoenaed two witnesses, both of whom are present. We have each taken the morning off from work, at substantial expense, to defend against this. I received no advance notice from anyone that the case would not proceed. Certainly if I failed to show up and the officer was present, I wouldn't be entitled to a last-minute postponement. So I respectfully ask that the court dismiss this case for lack of prosecution and in the interest of justice."*

Requests to dismiss under these circumstances are often granted. The judge will normally deny your request only if the officer has communicated to the court some really good reason for his failure to show up and for not notifying you in advance. Acceptable excuses might include law enforcement or medical emergencies. Unacceptable excuses include planned events like vacations and previously scheduled training or medical leave—reasons for which you could have been notified well in advance.

Excluding Multiple Witnesses

Occasionally the prosecution will have more than one witness. This is usually true in aircraft-patrol situations, because one officer must testify to clocking your vehicle from the air, the other to pulling you over and identifying you on the ground. This can also occur when two police officers were present at the time you were cited. In addition, if you were involved in an accident, other drivers or bystanders—in addition to the officer—may be asked to testify against you.

You never want to allow two or more prosecution witnesses to be in the courtroom at the same time during the trial, because doing so allows them an easy opportunity to coordinate their stories and present the same version of the facts. By contrast, if each officer or other prosecution witness testifies outside the presence of the others, you have the opportunity to exploit likely inconsistencies in their individual versions of events. To do this, say, *"Your Honor, I request that multiple witnesses be excluded from the courtroom."* Such a request is not impolite or hostile and will be routinely granted. (If your motion is granted, it will also mean any witnesses you have must also wait outside.)

Requesting a Continuance

If you feel a delay (continuance) would work in your favor (see Chapter 9 on how a continuance can help you), you have a final opportunity to ask for it just before trial actually starts. For example, a continuance might be needed if you've subpoenaed an essential witness who has not shown up. If you have subpoenaed a witness to produce certain documents—called a subpoena "duces tecum"—and the documents have not arrived, you may also want to ask for a delay.

But don't ask for a continuance until you see if the ticketing officer has arrived. Obviously, if the officer is not present, you'll want to ask for a dismissal.

Opening Statements

Before testimony is presented, both the prosecution and the defense have the right to make an opening statement briefly reviewing the violation and saying how they intend to prove each element of the case. It's important to realize that in doing this, neither you nor the prosecutor needs to prove anything. The point is to simply lay the groundwork for the officer (or maybe other witnesses as well) to testify later.

The Prosecution's Statement

Some prosecutors make an opening statement, but most are sensitive to the judge's desire for a quick trial and waive the opening statement, because their facts will come out during the testimony of the ticketing officer. When just the police officer shows up and there is no prosecutor, it's even rarer for an opening statement to be made. That's because most officers realize their role is to present evidence, not to act as an advocate for a guilty verdict or suggest to the judge how to view the testimony.

If a prosecutor chooses to make an opening statement, it may sound like this:

"Your Honor, the People (or State) will show, through the testimony of Officer Tim Ticketem of the Dayton Police Department, that the defendant, Sam Safespeed, was driving a red 1997 Corvette on Walnut Street, where posted speed limit signs indicate the speed limit to be 35 miles per hour. It will also show that Officer Ticketem, relying on his radar speed detection device, determined Mr. Safespeed drove in excess of 50 miles per hour, and he visually confirmed for over half a mile that Mr. Safespeed was weaving in and out of traffic."

Your Opening Statement

You also have the legal right to give an opening statement before any prosecution testimony or to "reserve" the right to make it until just before your defense begins. In many courts, the judge will assume you don't want to make an opening statement and simply ask the prosecutor or police officer to begin their presentation. At this point you will normally want to say, *"Your Honor, I would like to reserve the right to make a very brief opening statement until just before I testify."*

Why reserve your opening statement? Because by waiting you have the opportunity to tailor your remarks to what you learn in the officer's testimony. Also, by not giving your statement at the beginning, you avoid revealing your strategy in advance.

 TIP

You get an opening statement even if the prosecution waives it. Even when a prosecuting attorney does not make an opening statement or isn't even present, you still have the right to present—or reserve—an opening statement. But again, in some courtrooms you'll need to make sure the judge knows you wish to do so by politely speaking up.

The Prosecution's Testimony

After opening statements, the officer who cited you will explain why you are guilty of the violation you were ticketed for. In most traffic trials, he will testify by standing behind the counsel table (see the courtroom diagram at the beginning of this chapter). But in courts that prefer a more formal approach, he will testify from the witness stand.

If no prosecutor is present, the officer will recite what occurred and why he believes these facts justified issuing you a ticket. You have the right to interrupt the officer's presentation, but only if you identify a legitimate legal reason to "object" to a particular aspect of his testimony. Of course, you should never interrupt to say, *"He's lying! That's not true!"* or something similar. Instead, you must politely say *"Objection, Your Honor,"* and then briefly explain the legal basis for your objection.

> **TIP**
>
> **Don't object frivolously.** In a trial before a judge, without a jury, there is often little to be gained by making lots of objections. The judge almost surely knows the rules of evidence far better than you do and is likely to discount any testimony or documents the officer presents that are way out of bounds.

Most objections to testimony are made on one of the following four grounds.

The Witness Has Not Provided Enough Detail to Show Why He Has Personal Knowledge of His Testimony

This is called failing to provide a "foundation" or "legal basis" for the testimony. For example, if a police officer refers to a diagram, he must first say how he knows the diagram is an accurate reflection of the place you were stopped and ticketed. Usually this is done when the officer testifies that he drew the diagram after writing the ticket while still looking at the scene.

If he fails to do this, you could say, *"Objection, Your Honor. The officer has not provided a proper foundation for using the diagram. He apparently has no independent recollection of the incident and should not be allowed to refresh his memory with the diagram that may not even be of the proper area."*

This objection can be useful if you believe the officer really isn't prepared to lay the proper foundation, in which case the diagram could not be used against you. But, if you are pretty sure the officer will simply

explain facts and convince the judge his diagram accurately reflects the area where the ticket was given, it's a mistake to waste the judge's time with what he will likely consider to be a frivolous objection.

> **TIP**
>
> **Object to the officer's use of notes.** Watch the officer carefully during her testimony, to see if she's using notes. As discussed in Chapter 10, officers commonly testify by using notes scribbled on the back of their copy of the ticket. If the officer refreshes her memory in this way, you have a right to object on the basis she hasn't "laid the foundation" necessary to use the notes. This may discombobulate the officer, who may then have to admit she can't remember much without the notes. On cross-examination, you may then want to press this point home by asking the officer about details of what happened. Assuming she can't remember, you'll have a better shot at testifying to facts that raise a reasonable doubt as to whether you are really guilty. And then in your final argument, tell the judge that, based on the officer's poor recollection and your testimony, there is a reasonable doubt as to your guilt. (See Chapter 11 on when to object to testimony.)

The Officer Presents Evidence You Requested Well Before Trial But Never Received

Here you can say: *"Objection, Your Honor. The officer is referring to his notes, a copy of which I requested by way of discovery several weeks ago; my written request for those notes—which I'd like to show the court is right here—was never responded to. I ask that this evidence be excluded and the officer's testimony be disallowed."*

Then, you hand a copy of your written discovery request (see Chapter 9) to the clerk for the judge to see. If your objection is approved—or "sustained"—by the judge, you should ask for a continuance to study the notes. If granted, this means the officer must come back to court a second day (something he may be unable to do). At worst, the judge should give you the opportunity to study the notes right then— which may still be very helpful when you cross-examine the officer. For example, if they are cursory or sloppy (but the officer has already claimed he needs to refer to them to refresh his recollection), you may be able to get the cop to admit he can't recall other details not mentioned in his notes.

The Officer Says Something That Is Clearly Outside His Knowledge

If the cop testifies to what someone else saw or heard—called "hearsay"—you'll definitely want to object. This includes anything the officer testifies to that did not come from his direct observation. You can say, *"Objection, Your Honor. The officer's testimony as to how fast the officer in the aircraft told him my vehicle was going is hearsay."*

The point here is to begin to discredit any information the officer doesn't know firsthand, so that later you can argue that there is reasonable doubt as to your guilt. For example, if the officer says that another driver (perhaps after an accident) said you were going 70 mph, you'll want to object. Later you'll point out that this "hearsay" evidence does not prove that you were speeding.

The Testimony of an Officer Assumes Facts Not in Evidence

When an officer testifies that "the defendant's vehicle" exceeded the speed limit, but he hasn't testified how she knew it was your vehicle, she's assuming a fact—that *you* drove that vehicle—which hasn't been established yet. It is important to object here, particularly if you later plan to claim she may have stopped the wrong car. You can say, *"Objection, Your Honor. The officer has so far testified only that she observed a vehicle, not that she identified me as having driven it, and her reference to 'the defendant's vehicle' therefore assumes facts not in evidence."*

If your objection is approved ("sustained"), the officer will have to go back to square one and explain exactly how she determined that you were the driver of the vehicle. She will have to describe the vehicle, how she pulled it over, and how she identified you through your driver's license. Especially if she may have trouble doing this (your car was out of her sight briefly), this objection may throw her off balance (never a bad thing, because many officers are almost insultingly cocky in court) and remind her she's not out on the street where she runs the show. If the judge denies ("overrules") your objection, just let the officer continue testifying.

Your Cross-Examination

CROSS REFERENCE

In Chapter 11, we provide information on how to prepare for cross-examination.

After the officer is finished, you get to cross-examine him. (If you have not read Chapter 11 on preparing your cross-examination, do so now.) Remember to be polite and non-argumentative. Ask him simple questions that require short and direct answers. If he gives an unexpected answer, don't argue with him. If you think he is not being completely truthful or covering up important facts, ask a more detailed question. Otherwise, just go on.

Again, as discussed in Chapter 11, it's best not to ask vague questions that give the officer a chance to tell more of his story. If, despite your pointed questions, he tries to do that anyway, politely interrupt with *"Thank you"* or *"I think you've answered my question."* If all else fails, say to the judge, *"Objection, Your Honor. The latter part of his answer is nonresponsive, and I ask that it be stricken."*

Redirect Examination

If a prosecuting attorney handles the case, she has the chance to ask the officer more questions after you finish your cross-examination. This is called "redirect examination," and the questions asked are supposed to relate only to issues you brought up during your cross-examination.

If the prosecutor asks more questions, you too get another chance to ask more questions of the officer. Called "re-cross-examination," you must limit your questions to issues brought out by the prosecutor on redirect examination. If you start asking questions you have already asked earlier—or ask about new issues—the prosecutor will almost surely object, and the judge will probably ask you to sit down.

Reserved Opening Statements

You reserved your opening statement at the beginning of the trial, you'll want to make it now, just before you give your testimony. Why make an opening statement and then immediately set about testifying to the same facts? Because it allows you to get the judge's attention focused on what you intend to prove.

CAUTION

What if the judge asks you to waive your opening statement? Many judges will attempt to hurry you along by suggesting that you start your testimony by explaining what happened from your point of view and go on from there. Assuming you have prepared carefully, agreeing to do this may be a good idea. Not only does it keep the judge happy, but artfully done, you can make all the same points anyway.

If you do decide to make an opening statement, it should be short and to the point. Here the idea is to outline what you intend to prove, not to testify to the detailed facts that you claim back up these points (you do this next when you testify). Your opening statement should go more or less like this:

> "Your Honor, I will show facts that I believe will demonstrate that I am not guilty. Specifically, I will rely on my own testimony, and that of my passenger, that we both ascertained my speed to be approximately 35 miles per hour on Main Street at the time I was ticketed. I did this by occasionally glancing at my speedometer as I was driving, and my witness did it by checking my speed when she saw the reflection of the officer's colored lights on the windshield. I will also show my speedometer was accurate at that speed reading. Finally, I will testify to the fact that just before Officer Ticketem pulled up quickly behind me and used a radar gun, I saw a large truck pass in the 'fast' lane to my left."

Your Testimony

In most traffic court trials, you will simply stand up at the counsel table, look at the judge, and present your view of what happened. But in a few courts, you'll be asked to take the witness stand. Either way, as discussed in Chapter 10, you'll want to have practiced your presentation ahead of time. It's okay to glance briefly at notes, but don't read directly from them. Here is an abbreviated version of Sam Safespeed's testimony.

> "I was driving down Main Street at 35 mph, in the right-hand lane of two lanes in my direction. When I passed the speed limit sign just past Elm Street, I looked at my speedometer and it read between 32 and 35 mph. Because I was so surprised I was ticketed, later that same day I took my car to Spartan Speedo Shop and had my speedometer checked. I have proof of that certification, which says my speedometer was accurate, in this document, which I'd like to have marked and introduced as Defendant's Exhibit #1.
>
> "When I was driving, I also glanced in my rearview mirror from time to time. Just before the officer pulled me over, I looked and saw a vehicle, about a quarter mile behind, rapidly gaining on me, just as a large truck went by pretty fast in the left lane. I didn't recognize the car gaining rapidly on me from behind as a police vehicle until the officer activated his lights—which he did when he was fairly close to my rear bumper. At that point, I said to my passenger, 'Gee, Pam, there's an officer flashing his lights, maybe he's after that trucker, so I better pull over to let him pass.' I pulled over, but he stayed behind me."

At this point in the trial, you would want to refer to any diagrams, photos, or other evidence supporting your case. (See Chapter 10, on preparing your case for trial.) Once you have told your story and submitted all the evidence you have, the prosecutor (if present) may cross-examine you. (See Chapter 10.) She may ask a few questions or simply waive her right to cross-examine. The judge may also ask you some questions. But if the testifying police officer tries to question you, you should politely but promptly object on the ground that he is only a witness and not licensed to practice law. Say something like this: *"Objection, Your Honor. Officer Ticketem is not a lawyer, and therefore I do not believe it's proper for him to cross-examine me."* If your objection is overruled, you must answer the officer's questions.

All of your responses should be given courteously, truthfully, and as briefly as possible. Contrary to old Perry Mason episodes, you are not limited to only a "yes" or "no" answer. After all, what if the prosecutor asks you whether you knew you were speeding, in which case both "yes" and "no" are terrible answers. Far better—as is your right—to say, *"I know I wasn't speeding because I had just looked at my speedometer."*

Witness Testimony

Next will be your chance to present the testimony of any eyewitnesses. Depending on local court rules and customs, your witnesses will be expected to either testify in the same narrative fashion in which you testified, or you'll be expected to ask questions designed to allow the witness to explain what happened.

Here is what Pam Passenger, a passenger in Sam Safespeed's car, might say if allowed to simply explain what happened:

"Well, Your Honor, on March 15th at about 4:30 p.m., I was seated in the front passenger seat of Sam Safespeed's car. I recall just before Sam was pulled over by the officer that we were in the right or 'slow' traffic lane. Other cars were passing us on the left, including a large truck. Suddenly, I saw colored lights reflected on Sam's windshield and immediately glanced at the speedometer, and saw that we were going 35 mph. I am quite sure I did this before Sam had a chance to slow down."

 TIP

It pays to practice with your witness. It is both legal and sensible to ask your witness to practice giving her testimony. (If you don't know whether your court uses the narrative or question-and-answer style, practice both.) This will allow you to discuss and clear up any discrepancies in how you remember events.

The prosecutor will also have a chance to cross-examine your witnesses when each one is finished testifying.

Closing Statements

The final stage of your traffic court case is the closing arguments or statements. Each side has a chance to present its argument after both have presented their testimony and evidence and have been allowed to cross-examine any witnesses. This is the time when you must sum up the best arguments you have to be found not guilty.

How to Ask Questions of Your Own Witness

It's difficult for an inexperienced person to ask just the right questions. If you feel intimidated by this process, tell the judge, *"Your Honor, I haven't attended law school and I'm unfamiliar with technical rules. May I just ask Ms. Passenger to simply tell you what she saw?"*

If you choose—or are required—to have your witnesses respond to questions, particularly if a prosecuting attorney is opposing you, here are some hints that should make things go easier:

- Be sure to ask nonleading questions, which normally begin with "what," "who," "where," "when," or "how." Leading questions—which you may not use when questioning your own witness (but you may use when conducting cross-examination)—are questions that suggest or provide the answer you are seeking. For example, it is fine to ask, *"What color was the car?"* It is not acceptable to ask, *"Was the car red?"* or *"The car was red, wasn't it?"*

- Avoid irrelevant details. For example, if you are accused of running a red light, the judge will not care that you were on your way to help your Mom take your dog, Bonzo, to the vet to be cured of a severe flea infestation.

- Don't ask questions that assume facts that the witness hasn't testified to. This is another way of saying that your questions should help the witness explain what happened in chronological order. For example, don't ask, *"Did you see a truck pass my car?"* before the witness says anything about a truck being present. Instead, you could first ask, *"Did you see any other vehicles traveling in my direction?"* If the witness says, *"Yes, I saw a big truck,"* then it's time to ask her what it was doing.

- Don't ask your witness to recount what she was told by someone else. That is hearsay and cannot be used at a trial. But there is one big exception: A witness can testify to what the ticketing officer said to you and what you said to the officer, if the officer testified earlier about your conversation together.

- Make a list of the few key facts to which your witness will testify. Design a question calculated to get at each fact. Arrange them in chronological order. By asking your questions in chronological order, your goal is to build a logical foundation for later ones, using the expected answers from earlier questions. For example, you might start with, *"Where were you on March 15th at 2:30 p.m.?"* Assuming the witness says *"in your car,"* it makes sense to follow up with, *"Do you recall Officer Ticketem pulling me over?"* Only then is it time to ask, *"What did you observe before the officer pulled me over?"*

How to Ask Questions of Your Own Witness (continued)

For example:

Q: "On March 5th at 5:15 p.m., what were you doing?"

A: "I was traveling with you, in your car."

Q: "At that time, were you able to see which lane I was in?"

A: "Yes."

Q: "Which lane was that?"

A: "The right, or slow, lane."

Q: "Did you observe any other vehicles on the road?"

A: "Yes."

Q: "Where were they located?" (At this point, the witness should refer to the other cars she saw and explain where they were and in which direction they were going.)

A: "Traffic in our direction was passing on our left, and I think there was traffic in the other direction."

Q: "Do you recall seeing anything unusual?"

A: "Yes, I suddenly saw colored lights reflected on your windshield."

Q: "What, if anything, did you do then?"

A: "I looked over at your speedometer to see what it said."

Q: "Did you look at my speedometer before or after I started slowing down to pull over?"

A: "I looked so quickly, I'm sure it was before."

Q: "How fast was I going?"

A: "35 mph."

In most states, your goal is to make it clear that there is a reasonable doubt as to whether you committed the actual offense. (In a few states, you must prove your innocence—see the appendix.) If you have admitted the violation, you must explain that you had a very good legal reason for technically violating the law.

The Prosecution's Statement

If there is no prosecutor present, the case normally concludes after the officer's testimony and your cross-examination, unless you ask to make a final statement. In trials with a prosecuting attorney, she is allowed to summarize her case first. She will explain how the officer's testimony (and maybe some cross-examination testimony given by you or your witnesses) "proves beyond a reasonable doubt" each element of the offense and disproves any defenses you've raised. During the prosecutor's closing argument, remain calm and poker-faced. It is a mistake to express outrage, indignation, derision, or any other emotion. Remember, this is just another day in the office for the judge, who won't appreciate histrionics. But do listen carefully to the prosecution's arguments so that you can respond to them in your own closing argument, which comes next.

EXAMPLE:

Priscilla Prosecutor sums up the evidence, saying, *"Your Honor, Officer Ticketem, an officer with 20 years of traffic enforcement experience, testified as follows. He calibrated his radar unit with a tuning fork at the beginning of his shift. While parked northbound on Main Street, he observed a blue Plymouth Voyager van traveling about 45 mph in a 35-mph zone. Easy-to-read speed limit signs are posted every quarter of a mile in that area. He also testified that he aimed his radar gun within seconds after the vehicle had passed him, that he heard a strong Doppler tone, and that his radar unit read a speed of 49 mph. The officer testified he never lost sight of the vehicle, pulled it over, and ticketed Sam Safespeed. The evidence shows beyond a reasonable doubt that the defendant exceeded the posted speed limit by 10 mph."*

If a police officer tries to give a closing statement, you can object on the ground that this involves the practice of law. Do this by saying something like, *"Objection, Your Honor. The officer is a witness, not a lawyer or advocate. He's here to present evidence only, not to practice law by arguing which*

evidence is more believable, or how this Court should apply the law to the facts."

 TIP

Do not refer to new evidence or testimony in a closing statement. If the prosecutor or officer refers to any key fact not already brought out in court testimony, promptly object by saying, *"Objection, Your Honor. No evidence was presented on that point."*

Your Closing Statement

When you represent yourself in court, you have two roles—witness and advocate. In your role as witness, you have already testified to what you claim happened. Now, as your own attorney, you have a chance to review and summarize the main points you made during the trial and explain to the judge why you should be found not guilty. Making a closing argument is different than testifying. Your best approach is to act as if you were a third party, and summarize and comment on the evidence. The point, of course, is to convince the judge that there is at least a reasonable doubt as to your guilt.

Some judges—especially where no prosecutor represents the other side—will try to wrap up the case with no closing argument. Unless you are sure your case is hopeless—or the judge has all but said you have won—you'll want to politely request your right to make a final argument. With some judges, you'll need to insist by saying something like this: *"Your Honor, I believe it's my right to make a brief final statement.*

I'll be well organized and quick, but I do want to briefly explain why the evidence shows I'm not guilty."

To make an influential impression in final argument, you need to explain your position, convincingly and politely, usually in fewer than 15 sentences. Don't read a statement. Do outline your speech ahead of time and practice giving it several times in the days before your court date. If you have already obtained the officer's notes, study them carefully, looking for deficiencies in the evidence he cites or inconsistencies in the conclusions he draws. (See Chapter 9 on how to get the officer's notes.) You'll probably need to modify it a bit at the last minute to take into account what the officer says at trial, but this should be easy enough as long as you have a clear plan as to how to make your major points. Conclude with something like: *"And for these reasons, Your Honor, there is a reasonable doubt as to whether I committed the offense, and I therefore ask that you find me not guilty."*

TIP

Three closing argument no-nos:

- **Don't bring up new facts you or other witnesses haven't already testified to.** You are not allowed to refer to anything that was not brought up during the trial.
- **Don't make it personal.** Never insult the ticketing officer by suggesting he is lying or personally biased against you. But you may point out weaknesses in the officer's testimony—especially his failure to give convincing or thorough answers to your cross-examination questions.
- **Don't challenge the authority of the judicial system to charge you with a traffic offense or say you will ignore the court's ruling if you are found guilty.**

Your closing statement—given after the prosecution makes its closing statement—should emphasize that at least one of the elements of the offense hasn't been proven beyond a reasonable doubt. Or you can argue that you have presented some other legally sufficient defense. (See Chapter 3 on legal elements of a ticket and Chapters 5, 6, and 7 for defenses to various charges.)

To begin your closing argument, say to the judge: *"Your Honor, I would like to summarize how the evidence shows I'm not guilty."* Then explain how:

1. The officer's testimony failed to prove one or more of the necessary elements of the violation you are charged with, and/or

2. Your own testimony (and that of any other witness) has shown that you did not violate one or more elements, despite the officer's contrary testimony, and/or

3. Your testimony establishes a legally sufficient reason why you violated the statute, such as your legitimate mistake of fact or reaction to a dire emergency. (See Chapter 3.)

EXAMPLE:

Sam Safespeed's Closing Argument

"Your Honor, let me quickly summarize the evidence as part of telling you why I'm not guilty. First, Officer Ticketem never really established that I violated (the code section you are charged with violating) *when he relied heavily on his notes and didn't really remember what happened. When I cross-examined him, he honestly admitted:*

- *That he had not calibrated the radar unit with a tuning fork at the beginning and end of his shift, as is recommended in the radar unit's operating manual.*
- *That he was over 180 feet away from my vehicle when he activated his radar unit.*

"By contrast, both Pam Passenger, my witness, and I testified that I was in the right lane, the 'slow' lane, and that there was plenty of other traffic, in both directions, including a large truck quickly pulling ahead of me in the lane to my left. In addition, the officer testified that he took at least three seconds to aim the radar unit at my vehicle, meaning that my car was about 180 feet in front of his, and receding, when he activated it. He also conceded that at that distance the radar beam was at least 30 feet wide, which is the same width as two lanes. Finally, he also reluctantly conceded that his radar unit is more sensitive to a larger target, such as a large truck, and that it's quite possible to get a false reading in a situation like this.

"Finally, Ms. Passenger and I testified that I was going about 35 mph based on looking at my speedometer, which I proved was accurate. So to sum up, I think that in this situation there really is a reasonable doubt as to whether Officer Ticketem correctly determined my vehicle's speed, and I therefore respectfully ask that you find me not guilty."

Prosecution's Rebuttal Statement

Because the prosecution has the burden of proving you're guilty, it gets two shots to argue its case. The second one is intended to allow a rebuttal to the things you covered in your argument. Often, the prosecutor will choose not to make a rebuttal statement. If only an officer is present, he almost never will.

The Verdict

After all the evidence and closing statements have been presented, the judge must either announce his verdict or take the case "under advisement" or "under submission." This means the judge wants to think about it.

If the judge takes the case under advisement, it means you will be notified of the decision by mail. But if you are considering appealing if you lose, it's wise to call or visit the court about once a week to find out if the verdict has been filed. That's because in most places your appeal to a higher court must be made between five and 30 days from the time the judge files the verdict with the court clerk, and some court clerks don't get their paperwork in the mail on time. This can leave you with very little, or no, time in which to appeal.

If the judge finds you not guilty, you don't have to pay any fine and are entitled to a refund of any bail you may have posted.

The Sentence

In most places, for routine violations, judges state the amount of your fine immediately after announcing a guilty verdict. If you mounted a decent defense—but have not convinced the judge of your innocence—the judge may reduce, or even suspend, the fine. In a few states, if you are found guilty and fined, the judge may listen to a plea (or read a letter) from you requesting that your fine be suspended or reduced based on your good driving record (or for some other convincing reason). Or, the judge may agree to your request for a payment schedule, if you cannot afford to pay the amount all at once. (Talk to the court clerk if you wish to ask for a fine reduction.)

Appealing for a New Trial

If you haven't convinced a judge of your innocence at trial, your chances of overturning his decision by appealing are small. Even though every state gives a person the right to appeal, the process is almost always tedious, typically involving many hours and some expense. In short, before you seriously consider appealing, think long and hard about whether the time and effort is worth the outcome.

Very broadly speaking, there are two types of appeals. One type allows only an appeal on the record—that is, an appellate court will overturn the trial court only if the trial judge made a significant legal error. Another type—called "trial de novo"—allows you a second shot at a trial. Some states use one type of appeal, other states allow the other type, and a few states allow both types of appeals. It is generally easier to win when you are entitled to a new trial.

 TIP

Appeal rules vary widely, so check with a court clerk. Laws governing appeals vary considerably from state to state, so start by checking your state's entry in the appendix. Armed with this general information, it is then essential to also check with the clerk in the court where you were convicted for the specifics on your rights to a new trial. At the same time, ask the clerk how long you have to file a "notice of appeal," which starts the appeals process moving.

In most states where new trials are allowed, you will have to appear before a judge and plead your case again. There can be at least three reasons to consider this approach:

- If the judge in your first trial was a real "hanging" judge clearly biased against traffic court defendants. In this instance, you should check with the court clerk to see if judges are randomly selected or if a different court would handle your appeal. It's possible you could get a less-punitive judge the second time around.

- If you really did a lousy job presenting your case the first time. If you were nervous, unprepared, and railroaded by a good prosecutor or clever cop, you probably learned a lot about court procedure and how to present your case. You might want to give it a second try.
- In about a dozen states, a "de novo" trial is the first chance you have to appeal to a jury. Since it's probably fair to say juries are more friendly to defendants than judges are, you may get a better shot at acquittal the second time around in these states. (Note that in states allowing "de novo" jury trials there can be fees for the second trial, so be sure to check them out.)

But what about the majority of states (and the District of Columbia), where you are entitled to appeal a conviction only to an appellate court, claiming that the trial judge made a legal error? Here your chances of reversing the trial judge are usually somewhere between slim and slimmer. That's because the appellate court will almost always conclude that the traffic court judge ran your trial fairly and applied the law correctly. One reason this is true is that the appeals court has the power to ignore minor procedural glitches (like the trial judge let the officer glance at his notes) if they conclude that the errors were not significant.

 TIP

An appeal might delay or prevent a license revocation. One time when you might want to consider an appeal—even if your case is weak—is if you face the loss of your license because of the number of points that a new conviction will add to your record. If you are only a few points away from a license suspension—and some of those points are due to expire soon—the time it takes to appeal may keep you from losing your license, even if the appeals court eventually upholds your conviction.

The process of taking your case to an appellate court is also complicated and time-consuming—so much so that preparing and arguing an appeal is beyond the scope of this book. But if you are truly committed to your cause, you can consult a law librarian for reference books on appeals, or try to find a lawyer who shares your zeal and is willing to give you some pointers and support.

Jury Trials

Introduction 204

Try to Settle Your Case 204

    The Negotiation Process 205

    How a Deal Is Made 206

Selecting the Jury 206

    How Jury Selection Works 206

    Questions to Ask on "Voir Dire" 209

    How to Challenge a Juror 210

Trial Procedure 211

    Opening Statements 212

    The Prosecution's Testimony 212

    Your Cross-Examination 213

    Your Testimony 213

    Cross-Examination by the Prosecution 214

    Closing Arguments 214

Preparing Jury Instructions 216

The Judge Instructs the Jury 217

Appeals From a Jury Verdict 217

Introduction

SKIP AHEAD

Check the appendix to see if your state allows jury trials for routine traffic offenses. If the answer is no, read Chapter 12 on trial before a judge.

Defense lawyers will nearly always say that a jury trial is better for a defendant. This is true, but only if you prepare carefully to fight in a much more complicated legal arena. Not only will you need to pick a jury, but instead of just facing the arresting officer (as often happens when your trial is conducted without a jury), the state will likely send an experienced prosecutor against you, someone who knows the rules of presenting evidence. And since the judge may resent the time and trouble you are causing by insisting on a jury for a case involving a traffic ticket, he may insist on your following technical rules of evidence (something it can be hard to do without legal training or experience). So even in states that allow jury trials, many defendants will choose a trial by a judge only.

However, there can be good reasons to insist on a jury trial. The biggest one: If you make a convincing presentation, a jury is probably more likely than a judge to side with you. After all, at least some people on the jury are likely to feel they have been victimized by the traffic court system. In short, if you face serious consequences from a guilty verdict—like the risk of losing your license or an astronomical increase in your insurance premiums—you should at least

> ### Not All States Require 12 Jurors or a Unanimous Verdict
>
> Don't assume that because you demand a jury trial you must be convicted by the vote of 12 unanimous jurors. In traffic cases, some states provide for eight-member, six-member or even four-member juries. And other states allow jurors to reach a verdict on a 5–1 or 10–2 vote. Check with the court clerk for your state's rules.

consider requesting a jury trial where it is available.

The format of a jury trial is similar to a formal nonjury trial described in Chapter 12 except for one huge difference: You must participate in the process of choosing a jury. In this chapter, we go through the steps of a jury trial that are different from a trial in front of a judge. Where procedures are the same, we send you back to Chapter 12, which we assume you have already read.

Try to Settle Your Case

Jury trials are time-consuming for you, judges, prosecutors, and the police. This means once you ask for one, the system has some incentive to settle your case without going to trial. Deals can take many forms, depending on the situation. For example, if you are charged with speeding and running a stop sign, the prosecutor might offer to drop one of the charges if you plead guilty to the other. If you are trying to reduce the number of points against your license (or one ticket allows you to go to traffic school, but two don't), this can be a compromise you're willing to accept. In another case, the judge or prosecutor might be willing to offer you a chance to go to traffic school to keep your record clear.

The Negotiation Process

There's nothing to prevent you from approaching the prosecutor at any time to see if she is willing to make a deal to avoid a jury trial. Negotiations in jury-trial cases can take place in several locations, at a formal "pretrial" or "settlement" conference in the judge's chambers, informally by phone, or just before trial in a corner of the hallway outside the courtroom. But no matter the forum, the idea behind negotiating with the prosecutor is almost always to compromise on a better deal than you would get if you were found guilty and sentenced. It is seldom realistic to assume that you can get your case dismissed. Options that are more realistic often include:

- Allowing you to plead guilty to a less-serious offense than you are charged with. For example, in some states you could accept "simple" speeding rather than exceeding the speed limit by more than 30 mph.
- Dismissal of one charge against you, in exchange for a guilty plea to another. For example, dismissing the charge that you made an unsafe lane change and failed to stop at a signal

in exchange for your guilty plea to a speeding charge.

- Agreement that your sentence will not involve a high fine or license suspension. For example, in a situation where you can be fined $400 for deliberately running a red light and have your license suspended, you can bargain for an agreement to fine you $100 with no suspension.
- Approval of your attending traffic school (meaning the offense won't go on your record) where this otherwise wouldn't be an option.

Other points to remember while negotiating are:

- Be wary about agreeing to plead guilty to several offenses in exchange for the promise of a lesser fine. If you are entitled to a jury trial, you usually have more bargaining power than this. If the prosecutor won't dismiss at least one charge in exchange for pleading guilty (or nolo contendere), you may want to go to trial.
- Don't be bullied by a "hard ass" prosecutor into accepting a poor "take it or forget it" offer. No matter how much the prosecutor tries to intimidate you, if she makes one offer, she'll often be willing to eventually sweeten it up a little if you say "no."
- Never lay everything on the table by detailing your strategy to the prosecutor. If negotiations fail, you will have exposed your strategy to the opposition. Better to simply say you believe you can present a very strong

case as to why you are not guilty. If the prosecution's case really is weak, the prosecutor will spot it and be more willing to negotiate.

- Never—repeat—never admit guilt to a prosecutor or police official before a deal is formalized. If you do, your admission can be used against you in court.

EXAMPLE:

You talk to a prosecutor who says, *"Come on now—just between us—you were going 65 mph, weren't you?"* Never reply, *"Sure, but I think a jury will let me off."* If you fail to make a deal, the prosecutor can simply put himself on the stand and testify to what you said. Far better to respond, *"I don't think you can prove that"* and very briefly explain why. (But again, don't reveal the details of your defense strategy.)

 TIP

Never make a deal on trial day until you see the officer. If the police officer isn't present, the judge will probably dismiss the case. Knowing that the officer isn't going to make it, the prosecutor may propose a generous settlement immediately before court. Before going further, you should just ask the prosecutor if the officer is going to be present. Or, you could ask for a few minutes to think about any deal and, if the cop still hasn't appeared, just say no.

How a Deal Is Made

If you and the prosecutor orally agree to a compromise settlement, the two of you will then appear before the judge. The prosecutor will request permission to dismiss or reduce one or more charges against you "in the interests of justice" and tell the judge that you intend to plead guilty to the reduced charge. Depending on your agreement, sometimes the prosecutor will go on to recommend a particular punishment.

Although the judge does not have to agree to the prosecutor's proposal to dismiss or reduce the charges, or to impose the agreed punishment, he almost always will. If for some reason he doesn't, ask to withdraw your plea and proceed to trial.

Selecting the Jury

Here we look at the jury selection process, including:

- Basic jury selection procedures
- Good questions to ask potential jurors, and
- How to disqualify a hostile juror.

How Jury Selection Works

Many lawyers believe that selecting members of a jury is the single most important phase of the trial. As the defendant, this is because you want to send narrow-minded, police-oriented individuals straight home, since they will rarely vote for acquittal no matter how good a case you present. By contrast, you are hoping for jurors who are open-minded, willing to listen to both sides, and at least a little skeptical of police and prosecutorial power.

But realize that in an ordinary traffic case, many judges will already be annoyed that you are insisting on a jury. It follows that they will want to complete the jury selection process expeditiously, believing that any group of citizens is qualified to decide whether or not you rolled through a stop sign. Although, as discussed below, you'll want to protect your rights, it is almost always a big mistake to act as if your case is akin to "murder one" and try to insist on every technical procedural right. Or put another way, if you piss off a judge seriously enough, he has many ways to all but make sure the jury finds you guilty.

Jury selection normally begins as soon as the judge calls your case and after any preliminary motions are resolved. (See Chapter 12 for more on motions.) Potential jurors will normally wait in a "jury assembly room" where you will not have contact with them. In a few courts, they may be milling around in the corridors or seated inside the courtroom. In the unlikely event you find yourself talking with a potential juror, do not discuss your case, because this may be seen as attempting to tamper with the jury. Casual conversation about the weather or sports is okay.

When your case is called, the first group of potential jurors will be asked to take their seats. In some courts, you will be provided with a list of the names and occupations of the potential jurors. If so, write them down

MUNICPAL COURT JURY PANEL CHART			Peremptory Challenges								Only for offenses punishable by over 90 days in jail			
			No.	1	2	3	4	5	6	7	8	9	10	
Date	Case No.	People of State of Calif.	Plaintiff											
		vs.	Defendant											
1		2	3	4		5			6					
7		8	9	10		11			12					

on a chart that looks like the one above. Modify the chart if your jury has fewer than 12 members. If you don't get the names in advance, fill them in as you go along.

TIP

Use sticky paper notes. Removable sticky paper comes in handy to write jurors' names and place them in the appropriate place on your jury seating chart. That way, if a juror is removed and replaced, you can simply peel off the old note and write a new one.

The next step is to question jurors to see if any juror is biased or may view you in a negative way. This is called "voir dire," from the French words for "to speak the truth." In many states the judge will probably elect to ask all the questions himself. Usually the judge will direct questions at the entire panel, not to individual jurors. Often this will consist of only a few perfunctory questions relating to occupation, spouse's occupation, previous experience with the criminal justice system, and possible acquaintance with police officers and attorneys. For example, a judge might ask:

- *"Do any of you know any of the parties to this case, specifically Sam Safespeed, Pam Passenger, or Officer Ticketem?"*
- *"Do any of you work for the police, the district attorney's office, or any other law enforcement agency?"*
- *"Do any of you have relatives or close friends who work in law enforcement or in a district attorney's office?"*

- *"Does anyone on the jury panel know of any reason why he or she can't render an impartial decision in this case?"*

If a potential juror reveals a possibly significant prejudice that could bias him against you, the judge will probably quickly excuse that particular juror "for cause" without you even having to say anything. When the judge is done, he may allow you and the prosecutor to ask a few additional questions designed to ferret out a juror's prejudice or bias. (A sample list is shown below.) This lets you avoid using up your peremptory challenges. If a judge excuses a juror, a new juror will be called to sit in the jury box. At this point, the judge may ask additional questions of these new individuals or, if these people have already been in the courtroom, simply ask if they heard the questions and if they personally know any of the parties or anyone who does.

When the judge is finished questioning the jurors, it often makes sense to indicate that you accept the jury with no need to ask more questions. Again, in a garden variety traffic court case, you'll likely score more points by being fair and reasonable than you will by acting like Perry Mason (something you're likely not too good at anyway). That being said, there can, of course, be times when you'll want to ask jurors a few additional questions. This is particularly likely if the judge has done a half-baked job in attempting to determine if any jurors might be biased against you.

Questions to Ask on "Voir Dire"

Assuming you are given a chance to ask questions, don't repeat any of those the judge or prosecutor has already asked. Instead, follow up on any possibly unsatisfactory answers a particular juror already gave by asking for more detail. If you are told to ask questions directed at the whole panel, try these:

1. *"Do any of you have any objections to sitting here as jurors in a traffic-related case? Please raise your hand if you do."*

2. *"Do any of you object to the fact that I will be representing myself without an attorney?"*

3. *"Do any of you have trouble believing that a person is innocent until proven guilty beyond a reasonable doubt on the basis of the evidence?"*

4. *"Have any of you ever been employed as a law enforcement officer or security guard?"* (Note: Anyone with this background within the past ten years should probably be disqualified with a "peremptory" challenge if the judge has not already excused them for "cause.")

5. *"Do any of you have any close friends or relatives who have been employed as law enforcement officers, security guards, or in the district attorney's office?"* (Note: You should probably exercise "peremptory" challenges on spouses, parents, children, or siblings of anyone in law enforcement if the judge has not already excused them for "cause.")

6. *"Are there any among you who would believe the word of a police officer solely because he or she is a police officer, over my own testimony?"* (Note: Definitely exercise your "peremptory" challenge against anyone who even vaguely reeks of "bad vibes" when you ask this question.)

7. *"Do any of you believe that police officers are highly unlikely to make mistaken observations?"*

8. *"Do any of you believe a police officer always tells the entire truth?"*

9. *"Have any of you ever sat on a jury previously where the defendant was charged with the offense I'm charged with?"* (Note: If anyone answers "yes" to this question, follow up by asking, "Did that jury reach a verdict?" If they say "yes," you should assume the verdict was "guilty" and exercise your "peremptory" challenge.)

10. *"Have any of you ever been involved in an automobile accident that you believe was caused by someone breaking the law?"* (If a prospective juror answers "yes," be prepared to follow up by asking him to describe the accident, when it occurred, and how he thinks the other driver violated the law. If the accident was recent, and he says the other driver violated the same law you're charged with, you may want to exercise a "peremptory" challenge to excuse this juror.)

11. *"Are there any of you who don't drive or drive fewer than 5,000 miles each year?"* (Note: A person who mostly

takes public transit and drives only to church on Sundays may not be as sympathetic to your technical violation as a traveling salesman who drives 20,000 miles a year and gets frequent speeding tickets.)

12. *"Are there any among you who have never been cited for a moving traffic violation?"* (Note: You probably want to disqualify any juror who's never been subjected to the indignity.)

 TIP

What to do if you are unhappy with a juror's answer. If a juror says something that indicates to you that he might not be fair, be prepared to ask a follow-up question. For example, you might say, *"Mr. Jones, I noticed you seemed to nod slightly when I asked you if you had any friends or relatives who were police officers. Was that a 'yes' answer?"* Depending on the answer, you might want to ask further questions to expose a possible anti-defendant or pro-police prejudice. If you decide to excuse that particular person, either use one of your peremptory challenges or, if the juror's possible bias is obvious, ask the judge to excuse the juror for cause (see below).

How to Challenge a Juror

There are two reasons you may want to get a particular person off the jury:

- The person exposes a clear bias against you (says she hates people who drive fast), or

- You have a bad feeling about a juror for a vague, undefined reason.

Fortunately, there are also two ways to get rid of a juror you do not want.

Challenges for Cause

If a prospective juror strongly indicates that he can't be fair, the judge may disqualify him before you say anything. But if this doesn't occur, wait until you are given a chance to make a challenge and ask the judge to disqualify that person for cause. To do this, simply say, *"Your Honor, I respectfully challenge prospective juror Smith for cause on account of his statement that he would 'find it hard to be fair' in light of his statement that his mother was injured by someone who was speeding."*

Here are common reasons why a judge will agree to dismiss a juror for cause:

- The prospective juror, or his close friend or relative, was seriously injured by someone who committed the same type of offense you're charged with, and the juror admits he would "have a hard time" being objective.

- The prospective juror indicates he'd believe the word of a police officer over you, just because the witness was a police officer.

- The prospective juror is a close friend or relative of the officer or any other prosecution witness, or of the prosecuting attorney.

- The prospective juror learned of your case before being called to court as a juror, and has expressed some opinion about your guilt.

> ### 💡 TIP
>
> **It pays to be polite.** If you are nasty or sarcastic when you ask the judge to excuse a juror, you are likely to alienate the remaining jurors. As with most areas of life, it pays to be pleasant.

If the judge disagrees with you and refuses to remove the juror, you still have another way to get him off the panel.

Peremptory (Automatic) Challenges

In most states you have the right to excuse a certain specified number of prospective jurors for any reason, or for no given reason at all. How many of these automatic or "peremptory" challenges you are allowed varies from state to state (often depending on the offense you're charged with, and on the size of the jury). With a jury of 12, it would be typical for you and the prosecutor to each have anywhere from three to ten peremptory challenges. If the jury has only six members, you might be allowed only two to five such challenges. But since this is an area where each state does things a little differently, you'll want to ask in advance what your state's rules are.

Most experienced trial lawyers believe that, when considering whether or not to challenge a juror, it's wise to respect your instincts. If you get bad vibes from someone—even if you can't explain why—you'll want to remove her from the jury. But in addition to trusting your gut, if the judge does not excuse them himself, you probably would be wise to consider

exercising peremptory challenges to exclude the following types of people:

- Present and former police officers and security guards, their spouses, and children
- Anyone who has ever worked in a prosecutor's office, including lawyers, paralegals, and support staff
- Relatives or close friends of the above
- Anyone who has ever been involved in an accident, or had a relative involved in an accident, caused by someone who was charged with the offense you're charged with (assuming, of course, you've been able to get this information)
- People who don't drive much, or who have never received a traffic ticket
- People who, from gestures, body language, and a generally hostile attitude, obviously resent being called for jury duty
- People you feel uneasy about but don't know why, and
- (Possibly) people whose dress and/or lifestyles are very different from yours.

Again, when you exercise a peremptory challenge, be polite. Simply say something like this, *"Your Honor, the Defense would like to thank and request the court to excuse the fifth juror, Ms. Jones."*

Trial Procedure

After the jury is selected, the jurors will be "sworn in" by the judge or clerk. Then, the trial proceeds in much the same way as a trial before a judge. (See Chapter 11 on trial procedure).

Opening Statements

Though opening statements are often skipped during a ticket-related trial before a judge, it is unwise to waive your opening statement when a jury is present. That's because it is very important to get the jurors on your side right from the start. Remember, as discussed in Chapter 11, you have a choice to either give your opening statement after the prosecutor gives (or waives) hers, or you can reserve your opening statement until after you cross-examine the officer and just before you put on your testimony. But I advise making it as soon as possible in front of a jury. That's because jurors often make up their minds as to guilt or innocence very early in the trial, often right after opening statements. If you reserve your opening statement until later, jurors who hear only from the prosecution may have already decided you are guilty before you open your mouth.

Stand up behind your counsel table and make your opening statement facing the jury. Don't try to walk around the courtroom. Just stand straight, look right at the jury members and tell them briefly what evidence you will produce to show you are innocent. It's fine to quickly glance at notes, but since you should have already practiced your statement at home with friends, you should never need to read your statement. (See Chapter 11 on making your opening statement.)

TIP

Be straightforward. The important thing to remember is that your bearing and how you make your presentation will probably have a much greater effect on a jury than it would have on a judge. Never be sarcastic or insulting, even if the arresting officer treated you poorly. Instead assume the officer, acting in good faith, simply made an honest mistake that you now wish—with the help of the jury—to correct.

The Prosecution's Testimony

In jury trials, the officer will always take the witness stand and testify in response to the prosecutor's questions. You have the right to object to improper questions, but in a jury trial you should save your objections for issues that really are critical. That's because jurors typically resent anyone they think is trying to hide information from them and may rule against the side that objects the most. In addition, trying to keep evidence from a jury may backfire. Even if the judge agrees with your objection, jurors are likely to guess at what was excluded and give it more importance than if you just let it pass without objection. But despite this caution, if the prosecutor treads too far over the fairness line, you'll probably wish to object. (See Chapter 10 for tips and guidelines on objecting to testimony.)

Your Cross-Examination

When you cross-examine the prosecution's witnesses, be courteous but firm. If the officer tries to say more than you wish her to say, promptly but politely interrupt and direct her to, *"Please answer the question, you've already had a chance to tell your story. I'd appreciate it if you wouldn't try to influence the jury any further."* Otherwise, the cross-examination should follow the approach discussed in Chapter 12 with questions gleaned from Chapter 11.

Your Testimony

I recommend that you make your opening statement at the beginning of the trial. But if for some reason you have not, you should definitely make it before you start your testimony. Then, with several important exceptions, your testimony in a jury trial should proceed in the same way as before a judge (see Chapter 12).

Be sure to look directly at the jury from time to time while you explain key points. You want the jurors to see you as an honest, law-abiding citizen who has been mistakenly accused. But don't overact. People who suck up to the jury usually get what they deserve.

Judges often train themselves to remain totally expressionless even while listening to the most blatant nonsense. But most jurors are neither trained to do this nor particularly interested in appearing impartial. So, be alert for nonverbal signs that might suggest that one or more jurors is confused or skeptical about your testimony, and adjust

---

> ### You Don't Have to Ask Yourself Questions
>
> In a typical trial, lawyers ask the questions and witnesses answer them. But if you are acting as your own lawyer, most judges will allow you to dispense with this format and simply tell your story. If you come across a judge who insists on the question-and-answer format, you should object as follows: *"Your Honor, I just want to tell the jury what happened in my own words. I'm not a lawyer and I don't know how to ask myself questions. I assume that if I say something inappropriate, you will advise the jury to disregard it."* If after that, the judge still refuses to allow you to tell your story, you'll probably have to do your best to ask yourself pertinent questions before giving sensible answers. (Just in case this might happen, see Chapter 11 for tips on how to frame proper questions.) At the very least, you'll have obtained the jury's sympathy.

---

your conduct accordingly. For example, when questioning a not particularly believable witness, if you see jurors frowning or snickering, you probably won't want to rely heavily on what that witness said in making your closing statement.

When your testimony is completed, and after the prosecutor has cross-examined you, it's time to present any witnesses who will testify on your behalf. Depending on the preferences of the judge, your witnesses will either testify in narrative fashion as you probably did, or in response to your questions. If the judge indicates that you should question the witness, you may want to explain that because you're unfamiliar with the way such questions should be asked, you would prefer just to let your witness explain what they saw. But if the judge doesn't agree, be prepared to ask questions.

Cross-Examination by the Prosecution

When you have finished testifying, it's your time to be cross-examined by the prosecutor. Listen carefully to each question. If you don't fully understand a question, don't guess at the answer; instead, ask the prosecutor to repeat and clarify it. If you understand the question but just don't know the answer, say so, keeping in mind that you have a right to explain your answer, even when your answer is *"I don't know"* or *"I'm not sure."* On the other hand, do not purposely avoid answering reasonably clear questions. Otherwise, the jury will think you are being evasive.

Again, be polite. Sorry to belabor this point, but if you are obnoxious or impolite to the prosecutor, it may cause jurors to decide a close case against you. Your response to cross-examination should be the same as in non-jury trials, except that during your responses you should occasionally look at the jury as you might when explaining something to a group of friends (see Chapter 11).

Closing Arguments

After all the evidence is presented, both you and the prosecutor will have the opportunity to present a closing argument. Making a closing argument to a jury is much more important than making one to a judge in a nonjury trial. Judges pride themselves on deciding cases based on evidence—which they have already heard—not on the arguments from the opposing sides. Jurors, on the other hand, are usually far less sure of their legal judgments and will listen more carefully to your argument as to why there is reasonable doubt as to your guilt.

The Prosecutor's Closing Argument

During the prosecutor's closing argument, remain calm—poker-faced if you can. Never express outrage, indignation, derision, or any other emotion, no matter how much the prosecutor tortures the truth. Just listen carefully and take appropriate notes so that you can make any necessary modifications to the closing argument, which you should have already planned.

Your Closing Argument

Your closing argument should be designed to serve two purposes. First, you want to clearly explain how the evidence that has been presented at trial isn't sufficient to establish your guilt beyond a reasonable doubt, or actually disproves it. Second, you should rebut damaging statements made by the prosecutor in her arguments. For example, if the prosecutor says you entered an intersection when the light was already red, you'll want to discuss the fact that the officer had a lousy viewing angle and was doing something else at the time. Please refer to "Closing Statements" in Chapter 12. Much of the information set out there applies equally when making a closing argument before a jury.

It is essential to point out to the jurors, at both the beginning and end of your brief talk, that each element of the offense must be proven "beyond a reasonable doubt." Although legally this is something between a "great" doubt and an "insignificant" doubt, it is proper to state that a "reasonable" juror who has any doubt at all about any element of the offense must find you not guilty. Since everyone considers himself or herself reasonable, you hope that any juror who has any doubt about your guilt will vote not guilty. In states that allow jury trials for traffic offenses, most still require unanimous agreement for a verdict. In those states, if only one doubting juror sides with you, the result is a "hung" jury and no conviction.

Here is an example of how your argument might begin to a jury:

"Ladies and Gentlemen, because I know that I'm innocent of the offense(s) charged, I'm contesting it/them here. Attorneys are very expensive, and so I'm defending myself. Although I have no legal training, I've presented my case as best I know how to show you why I am not guilty. But there is one thing I do know about the American legal system— and it's something you know, too—the prosecution must prove every defendant, including me, guilty of each and

every element of an offense beyond a reasonable doubt. Now I want to explain exactly why the prosecutor has failed to do that in my case."

Now, describe the elements of the offense and how, in light of the evidence presented, and based on your testimony, evidence, and any witnesses, doubt as to your guilt remains. This is the most important part of your argument. See other examples in Chapter 12 under "Closing Statements."

"You have heard my evidence (and the statements of my witnesses). You have also heard from the police officer. These are conflicting versions of what happened. Please do not believe the officer's powers of observation are infallible just because she's a police officer. And please do not accept uncritically what the prosecutor just said when she repeated the officer's versions of events. The point is: Neither the prosecutor nor the police officer disproved any of the evidence my witnesses and I presented. Remember, if the law required you to believe law enforcement personnel are perfect, we wouldn't need trials at all! So again, please consider my side of the story—I've presented it as honestly as I can.

"When I am done speaking, the prosecutor is allowed another chance to undermine my argument. She may tell you that I have a lot to gain by being declared not guilty, and that therefore the officer's story is more believable than mine. I have no hard feelings toward the officer, and I know that part of the reason she's on

the roads is to protect us from hazardous drivers, but she's not infallible, and in this particular case, she was mistaken.

Finally, you will recall that in the beginning of this case, you each indicated you would honor my constitutional guarantee that I am not guilty until and unless the prosecution proves each element of the offense I'm charged with beyond a reasonable doubt. Indeed, in this case, the prosecution has come up far short in doing this. In retiring to the jury room, I ask you to do your duty in this regard and to enter a verdict of not guilty. Thank you."

This may seem a bit long-winded, but it goes pretty fast when you're talking. Feel free to change it to suit your particular case. It's wise to practice this sort of statement a number of times before you go to court.

The Prosecution's Rebuttal Argument

Because the prosecution has the burden of proof, it gets two shots to argue its case to the jury. The second one is intended to allow it to rebut any points you raised in your argument. Sometimes the prosecutor won't exercise this opportunity. Other times she will make a brief final statement.

Preparing Jury Instructions

After you have presented your evidence, you have an opportunity to submit proposed "jury instructions" to the judge to be read to the jury. Because most judges are required to—and do—a fairly decent job of doing this for routine cases, we normally recommend that you leave it to the judge. But if the judge is particularly hostile, you may want to take a shot at doing this.

Whole books have been written on how to prepare jury instruction. It's a very specialized skill, not something we can teach you in a couple of pages. But if you're determined, start by going to a law library and, with the help of the librarian, finding the jury instruction books judges most often use in your state. Then page through the instructions that relate to traffic offenses. A judge is required to give a jury instruction at your request, if there is evidence to support it. For example, if you testified you had to speed to the hospital with your wife, who was actually giving birth, the judge is probably required to read the jury instruction on the "necessity defense" (see Chapter 3).

The standard instructions, which the judge can usually be trusted to give on her own, include explaining to jurors how they are to understand the duties of the judge and jury, and how they are expected to consider different types of evidence and how to determine the credibility of witnesses. Finally, and most important, the judge will explain the presumption of innocence. Often she will say something like this:

"A defendant in a criminal action is presumed to be innocent until the contrary is proved, and in case of a reasonable doubt as to whether his guilt is proven, he is entitled to a verdict of not guilty. This presumption places on the State the burden of proving him

guilty beyond a reasonable doubt.
Reasonable doubt is defined as follows:
It is not a mere possible doubt, because
everything relating to human affairs,
and depending on moral evidence,
is open to some possible or imaginary
doubt. It is the state of the case that, after
the entire comparison and consideration
of the evidence, leaves the minds of
the jurors in that condition, such that
they cannot say they feel an abiding
conviction, to a certainty, of the truth of
the charge."

The Judge Instructs the Jury

Finally, the judge will instruct the jury from
the standard instructions, plus any the judge
accepted from you or the prosecutor. Then
the bailiff will take the jury into the jury
room to deliberate. When they come back,
they will announce a verdict. If you are
found guilty, the judge will set a later date
for you to appear for sentencing.

Appeals From a Jury Verdict

If you are convicted at a jury trial, your
chances of successfully appealing are very
small. That's because in the vast majority of
states, you do not have the right to a new
("de novo") trial (see the appendix for your
state's appeal rules). Instead, an appellate
court will simply look to make sure that the
trial court judge followed the law (called
an appeal "on the record" or "on the law").
Even then, the judge has to make a pretty
big error to catch the attention of an appeals
court and reverse your conviction. Given
the fact that, even for those who know how
to do it, the appeals process is complicated
and expensive, appeals rarely make sense
for traffic cases.

Traffic Court Rules for 50 States (and the District of Columbia)

Alabama..222

Alaska..222

Arizona..222

Arkansas..223

California...223

Colorado..224

Connecticut...225

Delaware..225

District of Columbia (Washington, D.C.)..226

Florida...226

Georgia..227

Hawaii...228

Idaho...228

Illinois...229

Indiana..229

Iowa...230

Kansas...230

Kentucky...231

Louisiana...231

Maine...232

Maryland...232

Massachusetts...232

Michigan...233

Minnesota...233

Mississippi 234

Missouri 234

Montana 235

Nebraska 236

Nevada 236

New Hampshire 236

New Jersey 237

New Mexico 237

New York 237

North Carolina 238

North Dakota 238

Ohio 239

Oklahoma 239

Oregon 240

Pennsylvania 240

Rhode Island 241

South Carolina 241

South Dakota 242

Tennessee 242

Texas 242

Utah 243

Vermont 243

Virginia 244

Washington 244

West Virginia 245

Wisconsin 245

Wyoming 246

Introduction

Here we list the courts where traffic cases are heard, along with other important legal information for the 50 states and Washington, D.C. We have made it as complete as possible. But rules and laws change, so it is important to check with your local court to make sure you are working with the most up-to-date information.

We list information under the following headings:

Court That Hears Traffic Violations: The courts where traffic violations are normally heard. The name of the court varies from state to state and sometimes within a state. For example, in Pennsylvania, traffic cases are heard in District Justice's Court in most parts of the state, but in that state's largest cities they are heard in Philadelphia Traffic Court and Pittsburgh City Magistrate's Court.

Court Websites: More and more courts are making information available via websites. However, only some of them have useful information on traffic cases.

State Statutes Online: For every state, there is a website where you can view your state's laws. We list them here.

Vehicle Laws and Speed Laws: State laws relating to the operation of motor vehicles (called "Vehicle Code" in most states) are listed here, along with where you can find your state's speed laws. Here we also indicate whether the speed limits are ABSOLUTE or PRESUMED. (See Chapter 5 for an explanation of this important distinction.)

Speed Detection Methods: The five most common methods police use to determine your speed, as listed in Chapter 6, are pacing, aircraft, VASCAR, radar, and laser. Here we list the methods allowed in your state.

Trial by Declaration: Some states allow you to present your defense in writing, without having to appear in court. (See Chapter 9 for more information.)

Jury Trial: Here, we indicate if your state allows jury trials for traffic violations. Among the states that do allow you a jury trial, most allow it only at a trial de novo after you are found guilty in a lower court.

Appeal Procedures: There are two different kinds of appeals to higher courts. In some states, you can automatically get a new trial, or "trial de novo." In other states (or in trial de novo states if you lose after your second trial), you can appeal only "on the record." That means your conviction is reversed only if you can convince a higher court that the traffic court judge committed a legal error. Here we list the type of appeal (de novo or on the record) allowed, and the name of the court to which you appeal.

DMV Website: Almost every state's motor vehicle agency has a website where you can find out about the effect of traffic violations on your driving privileges. We list those sites here.

ALABAMA

Court That Hears Traffic Violations

District Court, Municipal Court

Court Websites

www.judicial.state.al.us

State Statutes Online

www.legislature.state.al.us/Codeof
Alabama/1975/coatoc.htm

Vehicle Laws

Alabama Code, Title 32 (Motor Vehicles &
Traffic)

Speed Laws

Title 32, Ch. 5A (Rules of the Road),
§§ 32-5A-170 to 32-5A-177 (ABSOLUTE)

Speed Detection Methods

Pacing, aircraft, radar, laser

Trial By Declaration

No

Jury Trial

Not in lower court. Defendant has right
to jury trial de novo on appeal to Circuit
Court. § 15-14-30; *Thomas v. City of
Mobile*, 690 So. 2d 546 (1997).

Appeal Procedures

De novo appeal to Circuit Court. *Thomas
v. City of Mobile*, 690 So. 2d 546 (1997).

DMV Website

www.dps.state.al.us

ALASKA

Court That Hears Traffic Violations

District Court

Court Websites

www.state.ak.us/courts

State Statutes Online

www.legis.state.ak.us/folhome.htm
http://touchngo.com/lglcntr/akstats/
Statutes.htm

Vehicle Laws

Alaska Statutes, Title 28 (Motor Vehicles)

Speed Laws

Alaska Admin. Code Title 13, § 02.275
(ABSOLUTE). (Alaska's speed rules are
enacted as administrative regulations.)

Speed Detection Methods

Pacing, aircraft, radar, laser

Trial By Declaration

No

Jury Trial

No. § 28.40.050(d).

Appeal Procedures

Appeal on the record to Superior Court
(though Superior Court has discretion to
grant trial de novo). § 22.10.020.

Other

Traffic violations are civil infractions.
§ 28.40.050(c). Standard of proof is reasonable doubt, and all rules of criminal procedure apply, except for right to jury trial and
court-appointed lawyer. *State v. Clayton*, 584
P.2d 1111 (1978).

DMV Website

www.state.ak.us/dmv

ARIZONA

Court That Hears Traffic Violations

Justice Court (also known as Justice of
the Peace Court), Municipal Court (also
known as City Court or Magistrate Court)

Court Websites

www.supreme.state.az.us
Maricopa County Justice Courts information on traffic violations: www.superior
court.maricopa.gov/justiceCourts

State Statutes Online

www.azleg.state.az.us

Vehicle Laws

Arizona Revised Statutes, Title 28 (Transportation)

Speed Laws

Title 28, Ch. 3 (Traffic & Vehicle Registration), §§ 28-701 to 28-708 (PRESUMED in general, but ABSOLUTE on state and interstate highways)

Speed Detection Methods

Pacing, aircraft, VASCAR, radar, laser

Trial By Declaration

No

Jury Trial

No. Traffic violation hearings are "informal and without a jury." § 28-1596(D).

Appeal Procedures

Appeal to Superior Court on record only. § 28-1600; AZ Superior Ct Rules of Appellate Procedure – Civil.

Other

Traffic offenses are civil infractions. Burden of proof is preponderance of the evidence. § 28-1596.

DMV Website

www.dot.state.az.us/MVD/mvd.htm

ARKANSAS

Court That Hears Traffic Violations

District Court, City Court (Municipal Courts, Police Courts, and Justice of the Peace Courts were absorbed by the newly created District Courts in July 2001), Little Rock Traffic Court

Court Websites

www.courts.state.ar.us

Little Rock Traffic Court: www.geocities.com/~trafficcourt

State Statutes Online

www.arkleg.state.ar.us/data/ar_code.asp

Vehicle Laws

Ark. Code, Title 27 (Transportation)

Speed Laws

Title 27, Ch. 51 (Operation of Vehicles— Rules of the Road), §§ 27-51-201 to 27-51-214 (ABSOLUTE)

Speed Detection Methods

Pacing, aircraft, radar, laser

Trial By Declaration

No.

Jury Trial

No, but there is a right to jury trial during appeal (trial de novo) to Circuit Court. § 16-7-73; *State v. Roberts*, 900 S.W.2d 175 (1995).

Appeal Procedures

Appeal for jury trial de novo in Circuit Court. Ark. Constit. Amend. No. 80, § 7; § 16-17-703.

DMV Website

www.state.ar.us/dfa/motorvehicle

CALIFORNIA

Court That Hears Traffic Violations

Superior Court (Municipal Courts were consolidated into Superior Courts in 1998)

Court Websites

www.courtinfo.ca.gov

California Courts CAPs & Traffic Violator Fees Report: www.courtinfo.ca.gov/reference/documents/capstrafviofees.pdf

Many California Superior Courts have excellent websites. Below is a listing of the sites with the most useful sections on handling traffic tickets:

- Alameda County: www.alameda.courts.ca.gov/courts
- Los Angeles County: www.lasuperiorcourt.org
- Marin County: www.co.marin.ca.us/depts/MC/main/traffic.cfm
- Orange County: www.occourts.org/traffic
- Sacramento County: www.saccourt.com/index/traffic.asp
- San Diego County: www.sdcourt.ca.gov
- San Francisco City and County: www.sfgov.org/site/courts_index.asp
- Santa Clara county: www.scselfservice.org/traffic/default.htm

Links to each of California's Superior Court websites: www.courtinfo.ca.gov/courts/trial

State Statutes Online

www.leginfo.ca.gov/calaw.html

Vehicle Laws

Vehicle Code

Speed Laws

Veh. Code, Div. 11 (Rules of the Road), Ch. 7 (Speed Laws), §§ 22348-22366 (PRESUMED, except for the following zones, which are ABSOLUTE: 65-70 state highway limit and 55 limit on 2-lane undivided highways)

Speed Detection Methods

Pacing, aircraft, radar, laser

Trial By Declaration

Yes. If found guilty, defendant can request trial de novo. Veh. Code § 40902.

Jury Trial

No. Penal Code § 19.6.

Appeal Procedures

Appeal on record only to the Appellate Division of the Superior Court. Penal Code § 1466.

Other

- Traffic violations are infractions, but standard of proof is beyond a reasonable doubt.
- Under Vehicle Code §§ 40800-40808, VASCAR and aircraft timing between points (but not aircraft pacing) are illegal.

DMV Website

www.dmv.ca.gov

COLORADO

Court That Hears Traffic Violations

County Court, Municipal Court

Court Websites

www.courts.state.co.us

Denver County Traffic Court: www.denvergov.org/CountyCourt/Divisions/Divisions7/tabid/383399/Default.aspx

State Statutes Online

www.courts.state.co.us/chs/court/forms/selfhelpcenter.htm

Vehicle Laws

Colorado Revised Statutes, Title 42 (Vehicles & Traffic)

Speed Laws

Title 42, Article 4 (Regulations of Vehicles & Traffic), § 42-2-1101 (ABSOLUTE as 75 mph zone on highways; otherwise PRESUMED, except that cities and towns may adopt ordinances making local speed limits ABSOLUTE)

Speed Detection Methods

Pacing, aircraft, VASCAR, radar, laser

Trial By Declaration

No

Jury Trial

No. § 16-10-101. Traffic violation cases are heard before referees. Rule 11, Co. Rules for Traffic Infractions (CRTI)

Appeal Procedures

Appeal to District Court on record only. § 13-6-504; Rule 13, CRTI.

Other

Traffic violations are civil infractions. § 42-4-1701. Standard of proof is reasonable doubt. § 42-4-1708(3); Rule 7, CRTI. Rules of evidence do not apply at hearings. Rule 11, CRTI. No discovery allowed until the hearing, at which point defendant may ask to inspect the officer's records. Rule 8, CRTI.

DMV Website

www.mv.state.co.us

CONNECTICUT

Court That Hears Traffic Violations

Superior Court

Court Websites

www.jud.state.ct.us

Traffic violation FAQ: www.jud.state.ct.us/faq/traffic.html

State Statutes Online

www.cslib.org/psaindex.htm

Vehicle Laws

Conn. Gen. Stat., Title 14 (Motor Vehicles)

Speed Laws

Title 14, Ch. 248 (Vehicle Highway Use), §§ 14-218a to 14-219 (PRESUMED except for 55/65 highway limits, which are ABSOLUTE)

Speed Detection Methods

Pacing, aircraft, radar, laser

Trial By Declaration

No

Jury Trial

No. § 54-82b.

Appeal Procedures

Appeal de novo before a Superior Court judge if first trial was before a magistrate. § 51-193u; *State v. Torrance*, 738 A.2d 664 (1999). From Superior Court, appeal on record only to Appellate Court. § 54-82b.

Other

Traffic violations are classified as infractions. Payments are collected at Centralized Infractions Bureau, but trials are held at Superior Court and standard of proof is beyond a reasonable doubt. § 51-164n(g).

DMV Website

http://dmvct.org

DELAWARE

Court That Hears Traffic Violations

Justice of the Peace Court, Alderman's Court

Court Websites

http://courts.state.de.us/index.htm

State Statutes Online

www.michie.com (choose "Delaware" from the Legal Resources menu)

Vehicle Laws

Delaware Code, Title 21 (Motor Vehicles)

Speed Laws

Title 21, Part III (Operation & Equipment), Ch. 41 (Rules of the Road), Subch. VIII (Speed Restrictions), §§ 4168-4174 (ABSOLUTE)

Speed Detection Methods

Pacing, aircraft, VASCAR, radar, laser

Trial By Declaration

No

Jury Trial

There is a right to trial by jury in Court of Common Pleas; defendant making a request for jury will have his case transferred from lower court to Court of Common Pleas. Tit. 11, § 5301.

Appeal Procedures

Appeal de novo from Justice of the Peace and Alderman's Court to Court of Common Pleas, where fine exceeds $100 or punishment exceeds one month in jail. Tit. 11, § 5920. For cases tried in Court of Common Pleas, appeal is to Superior Court on record only. Tit. 11, § 5301.

DMV Website

www.dmv.de.gov

DISTRICT OF COLUMBIA (WASHINGTON, D.C.)

Court That Hears Traffic Violations

Traffic Adjudication Bureau (an administrative agency)

Court Websites

www.dccourts.gov/dccourts

State Statutes Online

http://government.westlaw.com/linkedslice/default.asp?SP=DCC-1000

Vehicle Laws

D.C. Code, Division VIII (General Laws), Title 50 (Motor and Non-Motor Vehicles & Traffic)

Speed Laws

Title 50, Subtitle VII (Traffic), Ch. 22 (Regulation of Traffic), § 50-2201.04 (ABSOLUTE)

Speed Detection Methods

Pacing, radar

Trial By Declaration

No

Jury Trial

No. Traffic violations are heard by an administrative hearing examiner. § 50-2301.04.

Appeal Procedures

Appeal on the law to the Appeals Board of the Adjudication Bureau. §§ 50-2304.02, 50-2304.03. From there, defendant can request review by the Superior Court. § 50-2304.05.

Other

- Traffic violations are decriminalized. § 50-2301.01. Standard of proof is clear and convincing evidence. § 50-2301.01.
- Radar detectors are illegal in D.C. D.C. Police Reg.: Art. 25, s 16; *Smith v. District of Columbia*, 436 A.2d 53 (1981).

DMV Website

http://dmv.washingtondc.gov/main.shtm

FLORIDA

Court That Hears Traffic Violations

Traffic Violations Bureau in County Court

Court Websites

www.flcourts.org
Miami-Dade traffic court: www.co.miami-dade.fl.us/clerk/TrafficCourt.htm
Traffic ticket FAQ on Volusia County's website: www.clerk.org/info/traffictickets.html

State Statutes Online

www.leg.state.fl.us/statutes/index.cfm

Vehicle Laws

Fla. Stats., Title XXIII (Motor Vehicles)

Speed Laws

Title XXIII, Ch. 316 (State Uniform Traffic Control), §§ 316.183-316.1895

Speed Detection Methods

Pacing, aircraft, VASCAR, radar

Trial By Declaration

Yes; in Florida it's called filing an Affidavit of Defense. Rule 6.340, Fla. Rules of Traffic Court.

Jury Trial

No. Traffic cases are decided before a hearing officer. § 318.14(5)

Appeal Procedures

Appeals of decision of hearing officer are on the record, to the Circuit Court. § 318.33.

Other

Traffic offenses are classified as civil infractions. Standard of proof is beyond a reasonable doubt. § 318.14(6).

DMV Website

www.hsmv.state.fl.us

GEORGIA

Court That Hears Traffic Violations

Georgia has a confusing array of trial level courts. Traffic cases may be heard in the following venues, depending on the party issuing the ticket (state, county, or local official) and the nature of the county or city's court structure:

- Atlanta Traffic Court (division of City Court of Atlanta)
- State Court
- County Recorder's Court
- Magistrate Court
- Probate Court

Court Websites

www.georgiacourts.org

State Statutes Online

www.lexis-nexis.com/hottopics/gacode/default.asp

Vehicle Laws

Ga. Code, Title 40 (Motor Vehicles & Traffic)

Speed Laws

Title 40, Ch. 6 (Uniform Rules of the Road), §§ 40-6-180 to 40-6-181 (ABSOLUTE)

Speed Detection Methods

Pacing, aircraft, VASCAR, radar

Trial By Declaration

No

Jury Trial

There is a statutory right to jury trial in misdemeanor traffic cases. § 40-13-23. (Traffic offenses such as speeding are mostly classified as misdemeanors in Georgia.) If defendant is charged in a court that doesn't hold jury trials, such as County Recorder's Court or Magistrate Court, defendant must either waive (give up the right to) jury trial or notify the court of her wish for a jury trial. If defendant asks for jury trial, case will then be transferred to court that does hold jury trials (State Court, Superior Court, Probate Court in counties with populations over 96,000, and Atlanta City Court).

Appeal Procedures

Appeal de novo to Superior Court from all trial level traffic courts listed above. § 5-3-29. Appeal from Magistrate Court can be to Superior Court or to State Court (appeal to State Court is also de novo). §§ 15-10-41, 5-3-30.

DMV Website

www.dmvs.ga.gov

HAWAII

Court That Hears Traffic Violations

District Court

Court Websites

Hawaii state judiciary's site has helpful self-help materials for traffic cases; go to www.courts.state.hi.us and under the "Self Help" heading, click on "Traffic Cases."

State Statutes Online

www.capitol.hawaii.gov/site1/docs/docs .asp?press1=docs

Vehicle Laws

Hawaii Revised Statutes, Title 17 (Motor & Other Vehicles)

Speed Laws

Title 17, Ch. 291C (Statewide Traffic Code), §§ 291C-101 to 291C-102 (ABSOLUTE)

Speed Detection Methods

Pacing, VASCAR, radar, laser

Trial By Declaration

Yes. § 291D-6(a)(2).

Jury Trial

No. Traffic offenses are decided at civil hearings. § 291D-8. No jury on de novo trial in district court. *State v. Shak*, 466 P.2d 422 (1970).

Appeal Procedures

If hearing officer finds that defendant committed the offense, defendant can ask for a trial in District Court. § 291D-13. Prosecutor is present at this trial, and

standard of proof is beyond a reasonable doubt. Hawaii Civil Traffic Rule 19.

Other

Traffic offenses in Hawaii are decriminalized. Officer does not have to appear at hearing, but court may subpoena him. § 291D-8(a)(1). Standard of proof is preponderance of the evidence. § 291D-8(a)(3). No prosecutor appears at the hearing. § 291D-14.

DMV Website

www.dmv.org/hi-hawaii/department-motor-vehicles.php

IDAHO

Court That Hears Traffic Violations

District Court, Magistrate Division

Court Websites

www.state.id.us/judicial

The Idaho Supreme Court has a publication you can download from its website called *Overview of the Idaho Court System* (at www.state.id.us/judicial/overview.pdf) that explains how traffic violations are handled within Idaho courts (at pp. 25-26). Idaho's Third Judicial District Court's FAQ on court trials in traffic cases: www .the3rdjudicialdistrict.com/itrials.htm

State Statutes Online

www.state.id.us/idstat

Vehicle Laws

Idaho Code, Title 49 (Motor Vehicles)

Speed Laws

Title 49, Ch. 6 (Rules of the Road), § 654 (ABSOLUTE)

Speed Detection Methods

Pacing, VASCAR, radar, laser

Trial By Declaration

No

Jury Trial

No. § 49-1502.

Appeal Procedures

Appeal from District Court Magistrate to District Court Judge, on record only. § 1-2213.

Other

Traffic violations are classified as infractions, but the burden of proof is beyond a reasonable doubt. Idaho Code § 49-1502.

DMV Website

www.state.id.us/itd/dmv

ILLINOIS

Court That Hears Traffic Violations

Circuit Court

Court Websites

www.state.il.us/court

Cook County traffic court information: www.cookcountycourt.org/traffic_court/index.html

Chicago Bar FAQ on traffic tickets: www.chicagobar.org/public/diallaw/12.asp

State Statutes Online

www.ilga.gov

Vehicle Laws

Ill. Comp. Stat., Chapter 625 (Vehicles)

Speed Laws

Ch. 625, Act 5 (Ill. Vehicle Code), Subchapter 11 (Rules of the Road), Art. VI (Speed Restrictions), §§ 5/11-601 to 5/11-605 (ABSOLUTE)

Speed Detection Methods

Pacing, VASCAR, radar, laser

Trial By Declaration

No

Jury Trial

Yes. 38 Ill. Comp. Stat. 5/103-6, *People v. Beil*, 395 N.E.2d 400 (1979).

Appeal Procedures

On record only, to Appellate Court. Ill. Const., Art. 6, § 6; Ill. Sup. Ct. Rule 603.

DMV Website

www.library.sos.state.il.us/services/services_motorists.html

INDIANA

Court That Hears Traffic Violations

Traffic Violations Bureau, County Court, City/Town Court, Circuit Court

Court Websites

www.state.in.us/judiciary

Indiana University Student Legal Services FAQ on traffic tickets: www.indiana.edu/~sls/traffic_violations.html

State Statutes Online

www.state.in.us/legislative/ic/code

Vehicle Laws

Indiana Code, Title 9 (Motor Vehicles)

Speed Laws

Title 9, Article 21 (Traffic Regulation), Ch. 5 (Speed Limits), §§ 9-21-5-1 to 9-21-5-6 (ABSOLUTE)

Speed Detection Methods

Pacing, aircraft, VASCAR, radar

Trial By Declaration

Yes (called "Trial By Affidavit")

Jury Trial

Yes, if defendant makes a timely request for jury. *Terpstra v. State*, 529 N.E.2d 839 (1988); Rule 38, Indiana Rules of Trial Procedure.

Appeal Procedures

Appeal from City or Town court to the Circuit or Superior Court of the county for trial de novo. § 33-10.1-5-9. Appeal from County Court or Circuit Court to Court of Appeals. § 33-10.5-7-10.

Other

Traffic violations are civil infractions. Standard of proof is preponderance of the evidence. Ind. Code § 34-28-5-1; Rule 5, Ind. Rules of Appellate Procedure.

DMV Website

www.ai.org/bmv

IOWA

Court That Hears Traffic Violations

District Court (Magistrate Division)

Court Websites

www.judicial.state.ia.us

State Statutes Online

www.legis.state.ia.us/IowaLaw.html

Vehicle Laws

Iowa Code, Title VIII (Transportation), Subtitle 2 (Vehicles)

Speed Laws

Tit. VIII, Ch. 321 (Motor Vehicles & Laws of the Road), §§ 321.285-321.293 (ABSOLUTE)

Speed Detection Methods

Pacing, aircraft, VASCAR, radar, laser

Trial By Declaration

No

Jury Trial

Yes, but defendant must make a timely demand for a jury trial. *Marzen v. Klousia*, 316 N.W.2d 688 (1982); Rule 2.64, Iowa Rules Crim. Pro.

Appeal Procedures

Appeal on record only, but judge hearing appeal has discretion to take further evidence. If case was tried before judicial magistrate, appeal is heard by district judge. If case was tried before district judge, appeal is heard by another district judge. Rule 2.73(3), Iowa Rules of Court.

DMV Website

www.dot.state.ia.us/mvd

KANSAS

Court That Hears Traffic Violations

District Court, Municipal Court

Court Websites

www.kscourts.org

State Statutes Online

www.kslegislature.org/cgi-bin/statutes/index.cgi

Vehicle Laws

Kansas Stats., Ch. 8 (Automobiles & Other Vehicles)

Speed Laws

Ch. 8, §§ 8-1557 to 8-1560 (ABSOLUTE)

Speed Detection Methods

Pacing, aircraft, VASCAR, radar, laser

Trial By Declaration

No

Jury Trial

No. § 22-3404(5), § 21-4502.

Appeal Procedures

On record only from Municipal Court to District Court. §§ 12-4602, 22-3610. Appeal from District Court magistrate judge to District Court judge on the record only. § 22-3609a.

Other

Kansas classifies traffic violations as infractions. §21-3105.

DMV Website

www.ksrevenue.org/dmv

KENTUCKY

Court That Hears Traffic Violations

District Court

Court Websites

www.kycourts.net

State Statutes Online

www.lrc.state.ky.us/statrev/frontpg.htm

Vehicle Laws

Kentucky Revised Statutes, Title XVI (Motor Vehicles).

Speed Laws

Title XVI, Ch. 189 (Traffic Regulations), § 189.390 (PRESUMED)

Speed Detection Methods

Pacing, VASCAR, radar, laser

Trial By Declaration

No

Jury Trial

Yes. § 29A.270, *Crone v. Commonwealth*, 680 S.W.2d 138 (1984).

Appeal Procedures

Appeal to District Court on record only. § 23A.080.

DMV Website

www.kytc.state.ky.us/mvl

LOUISIANA

Court That Hears Traffic Violations

City Court, Parish Court, Municipal Court, Justice of the Peace Court, Mayor's Court, Traffic Court (New Orleans only).

Court Websites

http://louisiana.gov/wps/wcm/connect/Louisiana.gov/Louisiana+Government/Judicial/

New Orleans Traffic Court: www.cityofno.com/Portals/Portal53/portal.aspx

State Statutes Online

www.legis.state.la.us

Vehicle Laws

Louisiana Revised Statutes, Title 32 (Motor Vehicles & Traffic Regulation)

Speed Laws

Title 32, Ch. 1, Part IV (Traffic Regulations), §§ 32:61 to 32:64 (55/65/70 zones are ABSOLUTE, otherwise PRESUMED)

Speed Detection Methods

Pacing, aircraft, VASCAR, radar

Trial By Declaration

Yes

Jury Trial

No. § 13:1450, La. Code Crim. Proc., Art. 779.

Appeal Procedures

Appeal de novo to District Court from Mayor's Court and Justice of the Peace Court. § 13:1896(A).

Appeal on record only to District Court from City, Parish or Municipal Court. § 13:1896(B).

On record only to District Court from New Orleans Traffic Court. La. Rev. Stat.

DMV Website

http://omv.dps.state.la.us

MAINE

Court That Hears Traffic Violations
District Court

Court Websites
www.courts.state.me.us

State Statutes Online
http://janus.state.me.us/legis/statutes

Vehicle Laws
Maine Revised Statutes, Title 29a (Motor Vehicles)

Speed Laws
Me. Rev. Stats., Tit. 29a, § 2074 (ABSOLUTE)

Speed Detection Methods
Pacing, aircraft, VASCAR, radar, laser

Trial By Declaration
No

Jury Trial
No. Tit. 29a, § 103.

Appeal Procedures
Appeal de novo to Superior Court. Tit. 4, §§ 105, 156; Rule 80F(j), Me. Rules of Civ. Pro.

Other
Traffic violations in Maine are "civil violations." Standard of proof is preponderance of the evidence. Rule 80F, Me. Rules of Civ. Proc. District attorney prosecutes the case. Me. Rev. Stats. Tit. 30-A, § 282.

DMV Website
www.state.me.us/sos/bmv

MARYLAND

Court That Hears Traffic Violations
District Court

Court Websites
www.courts.state.md.us

State Statutes Online
www.michie.com (choose "Maryland" from the Legal Resources menu)

Vehicle Laws
Md. Code. Ann., Transportation (Trans.), Titles 11-27 (Vehicle Laws)

Speed Laws
Md. Trans §§ 21-801 to 21-803.2

Speed Detection Methods
Pacing, aircraft, VASCAR, radar, laser

Trial By Declaration
No

Jury Trial
No. Cts. & Jud. Proc. § 4-302(e).

Appeal Procedures
Appeal for trial de novo from District Court to Circuit Court. Cts. & Jud. Proc., § 12-401(f).

DMV Website
http://mva.state.md.us

MASSACHUSETTS

Court That Hears Traffic Violations
District Court, Boston Municipal Court

Court Websites
www.state.ma.us/courts

State Statutes Online
www.state.ma.us/legis/laws/mgl

Vehicle Laws
Mass. General Laws, Part I, Title XIV, Chs. 89 (Law of the Road) and 90 (Motor Vehicles & Aircraft)

Speed Laws
Mass. Stat. 90, §§ 17, 17a (ABSOLUTE on interstates, otherwise PRESUMED)

Speed Detection Methods
Pacing, VASCAR, radar, laser

Trial By Declaration
No

Jury Trial
No. Mass. Stat. 90C § 3(A)(4).

Appeal Procedures

If the hearing is before a magistrate, either police officer or defendant can appeal for a de novo hearing in District Court. Thereafter, or if original hearing is in front of judge, then on record only to Appellate Division of District Court. 90C § 3(A)(4), 90C § 3(A)(5).

Other

- Traffic violations are "civil motor infractions" for which a defendant is found "responsible" or "not responsible." Procedure is called a "noncriminal hearing" where standard of proof is preponderance of the evidence. Mass. Stat. 90C § 3(A)(4).
- Massachusetts law says that the ticket itself is presumptive evidence of your guilt, and in practice that has meant that police officers have not been required to come to these hearings. But in 2001, the Appellate Division of the District Court ruled that the police officer must appear at the de novo appeal hearing or lose the case. *Boston Police Department vs. Moughalian*, 2001 Mass. App. Div 61 (No. 270257).

DMV Website

www.state.ma.us/rmv

MICHIGAN

Court That Hears Traffic Violations

District Court (Traffic Violations Bureau), Municipal Court

Court Websites

www.courts.michigan.gov
Michigan traffic court: www.courts
.michigan.gov/scao/selfhelp/intro/civil/
traffic.htm

State Statutes Online

www.michiganlegislature.org

Vehicle Laws

Mich. Stats., Ch. 257 (Motor Vehicles)

Speed Laws

Ch. 257, § 257.627 (PRESUMED)

Speed Detection Methods

Pacing, aircraft, VASCAR, radar, laser

Trial By Declaration

No

Jury Trial

No. *People v. Schomaker*, 323 N.W.2d 461 (1982).

Appeal Procedures

Appeal from District Court to Circuit Court on record only. § 660.8342. If defendant elects to have an informal hearing, then appeal is a de novo formal hearing in District Court. Rule 4.101, Mich. Rules of District Court.

Other

Traffic violations are civil infractions. §§ 257.627(10), 257.628(6). Defendant may elect an informal hearing before a magistrate or a formal hearing before a judge. §§ 600.8819, 600.8821. Burden of proof for a civil infraction is preponderance of the evidence. § 600.8821.

DMV Website

www.michigan.gov/sos

MINNESOTA

Court That Hears Traffic Violations

District Court

Court Websites

www.courts.state.mn.us

State Statutes Online

www.leg.state.mn.us/leg/statutes.htm

Vehicle Laws

Minn. Stats., Chs. 160-174a (Transportation)

Speed Laws

Ch. 169, § 169.14 (ABSOLUTE in munici-palities, otherwise PRESUMED)

Speed Detection Methods

Pacing, aircraft, VASCAR, radar, laser

Trial By Declaration

No

Jury Trial

No. § 169.89.

Appeal Procedures

Appeal on record only to Court of Appeals. Rule 28.01, Minn. Rules of Criminal Procedure.

DMV Website

www.dps.state.mn.us/dvs

MISSISSIPPI

Court That Hears Traffic Violations

Justice Court, Municipal Court, County Court

Court Websites

www.mssc.state.ms.us

State Statutes Online

www.michie.com (choose "Mississippi" from the Legal Resources menu) www.mscode.com/free/statutes/toc.htm

Vehicle Laws

Mississippi Code, Title 63 (Motor Vehicles & Traffic Regulation)

Speed Laws

Title 63, Ch. 3 (Traffic Regulations & Rules of the Road), §§ 63-3-501 to 63-3-516 (ABSOLUTE)

Speed Detection Methods

Pacing, aircraft, VASCAR, radar

Trial By Declaration

No

Jury Trial

Yes. § 99-3-9.

Appeal Procedures

From Justice Court and Municipal Court, appeal for de novo trial to County Court. On record only from County Court to Circuit Court. § 99-35-1; Rule 5.01, Miss. Unif. Rules of Circ. & County Ct. Practice.

DMV Website

www.dps.state.ms.us/dps/dps.nsf

MISSOURI

Court That Hears Traffic Violations

Municipal Court, Associate Division of Circuit Court

Court Websites

www.courts.mo.gov

St. Louis Municipal Court traffic ticket information: www.co.st-louis.mo.us/scripts/municourt/trafficticket

State Statutes Online

www.moga.state.mo.us/homestat.asp Missouri Bar guide to Your Rights in Traffic Court: www.mobar.org/4ddd6369-250f-4e5c-bc4e-46d5e7a1831d.aspx

Vehicle Laws

Mo. Rev. Stat. Title XIX (Motor Vehicles, Watercraft & Aviation)

Speed Laws

Title XIX, Ch. 304 (Traffic Regulations), § 304.010 (ABSOLUTE)

Speed Detection Methods

Pacing, aircraft, radar, laser

Trial By Declaration

No

Jury Trial

Yes, in third-class and fourth-class cities, for violations of municipal traffic ordinances, § 479.130. (The classification of cities under Missouri law has to do with the size of the city in addition to what classification the city elects. See §§ 72.030, 72.040.) Other types of cities may or may not provide for jury trial for violations of their ordinances. *City of Maplewood v. Marti*, 891 S.W.2d 500 (1995). Where charged by the State (as opposed to a municipality), there is a statutory right to a jury trial. § 543.200; *State ex rel. Cole v. Nigro*, 471 S.W.2d 933 (1971).

Appeal Procedures

If case was tried in Municipal Court before judge who is not a licensed attorney, or if case below was not a jury trial, appeal is trial de novo before a circuit judge. If case below was before licensed Municipal Court judge AND case was a jury trial, appeal is on record only. § 479.200.

Other

Speed over the limit by 5 mph or less is an infraction for which no points go on driving record. § 304.009.

DMV Website

www.dor.mo.gov/mvdl

MONTANA

Court That Hears Traffic Violations

Municipal Court, Justice's Court, City Court

Court Websites

www.montanacourts.org/default.asp

State Statutes Online

http://leg.state.mt.us/css/mtcode_const/laws.asp

Vehicle Laws

Montana Code, Title 61 (Motor Vehicles)

Speed Laws

Title 61, Ch. 8 (Traffic Regulation), Part 3 (Vehicle Operating Requirements), § 61-8-303 (ABSOLUTE)

Speed Detection Methods

Pacing, aircraft, radar

Trial By Declaration

No

Jury Trial

Yes. §§ 46-17-201, 46-17-403.

Appeal Procedures

Appeal de novo to District Court from City or Justice's Court; defendant may request jury trial. Mont. Code. Ann. § 46-17-11. From Municipal Court, appeal is on record only, to District Court. § 3-6-110.

Other

Up until 1999, Montana had no daytime speed limit on interstates, the only rule being to drive at a "reasonable and proper" speed. In 1998, the Montana Supreme Court overturned the "reasonable and proper" rule (also known as the "basic rule") as unconstitutionally vague. *State v. Stanko*, 974 P.2d 1132 (1998). The Montana legislature enacted a numerical speed limit in 1999.

DMV Website

www.doj.state.mt.us/department/motorvehicledivision.asp

NEBRASKA

Court That Hears Traffic Violations

County Court

Court Websites

http://court.nol.org

State Statutes Online

www.unicam.state.ne.us/web/public/
research

Vehicle Laws

Neb. Rev. Stat., Ch. 60 (Motor Vehicles)

Speed Laws

Ch. 60, Article 6(N) (Speed Restrictions),
§§ 60-6, 185 to 60-6, 195 (ABSOLUTE)

Speed Detection Methods

Radar, laser

Trial By Declaration

Yes

Jury Trial

No. § 25-2705.

Appeal Procedures

Appeal for trial de novo in District Court.
§ 25-1937.

DMV Website

www.dmv.state.ne.us

NEVADA

Court That Hears Traffic Violations

Municipal Court or Justice Court

Court Websites

Directory of local court websites: www
.nvsupremecourt.us/info/nvcourts/

State Statutes Online

www.leg.state.nv.us/law1.cfm

Vehicle Laws

Nev. Revised Stats., Title 43 (Public Safety;
Vehicles; Watercraft)

Speed Laws

Title 43, Ch. 484 (Traffic Laws), §§ 484.361
to 484.375 (ABSOLUTE)

Speed Detection Methods

Pacing, aircraft, radar, laser

Trial By Declaration

No

Jury Trial

No. § 266.550; *State v. Smith*, 672 P.2d 631
(1983).

Appeal Procedures

To District Court, on record only.
§§ 189.010, 266.595.

DMV Website

www.nevadadmv.state.nv.us

NEW HAMPSHIRE

Court That Hears Traffic Violations

District Court

Court Websites

www.courts.state.nh.us

State Statutes Online

http://gencourt.state.nh.us/rsa/html/
indexes/default.html

Vehicle Laws

N.H. Revised Statutes, Title 21 (Motor
Vehicles)

Speed Laws

Title 21, Ch. 265 (Rules of the Road),
§§ 265:60 to 265:63 (65 mph zone is
ABSOLUTE, otherwise PRESUMED)

Speed Detection Methods

Pacing, aircraft, radar, laser

Trial By Declaration

No

Jury Trial

No. § 595-A:2-b.

Appeal Procedures

On record, to Superior Court. §§ 599:1 to 599:4.

DMV Website

http://webster.state.nh.us/dmv/

NEW JERSEY

Court That Hears Traffic Violations

Municipal Court

Court Websites

www.judiciary.state.nj.us

State Statutes Online

www.njleg.state.nj.us

Vehicle Laws

N.J. Stats., Title 39 (Motor Vehicles & Traffic Regulation)

Speed Laws

Title 39, Ch. 4 (Traffic Regulation), §§ 39:4-98 to 39:4-100 (ABSOLUTE)

Speed Detection Methods

Pacing, aircraft, VASCAR, radar

Trial By Declaration

No

Jury Trial

No. § 2C:1-4.

Appeal Procedures

On record only, to Superior Court. § 39-5-2; NJ Rules of Court, Crim. Rule 3:23-8.

Other

Photo radar is illegal. § 39:4-103.1.

DMV Website

www.state.nj.us/mvc

NEW MEXICO

Court That Hears Traffic Violations

Magistrate Court, Municipal Court, Metropolitan Court (Bernalillo County only)

Court Websites

www.nmcourts.com

Bernalillo Metro Courts website: www.metrocourt.state.nm.us

State Statutes Online

http://legis.state.nm.us/lcs

Vehicle Laws

N.M. Revised Statutes, Ch. 66 (Motor Vehicles)

Speed Laws

Ch. 66, Art. 7 (Traffic Laws Generally), §§ 66-7-301 to 66-7-304 (ABSOLUTE)

Speed Detection Methods

Pacing, aircraft, VASCAR, radar, laser

Trial By Declaration

No

Jury Trial

No

Appeal Procedures

De novo appeal to district court (§§ 340-8a-6, 35-13-1, 35-13-2).

DMV Website

www.state.nm.us/tax/mvd/mvd_home.htm

NEW YORK

Court That Hears Traffic Violations

County Court; Town Court, City Court or Village Court; Traffic Violations Bureau (see "Other," below)

Court Websites

www.courts.state.ny.us

State Statutes Online

http://assembly.state.ny.us/leg

Vehicle Laws

N.Y. State Consolidated Laws, Ch. 71 (Vehicle & Traffic)

Speed Laws

V&T § 1180 (ABSOLUTE)

Speed Detection Methods

Pacing, aircraft, VASCAR, radar, laser

Trial By Declaration

No

Jury Trial

No. V&T § 155.

Appeal Procedures

De novo trial on appeal from Town, Village, or City Court to County Court. NY Constitution, Art. VI, § 11. From all other courts, appeal is on record only, to Appellate Term of Supreme Court (Supreme Court in New York is the county level trial court). Crim. Procedure Law, § 450.60.

Other

Traffic violations are classified as infractions, not crimes. V&T § 155. The Traffic Violations Bureau (TVB) handles non-criminal moving violations in these areas: the five boroughs of New York City; the cities of Buffalo and Rochester; and the towns of Babylon, Brookhaven, Islip, Riverhead, and Smithtown in western Suffolk County (for more information, see www.nysdmv.com/broch/c49.htm).

DMV Website

www.nydmv.state.ny.us

NORTH CAROLINA

Court That Hears Traffic Violations

District Court

Court Websites

www.nccourts.org

State Statutes Online

www.ncleg.net/gascripts/Statutes/Statutes.asp

Vehicle Laws

Gen. Stats. of N.C., Ch. 20 (Motor Vehicles)

Speed Laws

§ 20-141 (ABSOLUTE)

Speed Detection Methods

Pacing, VASCAR, radar

Trial By Declaration

No

Jury Trial

No jury trial in District Court. § 7a-196. Jury trial is available on appeal de novo to Superior Court.

Appeal Procedures

Appeal for trial de novo (no jury) from District Court magistrate to District Court judge, and then appeal for jury trial de novo from District Court judge to Superior Court. § 7a-290.

DMV Website

www.dmv.dot.state.nc.us

NORTH DAKOTA

Court That Hears Traffic Violations

Municipal Court, District Court (in areas with no Municipal Court)

Court Websites

www.court.state.nd.us

State Statutes Online

www.legis.nd.gov/information/statutes

Vehicle Laws

N.D. Century Code, Title 39 (Motor Vehicles)

Speed Laws

§§ 39-09-01 to 39-09-07.1 (PRESUMED)

Speed Detection Methods

Pacing, aircraft, radar, laser

Trial By Declaration

No

Jury Trial

No. § 39-06.1-03.

Appeal Procedures

De novo trial in district court. § 39-06.1-03(5).

Other

Traffic violations are civil ("decriminalized"), burden of proof is preponderance of the evidence. § 39-06.1-03.

DMV Website

www.dot.nd.gov

OHIO

Court That Hears Traffic Violations

County Court, Municipal Court, Mayor's Court

Court Websites

www.sconet.state.oh.us

State Statutes Online

http://codes.ohio.gov

Vehicle Laws

Ohio Revised Code, Title 45 (Motor Vehicles)

Speed Laws

Title 45, Ch. 4511 (Traffic Law—Operation of Motor Vehicles), §4511.21 (ABSOLUTE on interstate, otherwise PRESUMED)

Speed Detection Methods

Pacing, aircraft, VASCAR, radar, laser

Trial By Declaration

At discretion of each court

Jury Trial

No right to jury unless jail time is possibility or if penalty exceeds $100. § 2945.17. Where offense qualifies, defendant must make written demand for jury trial. Criminal Rule 23.

Appeal Procedures

Appeal is de novo from Mayor's Court to Municipal Court. § 1905.25. Appeal from Municipal Court and County Court is on record only, to Court of Appeals. §§ 1901.30, 1907.30.

DMV Website

http://ohiobmv.com

OKLAHOMA

Court That Hears Traffic Violations

Municipal Court

Court Websites

www.oscn.net

State Statutes Online

www.oscn.net (from home page, click on "Legal Research")

http://oklegal.onenet.net/statutes.basic .html

Vehicle Laws

Oklahoma Stats., Title 47 (Motor Vehicles)

Speed Laws

Title 47, Art. VIII (Speed Restrictions), Tit. 47, § 11-801 (ABSOLUTE as to 55/65/70/75 zones, school zones (25), and state parks (35); PRESUMED otherwise)

Speed Detection Methods

Pacing, aircraft, VASCAR, radar

Trial By Declaration

No

Jury Trial

No right to jury trial where punishment is by fine only that does not exceed $500. Tit. 22, § 601.

Appeal Procedures

Trial de novo in District Court. Tit. 11, § 27-129

DMV Website

www.dps.state.ok.us/dls

OREGON

Court That Hears Traffic Violations

Municipal Court, Justice Court, Circuit Court

Court Websites

http://bluebook.state.or.us/state/judicial/judicial.htm

Marion County Circuit Court website allows you to download forms for trial by affidavit: www.ojd.state.or.us/mar

State Statutes Online

www.leg.state.or.us/ors/home.html

Vehicle Laws

Oregon Revised Statutes, Chs. 801-826 (Vehicle Code)

Speed Laws

Ch. 811 (Rules of the Road for Drivers), §§ 811.100-811.124 (ABSOLUTE in urban areas, on interstates, and on ocean shore, otherwise PRESUMED)

Speed Detection Methods

Pacing, aircraft, VASCAR, radar, laser

Trial By Declaration

Yes. § 153.080.

Jury Trial

No. § 153.076.

Appeal Procedures

Appeal for trial de novo in Circuit Court where lower court (Justice, City or Municipal Court) was not court of record (courts of record are those that are required to keep a recorded version of proceedings); where lower court *was* court of record, appeal on record only. § 138.057.

Other

Traffic violations in Oregon are civil infractions. Prosecutor cannot appear at trial unless defendant has counsel;

regular discovery rules apply. Burden of proof is preponderance of the evidence. § 153.076.

DMV Website

www.oregon.gov/ODOT/DMV

PENNSYLVANIA

Court That Hears Traffic Violations

District Justice's Court, Pittsburgh Magistrate's Court, Philadelphia Traffic Court

Court Websites

Philadelphia Traffic Court website: http://courts.phila.gov/traffic-court

Pittsburgh City Courts Building's website: www.city.pittsburgh.pa.us/maps/html/city_courts_building.html

State Statutes Online

www.legis.state.pa.us

Vehicle Laws

Pa. Consolidated Statutes, Title 75 (Vehicles)

Speed Laws

Title 75, Part III, Ch. 33 (Rules of the Road in General), §§ 3361-3368 (ABSOLUTE)

Speed Detection Methods

Pacing, aircraft, VASCAR, radar

Trial By Declaration

No

Jury Trial

No. *Bacik v. Commonwealth*, 434 A.2d 860 (1981).

Appeal Procedures

Appeal for jury trial de novo in the Court of Common Pleas. Tit. 42, § 1123(a)(2).

Other

- Radar may be used by State Police only. Radar and VASCAR cannot be used to prove speeding unless violator exceeds speed limit by 6 mph or more. Where speed limit is under 55 mph, VASCAR cannot be used to prove speeding unless violator exceeds speed limit by 10 mph or more. But these limits on use of VASCAR do not apply in a school zone. Tit. 75, § 3368.

- Officer is not required to appear at summary proceeding (first trial); Rule 454, Pa. Rules Crim. Pro. But officer is required to appear at trial de novo on appeal. Rule 462(C), Pa. Rules Crim. Pro.

DMV Website

www.dmv.state.pa.us

RHODE ISLAND

Court That Hears Traffic Violations

Traffic Tribunal

Court Websites

www.courts.state.ri.us

State Statutes Online

www.rilin.state.ri.us/statutes/statutes.html

Vehicle Laws

General Laws of Rhode Island, Title 31 (Motor & Other Vehicles)

Speed Laws

Ch. 31-14 (Speed Restrictions), §§ 31-14-1 to 31014-8 (PRESUMED)

Speed Detection Methods

Pacing, aircraft, radar, laser

Trial By Declaration

No

Jury Trial

No

Appeal Procedures

Appeal goes to three-judge appellate panel within the Traffic Tribunal, and from

there to District Court. Rule 21, Traffic Tribunal Rules of Procedure (www.courts. state.ri.us/traffic/rulesofprocedure.htm).

Other

Rhode Island traffic violations are decriminalized and handled by an administrative agency called the Traffic Tribunal. Standard of proof is clear and convincing evidence. Rule 17, RI Traffic Tribunal Rules of Procedure.

DMV Website

www.dmv.state.ri.us

SOUTH CAROLINA

Court That Hears Traffic Violations

Magistrate Court (also called Summary Court) or Municipal Court

Court Websites

www.judicial.state.sc.us

State Statutes Online

www.scstatehouse.net/code/statmast.htm

Vehicle Laws

S.C. Code of Laws, Title 56 (Motor Vehicles)

Speed Laws

Title 56, Ch. 5, Art. 11, §§ 56-5-1520 to 56-5-1570 (ABSOLUTE)

Speed Detection Methods

Pacing, VASCAR, radar, laser

Trial By Declaration

No

Jury Trial

Yes. § 14-25-125.

Appeal Procedures

On record only to Circuit Court (Court of Common Pleas). §§ 14-25-105, 18-3-70.

DMV Website

www.scdps.org/dmv

SOUTH DAKOTA

Court That Hears Traffic Violations

Magistrate Court

Court Websites

www.state.sd.us/state/judicial

State Statutes Online

http://legis.state.sd.us/index.cfm

Vehicle Laws

S.D. Codified Laws, Title 32 (Motor Vehicles)

Speed Laws

Title 32, Ch. 25 (Speed Regulation), §§ 32-25-1.1 to 32-25-21 (ABSOLUTE)

Speed Detection Methods

Pacing, aircraft, radar, laser

Trial By Declaration

No

Jury Trial

No right to jury trial where judge assures defendant at time of request for jury trial that judge will not impose jail time (even if traffic statute under which defendant is charged authorizes jail time of up to six months). *State v. Auen*, 342 N.W.2d 236 (1984).

Appeal Procedures

To Circuit Court on record only, if Magistrate Court proceedings are recorded. Where not recorded, trial de novo in Circuit Court. §§ 16-12A-26, 16-12A-27.

DMV Website

www.state.sd.us/dps/dl

TENNESSEE

Court That Hears Traffic Violations

General Sessions Court or Municipal Court (sometimes also called City Court)

Court Websites

www.tsc.state.tn.us

State Statutes Online

www.michie.com (choose "Tennessee" from the Legal Resources menu)

Vehicle Laws

Tennessee Code, Title 55 (Motor & Other Vehicles)

Speed Laws

§§ 55-8-152 to 55-8-157 (ABSOLUTE)

Speed Detection Methods

Pacing, aircraft, radar, laser

Trial By Declaration

No

Jury Trial

Yes, where defendant faces fine of $50 or more, or possibility of confinement. *State v. Dusina*, 764 S.W.2d 766 (1989).

Appeal Procedures

Appeal for trial de novo to Circuit Court or Criminal Court; defendant must make request for jury trial at time of filing his appeal. § 27-3-131.

DMV Website

www.state.tn.us/safety

TEXAS

Court That Hears Traffic Violations

Municipal Court or Justice of the Peace Court

Court Websites

www.courts.state.tx.us

State Statutes Online

www.courts.state.tx.us/

Vehicle Laws

Tex. Transportation Code, Title 7 (Vehicles & Traffic)

Speed Laws

Tex. Transp. Code, Title 7, Subtitle C (Rules of the Road), §§ 545.351-545.362 (PRESUMED)

Speed Detection Methods

Pacing, radar, laser

Trial By Declaration

No

Jury Trial

Yes

Appeal Procedures

For appeals from a municipal court of record, appeal is on the record only, under jurisdiction of County Court. For appeals from justice courts and municipal courts not of record, trial de novo, under jurisdiction of County Court. Govt. Code § 30.00014; Code of Crim. Procedure, Articles 44.17 and 45.042.

Other

A law prohibiting open containers in cars (previously open alcoholic beverages in vehicles were allowed) went into effect in 2001.

DMV Website

www.txdps.state.tx.us

UTAH

Court That Hears Traffic Violations

Justice Court, District Court (in jurisdictions with no Justice Court)

Court Websites

http://courtlink.utcourts.gov/
Useful FAQ on traffic violations at http://courtlink.utcourts.gov/howto/trafficn.htm.

State Statutes Online

www.le.state.ut.us/Documents/code_const.htm

Vehicle Laws

Utah Code, Title 41 (Motor Vehicles)

Speed Laws

Utah Code, Title 41, Ch. 6 (Utah Code §§ 41-6-46 to 41-6-48.5) (ABSOLUTE in school zones, otherwise PRESUMED)

Speed Detection Methods

Pacing, aircraft, VASCAR, radar, laser

Trial By Declaration

No

Jury Trial

Yes

Appeal Procedures

Appeal for trial de novo from Justice Court to District Court (§ 78-5-120); from District Court, appeal is on record only to Court of Appeals.

DMV Website

http://driverlicense.utah.gov

VERMONT

Court That Hears Traffic Violations

Judicial Bureau

Court Websites

www.vermontjudiciary.org

State Statutes Online

www.leg.state.vt.us/statutes/statutes2.htm

Vehicle Laws

Vermont Statutes, Title 23 (Motor Vehicles)

Speed Laws

Vermont Statutes, Title 23, Chapter 13 (Operation of Vehicles), § 1081 (ABSOLUTE)

Speed Detection Methods

Pacing, radar, laser

Trial By Declaration

No

Jury Trial

No, first proceeding is before a hearing officer. Tit. 4, § 1106. Yes on trial de novo. Tit. 4, § 1107.

Appeal Procedures

A jury trial is allowed on de novo appeal at driver's option, or the court can solely consider questions of law. Tit. 4, § 1107.

Other

Traffic violations are handled by an administrative agency, the Judicial Bureau. Standard of proof is clear and convincing. Hearing officers preside over cases. Officer must appear; no prosecutor is present. Tit. 4, §§ 1102-1108, Tit. 23, § 2302-2305.

DMV Website

www.aot.state.vt.us/dmv/dmvhp.htm

VIRGINIA

Court That Hears Traffic Violations

General District Court

Court Websites

Virginia Judicial System website has links to General District Court websites across the state: www.courts.state.va.us/courts/courts.html#gd

State Statutes Online

http://leg1.state.va.us/000/src.htm

Vehicle Laws

Code of Virginia, Title 46.2 (Motor Vehicles)

Speed Laws

Title 46.2, Subtitle III (Operation), Ch. 8 (Regulation of Traffic)
Va. Code §§ 46.3-862, 46.2-870 to 46.2-876 (ABSOLUTE)

Speed Detection Methods

Pacing, VASCAR, Radar

Trial By Declaration

No

Jury Trial

No, at first trial. Yes, on de novo appeal to Circuit Court. § 16.1-136.

Appeal Procedures

Appeal to Circuit Court for trial de novo. §§ 16.1-132, 16.1-136.

Other

Radar detectors are illegal. § 46.2-1079.

DMV Website

www.dmv.state.va.us

WASHINGTON

Court That Hears Traffic Violations

Municipal Court, District Court (in areas that don't have a Municipal Court)

Court Websites

www.courts.wa.gov

State Statutes Online

http://apps.leg.wa.gov/rcw

Vehicle Laws

Revised Code of Washington, Title 46 (Motor Vehicles)

Speed Laws

§§ 46.61.400 to 46.61.475 (ABSOLUTE)

Speed Detection Methods

Pacing, aircraft, VASCAR, radar, laser

Trial By Declaration

No

Jury Trial

No. Rev. Code Wash. § 46.63.090

Appeal Procedures

On record only, to Superior Court. § 46.63.090. Superior Court has discretion to refuse to consider the appeal. Rule 2.3, Wash. Rules Appellate Procedure.

Other

- Traffic violations decriminalized; burden of proof by preponderance of the evidence. No prosecutor. Court will consider written statement of officer in lieu of personal appearance, but defendant has right to subpoena officer. §§ 46.63.010 to 46.63.151.
- Moving VASCAR illegal. Stationary VASCAR allowed if distance "accurately measured off." Distances for VASCAR and aircraft speed timing must be at least a quarter mile. § 46.61.470.

DMV Website

www.wa.gov/dol

WEST VIRGINIA

Court That Hears Traffic Violations

Magistrate Court or Municipal Court

Court Websites

www.state.wv.us/wvsca

The West Virginia Supreme Court of Appeals website has some helpful material for people who don't have lawyers: www .state.wv.us/wvsca/ProSe/self_help.htm

State Statutes Online

www.legis.state.wv.us

Vehicle Laws

West Virginia Code, Chapter 17C (Traffic Regulations and Rules of the Road)

Speed Laws

West Virginia Code, Chapter 17C (Traffic Regulations and Rules of the Road), §§ 17C-6-1 to 17C-6-5 (ABSOLUTE)

Speed Detection Methods

Pacing, aircraft, VASCAR, radar, laser

Trial By Declaration

No

Jury Trial

Defendant may request a jury trial but right to jury trial is not guaranteed where there is no possibility of jail time. §§ 8-10-2, 50-5-1; *Champ v. McGhee*, 270 S.E. 2d 445 (1980).

Appeal Procedures

Appeal from Magistrate Court or Municipal Court goes to Circuit Court. If lower court trial was by jury, appeal to Circuit Court is on the record. If lower court trial was without jury, appeal to Circuit Court is trial de novo before a judge (not a jury). §§ 8-34-1, 50-5-1.

DMV Website

www.wvdot.com/6_motorists/dmv/6G_ DMV.HTM

WISCONSIN

Court That Hears Traffic Violations

Municipal Court or Circuit Court

Court Websites

www.courts.state.wi.us

State Statutes Online

www.legis.state.wi.us/rsb/stats.html

Vehicle Laws

Wisconsin Statutes, Vehicles, Chapters 340-351

Speed Laws

§§ 346.57 to 346.60 (ABSOLUTE)

Speed Detection Methods

Pacing, aircraft, VASCAR, radar, laser

Trial By Declaration

No

Jury Trial

Yes. Written demand and fee required. § 345.43.

Appeal Procedures

Appeal from Municipal Court to Circuit Court. Appeal is de novo upon request of either party; otherwise, appeal is on the record. § 800.14. Appeal from Circuit Court is to Court of Appeals.

Other

Standard of proof in a traffic violation is "clear, satisfactory and convincing." § 345.45.

DMV Website

www.dot.state.wi.us/drivers

WYOMING

Court That Hears Traffic Violations

Circuit Court or Justice of the Peace Court

Court Websites

http://courts.state.wy.us

State Statutes Online

http://legisweb.state.wy.us/titles/statutes.htm

Vehicle Laws

Wyoming Statutes, Title 31 (Motor Vehicles)

Speed Laws

Title 31, Ch. 5, Article III (Speed Regulations), §§ 31-5-301 to 31-5-306 (ABSOLUTE)

Speed Detection Methods

Pacing, radar

Trial By Declaration

Some courts allow this.

Jury Trial

Yes

Appeal Procedures

On record only, to District Court. §§ 5-4-119, 5-9-41.

DMV Website

http://dot.state.wy.us/web/driver_services/index.html

Index

A

Absolute speed limits, 35
  testimony about exceeding, 147–148
Accidents
  civil suits and pleas, 126
  nolo contendere plea, 126–127
  tickets issued after, 40, 69
Administrative offenses
  traffic violations as, 16–17
  See also Decriminalized traffic offenses
Affidavit, trial by, 130–134
Aircraft speed detection, 47–50
  cross-examination questions, 165–169
Alabama, court rules, 222
Alaska, court rules, 222
Alcohol and the body, 103–107
  See also Blood alcohol content
Alcohol-related (non-DUI/DWI) offenses,
  92–94
Appeals
  case under advisement and, 199–200
  jury verdict, 217
  for new trial, 200–201
Arizona, court rules, 222–223
Arkansas, court rules, 223
Arraignment
  DUI arrests, 117–118
  procedures, 127–130
  reasons for insisting on, 127
Assuming facts not in evidence, 155–156, 191
Attorneys. *See* Lawyers

B

BAC. *See* Blood alcohol content (BAC)
"Basic" speed law, 39–40
"Blind" passing, 91–92
Blood alcohol content (BAC)
  BAC 0.08% or higher, 101–102
  blood tests, 109–110
  breath tests, 110–112
  calculating, 104–106
  effects of, 106–107
  levels and "under the influence," 100–101
  urine tests, 112–113
Breath tests, 110–112
Business district, U-turns in, 76–77

C

California, court rules, 223–224
Cameras, photographic automated enforcement
  devices, 73–74
Cause, challenges for, 210–211
Challenging a juror, 210–211
Civil lawsuits and pleas, 126
Civil offenses
  traffic violations as, 16–17
  See also Decriminalized traffic offenses
Closing statements
  trial by judge, 194, 196–199
  trial by jury, 214–216
Colorado, court rules, 224–225
Connecticut, court rules, 225
Continuance, 140–142, 188
Courtroom
  diagram, 183

overview, 182–185

Court rules for all states, 221–246

Courts, contacting for information, 124–125

Criminal offenses, traffic violations as, 17–18

Cross-examination by prosecutor

preparing for, 151–152

trial by jury, 214

Cross-examination of officer

illegal turn questions, 180

judge asks you to waive right to, 185

nonresponsive answers, 159–160

officer's power of observation, 160

preparing for, 157–159

presumed speed limit questions, 176–177

sample questions, 160–162

speed violations generally, 163–176

stoplight running questions, 178–179

stop sign running questions, 179–180

trial by judge, 192

trial by jury, 213

Curves, "blind" passing, 91–92

D

Declaration, trial by, 130–134

Decriminalized traffic offenses, 16–17

informal procedures in some states, 184

Delaware, court rules, 225–226

Delays

arraignment dates, 129–130

trial dates, 129–130, 140–142, 188

"De novo" jury trials, 201

Diagrams, preparing for trial, 142–144

Discovery procedures, 134–138

ignoring request, 134, 136–137, 190–191

written request, 135

Dismissal of case

discovery request ignored, 134, 136–137, 187

officer fails to appear, 22, 187

speedy trial rules ignored, 141–142, 187

Distance rules, for witnesses, 151

District of Columbia, court rules, 226

Drinking alcohol in moving vehicle, 94

Driving too slowly, 86–88

Driving Under the Influence (DUI), 98–122

BAC 0.08% or higher, 101–102

blood alcohol levels, 100–101, 104–106

drugs and, 101

effects of alcohol, 106–107

elements of DUI, 99–101

evaluating your case, 114–116

felony DUI, 103

impairment chart, 106

implied consent law, 108–109

lawyers and, 116

license suspension, 113–114

overview, 98

penalties, 102

plea bargaining, 116–117

pretrial court proceedings, 117–119

state DUI/DWI laws compared, 120–122

tests for alcohol, 108–113

"under the influence," 100

Drugs

illegal drugs in car, 95

under the influence of, 101

See also Driving Under the Influence

DUI/DWI. *See* Driving Under the Influence (DUI)

F

Felonies, 18
  felony DUI, 103
Fighting a ticket
  considerations about, 21–24
  defenses that rarely work, 24
  overview, 4–6
Fines, 18–19
  paying (forfeiting bail), 125–126
Florida, court rules, 226–227
Forfeiting bail (paying the fine), 125–126

G

Georgia, court rules, 227–228
Group legal practices, 30–31
Guilty with an explanation plea, 126

H

Hawaii, court rules, 228
Hearsay evidence, 42, 156–157, 191
Highways, U-turns and, 78
Hills, "blind" passing, 91–92
Hostile witnesses, 151

I

Idaho, court rules, 228–229
Illegal drugs
  in car, 95
  See also Driving Under the Influence
Illinois, court rules, 229
Impeding traffic violations, 87–88
Implied consent law, 108–109
Improper passing, 91–92
Improper turning, 74–81
  failing to signal, 81
  failing to stay at edge of road, 75
  officer cross-examination questions, 180
  prohibited by signs or lanes, 75–76
  unsafe turns and lane changes, 79–81
  U-turn violations, 76–79
Indiana, court rules, 229–230
Infractions, 17
Insurance rates, 19
Internet resources, researching traffic laws, 9
Intersections, right of way at, 82–86
Iowa, court rules, 230

J

Judge, trial by
  appeals, 200–201
  overview, 182–186
  procedure, 186–200
Jury instructions, 216–217
Jury trials, 204–217
  challenging a juror, 210–211
  "de novo" trials, 201
  insisting on having, 128
  number of jurors, 204
  overview, 204
  procedures, 211–217
  selection of jury, 206–211
  "voir dire" questions for jurors, 208–210

K

Kansas, court rules, 230–231
Kentucky, court rules, 231

L

Lane changes, unsafe lane changes, 90–91
Laser speed detection, 64–65
  cross-examination questions about, 175–176
Lawsuits and pleas, 126
Lawyers
  DUI charges and, 116
  firing, 32

services provided by, 28–29

types of, 29–31

when to hire, 28

Left turns, failure to yield, 83–84

Legally justified conduct, 23–24

Legal research

  analyzing court decisions, 12

  citation formats, 12

  finding case law, 10–11

  finding traffic laws, 8–10

  interpretation of other laws, 12–13

License suspensions, 19–20

  appeals and delaying of, 201

  drug convictions and, 95

  DUI arrests and, 113–114

Limit line faded, 71

Louisiana, court rules, 231

M

Maine, court rules, 232

Maps, preparing for trial, 142–144

Maryland, court rules, 232

Massachusetts, court rules, 232–233

Michigan, court rules, 233

Minnesota, court rules, 233–234

Misdemeanors, 17

Mississippi, court rules, 234

Missouri, court rules, 234–235

Mistake-of-fact defense, 23

  new stop sign, 71

  obscured stop sign, 70–71

Montana, court rules, 235

Motions

  to compel discovery, 134, 136

  for continuance, 140–142, 188

  excluding multiple witnesses from

    courtroom, 188

  to strike a prior in DUI cases, 118

  to suppress evidence in DUI case, 118

  See also Dismissal of case

Motor Vehicle Laws, finding, 8–10

Moving violations

  alcohol-related (non-DUI/DWI) offenses,
    92–94

  driving too slowly, 86–88

  improper passing, 91–92

  improper turning, 74–81

  not stopping at stoplights, 71–74

  not stopping at stop signs, 69–71

  point system, 20

  right-of-way violations, 81–86

  tailgating, 88–89

  unsafe lane changes, 90–91

  See also Driving Under the Influence;
    Speed violations

N

Nebraska, court rules, 236

Necessity defense, 24

Nevada, court rules, 236

New facts, closing statements and, 197, 198

New Hampshire, court rules, 236–237

New Jersey, court rules, 237

New Mexico, court rules, 237

New York, court rules, 237–238

Nolo contendere plea, 126–127

North Carolina, court rules, 238

North Dakota, court rules, 238–239

Notes of police officer

  discovery and, 134–138

  objecting to reading from, 154–155, 190

Not guilty plea, 127, 128

Number of jurors, 204

O

Objecting to testimony, 154–157
  assuming facts not in evidence, 155–156, 191
  discovery request ignored, 190–191
  foundation not provided, 190
  hearsay evidence, 156–157, 191
  officer reading from notes, 154–155, 190
Obscured stop sign, 70–71
Officer. *See* Police officer
Ohio, court rules, 239
Oklahoma, court rules, 239
Open alcohol container in car, 92–94
Opening statements
  trial by judge, 188–189, 192–193
  trial by jury, 212
Oregon, court rules, 240

P

Pacing by police officer
  aircraft speed detection, 47–50
  cross-examination questions about, 163–169
  in police car, 43–46, 163–165
Passing, improper passing, 91–92
Pedestrians, failure to yield, 85–86
Pennsylvania
  court rules, 240–241
  VASCAR speeding conviction limits, 53
Peremptory challenges, 211
Perjury, 150
Petty offenses, 17
Photographic automated enforcement devices, 73–74
Photographs, preparing for trial, 145
Plea bargaining
  DUI cases and, 116–117
  settlement before jury trial, 205
Pleas, deciding on options, 125–127

Point system for moving violations, 20
  See also License suspensions
Police officer
  challenging in court, 22–23
  discovery request for notes, 134–137
  failing to come to court, 22, 187
  reviewing officer's notes, 137–138
Prepaid legal services, 30–31
Preparing for trial. *See* Trial preparations
Presumed speed limits, 35–39
  officer cross-examination questions, 176–177
  testimony about exceeding, 148–149
Pretrial conference
  DUI cases and, 118–119
  settlement negotiation, 205–206
Pretrial court proceedings, DUI arrests, 117–119
Prosecutors
  closing statement, 196–197, 214
  negotiating a settlement with, 205–206
  opening statement, 188–189, 212
  preparing for cross-examination by, 151–152
  rebuttal statement, 199, 216
  trials by judge and, 185–186
  See also Plea bargaining
Public defenders, 31

Q

Questions for jurors, 208–210

R

Radar detectors, 63–64
Radar speed detection, 56–64
  cross-examination questions about, 173–175
Reasonable doubt, 140
Rebuttal statement, 199, 216
Redirect examination, 192

Red light cameras, 73–74
Reserved opening statements, 192–193
Residence district, U-turns in, 77–78
Rhode Island, court rules, 241
Right, passing on, 92
Right-of-way violations, 81–86
Rough pavement, driving slowly and, 88

S

Selection of jury, 206–211
Selective enforcement defense, 25
Sentence, trial by judge, 200
Settlement conference
    DUI cases and, 118–119
    negotiating with the prosecutor, 205–206
Signal violations, turns, 81
Slow driving violations, 86–88
South Carolina, court rules, 241
South Dakota, court rules, 242
Speed detection
    aircraft detection, 47–50
    laser, 64–65
    officer cross-examination questions, 163–176
    overview of methods, 42
    pacing, 43–46
    radar, 56–64
    VASCAR, 50–56
Speed violations, 34–40
    absolute speed limits, 35
    "basic" speed law, 39–40
    officer cross-examination questions, 176–177
    presumed speed limits, 35–39
    testimony, absolute speeding limit, 147–148
    testimony, presumed speeding limit, 148–149
    types of, 34

Speedy trial rules, 129, 141–142
Standards of proof, decriminalized traffic offenses, 17
State laws
    DUI/DWI comparison chart, 120–122
    traffic court rules for all states, 221–246
Stoplights
    not stopping at, 71–73
    officer cross-examination questions, 178–179
    photographic automated enforcement devices, 73–74
    testimony about running, 149–150
Stop signs
    elements of violation, 69–70
    failing to yield at, 84–85
    four-way stops and failure to yield, 82–83
    limit line faded, 71
    new sign, 71
    not stopping at, 69–71
    obscured sign, 70–71
    officer cross-examination questions, 179–180
    stopping further back, 70
Subpoenaing witnesses, 151
Summary offenses, 17
Suspensions. *See* License suspensions

T

Tailgating, 88–89
Tennessee, court rules, 242
Testimony
    by prosecution, 189–191, 212
    by you, 193–194, 213–214
    by your witnesses, 194, 195–196
Texas, court rules, 242–243
Traffic islands, U-turns and, 78–79
Traffic laws, finding, 8–10
Traffic offenses

as civil or administrative offenses, 16–17
as criminal offenses, 17–18
negative consequences, 18–20
Traffic school, 20–21
Transportation Code, finding, 8–10
Trial preparations, 140–152
  cross-examination by prosecutor, 151–152
  cross-examination of the officer, 157–180
  delaying date of, 129–130, 140–142
  diagrams and maps, 142–144
  notes and research, 142
  objecting to testimony, 154–157
  photographs, 145
  testimony by witnesses, 150–151
  testimony by you, 146–150
  witness preparation, 150–151
Trials
  by declaration or affidavit, 130–134
  delaying date of, 129–130, 140–142
  by judge, 182–200
  by jury, 204–217
Turning violations. *See* Improper turning
Turnouts, failing to use, 88

U

Unanimous jury verdict not always required, 204
Uncontrolled intersections, failure to yield, 82–83
"Under the influence," 100
  See also Driving Under the Influence
Unsafe lane changes, 90–91
Unsafe turns and lane changes, 79–81
Urine tests, 112–113
Utah, court rules, 243
U-turn violations, 76–79

V

VASCAR, 50–56
  cross-examination questions, 169–173
Vehicle Code, finding, 8–10
Verdict
  trial by judge, 199–200
  unanimous jury verdict not always required, 204
Vermont, court rules, 243–244
Visual Average Speed Computer and Recorder (VASCAR), 50–56, 169–173
"Voir dire" questions for jurors, 208–210

W

Waiving right to cross-examination of officer, 185
Waiving right to speedy trial, 129
Washington, court rules, 244–245
West Virginia, court rules, 245
Wisconsin, court rules, 245–246
Witnesses
  questioning procedures, 195–196
  subpoenaing, 151
  testimony by, 150–151, 194
Wyoming, court rules, 246

Y

Yellow light duration, 73
Yielding right of way, violations, 82–86
Yield signs, failing to yield at, 84–85

CATALOG
...more from Nolo

BUSINESS	PRICE	CODE
Business Buyout Agreements (Book w/CD-ROM)	$49.99	BSAG
The California Nonprofit Corporation Kit (Binder w/CD-ROM)	$69.99	CNP
California Workers' Comp: How to Take Charge When You're Injured on the Job	$34.99	WORK
The Complete Guide to Buying a Business (Book w/CD-ROM)	$24.99	BUYBU
The Complete Guide to Selling a Business (Book w/CD-ROM)	$24.99	SELBU
Consultant & Independent Contractor Agreements (Book w/CD-ROM)	$29.99	CICA
The Corporate Records Handbook (Book w/CD-ROM)	$69.99	CORMI
Create Your Own Employee Handbook (Book w/CD-ROM)	$49.99	EMHA
Dealing With Problem Employees	$44.99	PROBM
Deduct It! Lower Your Small Business Taxes	$34.99	DEDU
Effective Fundraising for Nonprofits	$24.99	EFFN
The Employer's Legal Handbook	$39.99	EMPL
Essential Guide to Federal Employment Laws	$39.99	FEMP
Form a Partnership (Book W/CD-ROM)	$39.99	PART
Form Your Own Limited Liability Company (Book w/CD-ROM)	$44.99	LIAB
Home Business Tax Deductions: Keep What You Earn	$34.99	DEHB
How to Form a Nonprofit Corporation (Book w/CD-ROM)—National Edition	$49.99	NNP
How to Form a Nonprofit Corporation in California (Book w/CD-ROM)	$49.99	NON
How to Form Your Own California Corporation (Binder w/CD-ROM)	$59.99	CACI
How to Form Your Own California Corporation (Book w/CD-ROM)	$34.99	CCOR
How to Write a Business Plan (Book w/CD-ROM)	$34.99	SBS
Incorporate Your Business (Book w/CD-ROM)	$49.99	NIBS
Investors in Your Backyard (Book w/CD-ROM)	$24.99	FINBUS
The Job Description Handbook	$29.99	JOB
Legal Guide for Starting & Running a Small Business	$34.99	RUNS
Legal Forms for Starting & Running a Small Business (Book w/CD-ROM)	$29.99	RUNSF
LLC or Corporation?	$24.99	CHENT
The Manager's Legal Handbook	$39.99	ELBA
Marketing Without Advertising	$20.00	MWAD
Music Law (Book w/CD-ROM)	$39.99	ML
Negotiate the Best Lease for Your Business	$24.99	LESP
Nolo's Guide to Social Security Disability (Book w/CD-ROM)	$29.99	QSS
Nolo's Quick LLC	$29.99	LLCQ
The Performance Appraisal Handbook	$29.99	PERF
The Small Business Start-up Kit (Book w/CD-ROM)	$24.99	SMBU
The Small Business Start-up Kit for California (Book w/CD-ROM)	$24.99	OPEN
Starting & Running a Successful Newsletter or Magazine	$29.99	MAG
Tax Deductions for Professionals	$34.99	DEPO
Tax Savvy for Small Business	$36.99	SAVVY
Whoops! I'm in Business	$19.99	WHOO
Working for Yourself: Law & Taxes for Independent Contractors, Freelancers & Consultants	$39.99	WAGE
Working With Independent Contractors (Book w/CD-ROM)	$29.99	HICI
Your Crafts Business: A Legal Guide (Book w/CD-ROM)	$26.99	VART
Your Limited Liability Company: An Operating Manual (Book w/CD-ROM)	$49.99	LOP
Your Rights in the Workplace	$29.99	YRW

Prices subject to change.

ORDER 24 HOURS A DAY @ www.nolo.com
Call 800-728-3555 • Mail or fax the order form in this book

CONSUMER	PRICE	CODE
How to Win Your Personal Injury Claim	$29.99	PICL
Nolo's Encyclopedia of Everyday Law	$29.99	EVL
Nolo's Guide to California Law	$24.99	CLAW

ESTATE PLANNING & PROBATE	PRICE	CODE
8 Ways to Avoid Probate	$19.99	PRAV
Estate Planning Basics	$21.99	ESPN
The Executor's Guide: Settling a Loved One's Estate or Trust	$34.99	EXEC
How to Probate an Estate in California	$49.99	PAE
Make Your Own Living Trust (Book w/CD-ROM)	$39.99	LITR
Nolo's Simple Will Book (Book w/CD-ROM)	$36.99	SWIL
Plan Your Estate	$44.99	NEST
Quick & Legal Will Book (Book w/CD-ROM)	$19.99	QUIC
Special Needs Trust: Protect Your Child's Financial Future (Book w/CD-ROM)	$34.99	SPNT

FAMILY MATTERS	PRICE	CODE
Always Dad	$16.99	DIFA
Building a Parenting Agreement That Works	$24.99	CUST
The Complete IEP Guide	$34.99	IEP
Divorce & Money: How to Make the Best Financial Decisions During Divorce	$34.99	DIMO
Divorce Without Court	$29.99	DWCT
Do Your Own California Adoption: Nolo's Guide for Stepparents & Domestic Partners (Book w/CD-ROM)	$34.99	ADOP
Every Dog's Legal Guide: A Must-Have for Your Owner	$19.99	DOG
Get a Life: You Don't Need a Million to Retire Well	$24.99	LIFE
The Guardianship Book for California	$34.99	GB
A Legal Guide for Lesbian and Gay Couples	$34.99	LG
Living Together: A Legal Guide (Book w/CD-ROM)	$34.99	LTK
Nolo's IEP Guide: Learning Disabilities	$29.99	IELD
Parent Savvy	$19.99	PRNT
Prenuptial Agreements: How to Write a Fair & Lasting Contract (Book w/CD-ROM)	$34.99	PNUP
Work Less, Live More	$17.99	RECL

GOING TO COURT	PRICE	CODE
Beat Your Ticket: Go To Court & Win (National Edition)	$21.99	BEYT
The Criminal Law Handbook: Know Your Rights, Survive the System	$39.99	KYR
Everybody's Guide to Small Claims Court (National Edition)	$29.99	NSCC
Everybody's Guide to Small Claims Court in California	$29.99	CSCC
Fight Your Ticket & Win in California	$29.99	FYT
How to Change Your Name in California	$29.99	NAME
Nolo's Deposition Handbook	$29.99	DEP
Represent Yourself in Court: How to Prepare & Try a Winning Case	$39.99	RYC
Win Your Lawsuit: A Judge's Guide to Representing Yourself in California Superior Court	$29.99	SLWY

HOMEOWNERS, LANDLORDS & TENANTS	PRICE	CODE
California Tenants' Rights	$27.99	CTEN
Deeds for California Real Estate	$24.99	DEED
Every Landlord's Legal Guide (National Edition, Book w/CD-ROM)	$44.99	ELLI
Every Landlord's Guide to Finding Great Tenants (Book w/CD-ROM)	$19.99	FIND
Every Landlord's Tax Deduction Guide	$34.99	DELL
Every Tenant's Legal Guide	$29.99	EVTEN
For Sale by Owner in California	$29.99	FSBO
How to Buy a House in California	$29.99	BHCA
The California Landlord's Law Book: Rights & Responsibilities (Book w/CD-ROM)	$44.99	LBRT
The California Landlord's Law Book: Evictions (Book w/CD-ROM)	$44.99	LBEV
Leases & Rental Agreements	$29.99	LEAR

	PRICE	CODE
Neighbor Law: Fences, Trees, Boundaries & Noise	$26.99	NEI
Renters' Rights (National Edition)	$24.99	RENT

IMMIGRATION

	PRICE	CODE
Becoming A U.S. Citizen: A Guide to the Law, Exam and Interview	$24.99	USCIT
Fiancé & Marriage Visas (Book w/CD-ROM)	$34.99	IMAR
How to Get a Green Card	$29.99	GRN
Student & Tourist Visas	$29.99	ISTU
U.S. Immigration Made Easy	$39.99	IMEZ

MONEY MATTERS

	PRICE	CODE
101 Law Forms for Personal Use (Book w/CD-ROM)	$29.99	SPOT
Chapter 13 Bankruptcy: Repay Your Debts	$39.99	CHB
Credit Repair (Book w/CD-ROM)	$24.99	CREP
How to File for Chapter 7 Bankruptcy	$29.99	HFB
IRAs, 401(k)s & Other Retirement Plans: Taking Your Money Out	$34.99	RET
Solve Your Money Troubles	$19.99	MT
Stand Up to the IRS	$29.99	SIRS

PATENTS AND COPYRIGHTS

	PRICE	CODE
All I Need is Money: How to Finance Your Invention	$19.99	FINA
The Copyright Handbook: How to Protect and Use Written Works (Book w/CD-ROM)	$39.99	COHA
Copyright Your Software (Book w/CD-ROM)	$34.95	CYS
Getting Permission: How to License & Clear Copyrighted Materials Online & Off (Book w/CD-ROM)	$34.99	RIPER
How to Make Patent Drawings	$29.99	DRAW
The Inventor's Notebook	$24.99	INOT
Nolo's Patents for Beginners	$24.99	QPAT
Patent, Copyright & Trademark	$39.99	PCTM
Patent It Yourself	$49.99	PAT
Patent Pending in 24 Hours	$34.99	PEND
Patenting Art & Entertainment: New Strategies for Protecting Creative Ideas	$39.99	PATAE
Profit from Your Idea (Book w/CD ROM)	$34.99	LICE
The Public Domain	$34.99	PUBL
Trademark: Legal Care for Your Business and Product Name	$39.99	TRD
Web and Software Development: A Legal Guide (Book w/ CD-ROM)	$44.99	SFT
What Every Inventor Needs to Know About Business & Taxes (Book w/CD-ROM)	$21.99	ILAX

RESEARCH & REFERENCE

	PRICE	CODE
Legal Research: How to Find & Understand the Law	$39.99	LRES

SENIORS

	PRICE	CODE
Long-Term Care: How to Plan & Pay for It	$19.99	ELD
Social Security, Medicare & Goverment Pensions	$29.99	SOA

SOFTWARE Call or check our website at www.nolo.com for special discounts on Software!

	PRICE	CODE
Incorporator Pro	89.99	STNC1
LLC Maker—Windows	$89.95	LLP1
Patent Pending Now!	$199.99	PP1
PatentEase—Windows	$349.00	PEAS
Personal RecordKeeper 5.0 CD—Windows	$59.95	RKD5
Quicken Legal Business Pro 2007—Windows	$109.99	SBQB7
Quicken WillMaker Plus 2007—Windows	$79.99	WQP7

Special Upgrade Offer
Save 35% on the latest edition of your Nolo book

Because laws and legal procedures change often, we update our books regularly. To help keep you up-to-date, we are extending this special upgrade offer. Cut out and mail the title portion of the cover of your old Nolo book and we'll give you 35% off the retail price of the New Edition of that book when you purchase directly from Nolo. This offer is to individuals only. Prices and offer subject to change without notice.

ORDER 24 HOURS A DAY @ www.nolo.com
Call 800-728-3555 • Mail or fax the order form in this book

Order Form

Name		
Address		
City		
State, Zip		
Daytime Phone		
E-mail		

Item Code	Quantity	Item	Unit Price	Total Price

Method of payment

☐ Check   ☐ VISA
☐ American Express
☐ MasterCard
☐ Discover Card

Subtotal	
Add your local sales tax (California only)	
Shipping: RUSH $12, Basic $9 (See below)	
"I bought 3, ship it to me FREE!"(Ground shipping only)	
TOTAL	

Account Number

Expiration Date

Signature

Shipping and Handling

Rush Delivery—Only $12

We'll ship any order to any street address in the U.S. by UPS 2nd Day Air* for only $12!

* Order by noon Pacific Time and get your order in 2 business days. Orders placed after noon Pacific Time will arrive in 3 business days. P.O. boxes and S.F. Bay Area use basic shipping. Alaska and Hawaii use 2nd Day Air or Priority Mail.

Basic Shipping—$9

Use for P.O. Boxes, Northern California and Ground Service.

Allow 1-2 weeks for delivery.

U.S. addresses only.

For faster service, use your credit card and our toll-free numbers

Call our customer service group Monday thru Friday 7am to 7pm PST

 Phone
1-800-728-3555

 Fax
1-800-645-0895

 Mail
Nolo
950 Parker St.
Berkeley, CA 94710

Order 24 hours a day @ www.nolo.com

Get the Latest in the Law

Nolo's Legal Updater
We'll send you an email whenever a new edition of your book is published!
Sign up at **www.nolo.com/legalupdater**.

Updates at Nolo.com
Check **www.nolo.com/update** to find recent changes in the law that
affect the current edition of your book.

Nolo Customer Service
To make sure that this edition of the book is the most recent one, call us at
800-728-3555 and ask one of our friendly customer service representatives
(7:00 am to 6:00 pm PST, weekdays only). Or find out at **www.nolo.com**.

Complete the Registration & Comment Card ...
... and we'll do the work for you! Just indicate your preferences below:

Registration & Comment Card

NAME   DATE

ADDRESS

CITY   STATE   ZIP

PHONE   EMAIL

COMMENTS

WAS THIS BOOK EASY TO USE?   (VERY EASY)   5   4   3   2   1   (VERY DIFFICULT)

☐ Yes, you can quote me in future Nolo promotional materials. *Please include phone number above.*

☐ Yes, send me **Nolo's Legal Updater** via email when a new edition of this book is available.

Yes, I want to sign up for the following email newsletters:

   ☐ **NoloBriefs** (monthly)
   ☐ **Nolo's Special Offer** (monthly)
   ☐ **Nolo's BizBriefs** (monthly)
   ☐ **Every Landlord's Quarterly** (four times a year)

☐ Yes, you can give my contact info to carefully selected
partners whose products may be of interest to me.

BEYT 5.0

Nolo
950 Parker Street
Berkeley, CA 94710-9867
www.nolo.com

- -